Hegel on Second Nature in Ethical Life

What does it take to be subjectively free in an objectively rational social order? In this book Andreja Novakovic offers a fresh interpretation of Hegel's account of ethical life by focusing on his concept of habit or "second nature." Novakovic addresses two central and difficult issues facing any interpretation of Hegel's *Philosophy of Right*: why Hegel thinks that it is better to relate unreflectively to the laws of ethical life, and which forms of reflection, especially critical reflection, remain available within ethical life. Her interpretation draws on numerous parts of Hegel's system, particularly on his "Anthropology" and his *Phenomenology of Spirit*, and also explores connections between his account and those of other philosophers. Her aim is to argue that Hegel has a compelling conception of the ordinary ethical standpoint that takes seriously both the virtues and the perils of reflection.

ANDREJA NOVAKOVIC is Assistant Professor of Philosophy at the University of California, Riverside.

Hegel on Second Nature in Ethical Life

Andreja Novakovic
University of California, Riverside

CAMBRIDGE
UNIVERSITY PRESS

University Printing House, Cambridge CB2 8BS, United Kingdom

One Liberty Plaza, 20th Floor, New York, NY 10006, USA

477 Williamstown Road, Port Melbourne, VIC 3207, Australia

4843/24, 2nd Floor, Ansari Road, Daryaganj, Delhi – 110002, India

79 Anson Road, #06-04/06, Singapore 079906

Cambridge University Press is part of the University of Cambridge.

It furthers the University's mission by disseminating knowledge in the pursuit of education, learning, and research at the highest international levels of excellence.

www.cambridge.org
Information on this title: www.cambridge.org/9781107175969
DOI: 10.1017/9781316809723

© Andreja Novakovic 2017

This publication is in copyright. Subject to statutory exception and to the provisions of relevant collective licensing agreements, no reproduction of any part may take place without the written permission of Cambridge University Press.

First published 2017

Printed in the United Kingdom by Clays, St Ives plc

A catalogue record for this publication is available from the British Library.

ISBN 978-1-107-17596-9 Hardback

Cambridge University Press has no responsibility for the persistence or accuracy of URLs for external or third-party internet websites referred to in this publication and does not guarantee that any content on such websites is, or will remain, accurate or appropriate.

For my family:
Lidija, Ivo, and Matthew Novakovic

Contents

Acknowledgments		*page* ix
List of Abbreviations		xi
	Introduction	1
	I.1 Reflection	5
	I.2 *Phenomenology of Spirit*	12
	I.3 Overview	15
1	Habit	20
	1.1 Pragmatic Point of View	27
	1.2 Habit in the "Anthropology"	32
	1.3 True Conscience	38
	1.4 Ethical Disposition	44
	1.5 Principled Habits	56
	1.6 Death by Habit	64
2	Culture	69
	2.1 *Bildung* in the *Phenomenology*	76
	2.2 Self-Cultivation	80
	2.3 Work	86
	2.4 Civil Society	93
	2.5 Cultural Identity	103
3	Critique	106
	3.1 Critical Criticism	110
	3.2 Immanent Critique	115
	3.3 Beautiful Ethical Life	126
	3.4 Modern Contradictions	133
	3.5 Theory and Criticism	147
4	Science	161
	4.1 Theories of Right	167
	4.2 The *Doppelsatz*	174
	4.3 Science and Right	179
	4.4 Recollection	188
	4.5 Objective and Absolute Spirit	204
Works Cited		209
Index		215

Acknowledgments

My greatest gratitude goes to Fred Neuhouser, who taught me how to practice history of philosophy. I am likewise indebted to my dissertation committee at Columbia University – Wolfgang Mann, Katja Vogt, and Axel Honneth – for invaluable input during an earlier iteration of this project. Rahel Jaeggi has been a source of inspiration and support since I first met her, and she has given me numerous occasions for feedback from her and her colloquium at the Humboldt University in Berlin. Terry Pinkard has also lent vital inspiration and support. Dean Moyar has offered careful and generous comments on the book as a whole. And a very special thanks to Rolf Horstmann for helping me understand my thoughts better than I am able to do on my own.

I have benefited from conversations with many friends and colleagues over the years, especially from the enduring exchanges with Katie Gasdaglis, Oksana Maksymchuk, Karen Ng, and Nandi Theunissen, and from the support of the College of William & Mary and the University of California, Riverside. I am grateful to Hilary Gaskin for her faith in this project and to the reviewers at Cambridge University Press for their helpful feedback. This book is dedicated to my parents, Lidija and Ivo Novakovic, and my brother, Matthew, who have taught me courage and focus through the example they set.

Abbreviations

German

DS   *Differenz des Fichteschen und Schellingschen Systems der Philosophie*, in *Jenaer Schriften* (Frankfurt am Main: Suhrkamp)

Enz. I   *Enzyklopädie der philosophischen Wissenschaften I* (Frankfurt am Main: Suhrkamp)

Enz. III   *Enzyklopädie der philosophischen Wissenschaften III* (Frankfurt am Main: Suhrkamp)

GW   *Gesammelte Werke*, ed. Rheinische-Westfälische Akademie der Wissenschaften (Hamburg: F. Meiner)

PR   *Grundlinien der Philosophie des Rechts* (Frankfurt am Main: Suhrkamp)

PG   *Phänomenologie des Geistes* (Frankfurt am Main: Suhrkamp)

NR   *Ueber die wissenschaftliche Behandlungsarten des Naturrechts*, in *Jenaer Schriften* (Frankfurt am Main: Suhrkamp)

VPG   *Vorlesungen über die Philosophie der Geschichte* (Frankfurt am Main: Suhrkamp)

VPR   *Vorlesungen über die Philosophie des Rechts: Berlin 1819/1820* (Hamburg: F. Meiner)

VRP   *Vorlesungen über Rechtsphilosophie: 1818–1831* (Band 1), edited by Karl Ilting (Stuttgart: Frommann-Holzboog)

WL II   *Wissenschaft der Logik* II (Frankfurt am Main: Suhrkamp)

English

PhR   *Elements of the Philosophy of Right*, ed. by Allen Wood (Cambridge University Press)

PhS   *Hegel's Phenomenology of Spirit*, trans. by A. V. Miller (Oxford University Press)

LNR   *Lectures on Natural Right and Political Science: The First Philosophy of Right*, trans. by J. M. Stewart and P. C. Hodgson (University of California Press)

NL   *Natural Law: The Scientific Ways of Treating Natural Law, Its Place in Moral Philosophy, and Its Relation to the Positive Sciences of Law*, trans. by T. M. Knox (University of Pennsylvania Press)

Note: The quoted passages are my own translations, unless otherwise noted. I translated the passages from the *Philosophy of Right*, *The Phenomenology of Spirit*, and the "Natural Law" essay with the assistance of those done by H. B. Nisbet, A. V. Miller, and T. M. Knox, respectively.

Introduction

"The familiar in general is, just because it is *familiar*, not *recognized*."[1]

The question that I pose to Hegel is at first sight not one that Hegel himself seems to ask, at least not in its initial formulation. I want to know how Hegel conceives of our ordinary perspective when we are faced with the mundane task of finding our way about in our social world.[2] Hegel is very interested in grasping our social world, but he approaches it from a highly detached, philosophical standpoint. Whatever it is that he thinks this standpoint can contribute, it seems to differ from the one we occupy when we engage in various forms of evaluation, whether in order to determine what to do or what to continue doing, or even when we simply go about our business without engaging in overt evaluation at all. At the same time, it is not a question that falls outside of Hegel's project, especially not outside of the *Philosophy of Right*, where Hegel delivers such a philosophical account. As unparalleled as his ambitions there may be, he claims that he is merely explicating what social participants already know. In fact, he suggests that it is only philosophy of the sort he himself practices that can explicate this perspective in a way that does not distort it beyond recognition. Upon closer examination we discover a surprising thesis spanning this text, namely, that it is only the most embedded perspectives, as well as the most philosophical, that can adequately capture the rationality of what he calls modern "ethical life" (*Sittlichkeit*). Everything else is a product of the "restless activity of reflection and vanity" (PR, 17).

Hegel introduces what looks like a hierarchy in our ways of relating to ethical life, a hierarchy determined by the degree to which we reflectively relate to its laws. At the bottom is an immediate relationship, in which ethical laws "are

---

[1] PG ¶31 ["Das Bekannte überhaupt ist darum, weil es *bekannt* ist, nicht *erkannt*."]
[2] I will frequently speak about "we" and "us." In doing this, I am imagining Hegel as addressing a contemporary audience and as articulating a view that continues to be of relevance today. It is important to keep in mind that the ordinary standpoint that Hegel seeks to capture is contingent on inhabiting an objectively rational social order. So there is an open question about who, if anyone, does in fact inhabit such an order. But I think that certain aspects of Hegel's view, specifically the function of critical reflection, apply even to those who do not inhabit such an order. This is all to say that the boundaries of the "we" are left deliberately hazy.

not something alien to the subject, rather the subject bears *a witness of spirit* to them as to its own essence, in which it has its *self-feeling* and wherein it lives as in an element indistinguishable from itself – a relation that is more identical than even *belief* and *trust*" (PR §147).

> That relationship, or rather that relation-less identity, in which the ethical is the actual vitality [*Lebendigkeit*] of self-consciousness, may indeed turn into a relationship of belief and trust, or a relationship mediated by *further reflection* into insight through reasons, which may also begin with certain particular ends, interests, and considerations, with hope or fear, or with historical presuppositions. But *adequate cognition* of [this relationship] belongs to conceptual thought [*dem denkenden Begriffe*]. (PR §147)

Given his order of presentation, we might assume that Hegel is telling a progressive story in which we advance to higher stages by adopting an increasingly reflective relation to ethical life. The lowest would be the one in which we fully identify with the laws we live by, in fact identify with them so thoroughly that these laws simply are our way of life. A more advanced attitude is one that is also more reflective, first attaining to the level of belief or conviction in their goodness, and next rising even higher, to an insight grounded in reasons as to why we should consider them good. The highest would be the cognition that belongs to conceptual thought, a form Hegel associates with philosophical comprehension.

But it would be a mistake to assume that mediation through *further reflection* constitutes an advance in Hegel's eyes. There are even reasons to suspect that these reflective stages mark levels of distortion that only a philosophical account can mend.[3] It would also be a mistake to think that Hegel thinks these different levels can be neatly distinguished, that they constitute discrete developmental stages. As it turns out, even this immediate relationship is already an expression of conviction and of insight and so is permeated by those attitudes that reflection can at best make explicit. Finally, this hierarchy is perhaps better described as a circle, for what the philosophical account is ultimately an

---

[3] It may be difficult to see how an insight based on reasons could *not* constitute an advance over an unreflective attitude. But note the kinds of reasons Hegel associates with this supposed insight – reasons such as particular ends, interests, hope, fear, and historical presuppositions. This suggests that Hegel thinks this stage of "further reflection" introduces considerations that are external to the law in question. It provokes us to answer the question as to why we should follow this law, not by looking at its internal justification, but by searching out ways it promotes our self-interest. Nonetheless, Hegel does consider questions of self-interest to be legitimate ones to ask, for he insists that modern subjects demand, and have a right to demand, that their "particularity" be satisfied. See, for example, PR §124 on his gloss on the right of subjectivity, and PR §268 on his characterization of patriotism. So reflection of this sort could, again under certain circumstances, count as a legitimate exercise of this right – namely, under circumstances when this right is not already being satisfied. We usually form our particular ends, interests, hopes, etc. in a social context by situating them within institutional roles. So the two do not ordinarily conflict in a way that would call for explicit reflection.

account *of* is our embedded starting point, so the relation we had to our social world prior to explicit reflection. Hegel calls it a relation-less identity and suggests that conceptual thought is the only form that can capture it in a way that is adequate to it.

This study is an effort to understand these two ends of the spectrum, so to explain what kind of relation to ethical life each of them involves, by focusing on the status of reflection in ethical life. Its angle thus differs from studies that focus on Hegel's conception of freedom, which is usually (and rightly) taken to be the hallmark of Hegel's practical philosophy.[4] As Hegel states in the opening pages of the Introduction: "The ground of right is the *spiritual* in general and its closest location and point of departure is the *will*, which is *free*, so that freedom constitutes its substance and determination and the system of right is the realm of actualized freedom, the world of spirit produced within itself as a second nature" (PR §4). Hegel frames the *Philosophy of Right* as an investigation into "actualized freedom": what are the conditions that make it possible for the will to be free? And he brings this question into connection with that of "right": what kind of social order actualizes a free will? This tracks "Objective Spirit" because it is concerned with delineating the objective conditions that actualize freedom, conditions such as social relations and institutions that free wills inhabit. But within this account of Objective Spirit Hegel argues that a free will must also be subjectively free. It is not enough that I inhabit an objectively freeing order, if I do not know myself to be free in it, so if I do not find my "knowledge and volition" satisfied in it. Thus Hegel can be read as investigating actualized freedom under its objective and subjective guises.

My focus on reflection is not at odds with approaches to the *Philosophy of Right* that foreground his conception of freedom, since the question of reflection is undeniably bound up with the question of freedom, especially with that of subjective freedom. Hegel frequently identifies reflection with abstraction, with the activity of detaching oneself from one's social roles for the sake of evaluation, or the activity of detaching one standard of evaluation from the social context in which it is generally found. He regards this capacity for reflection as one essential feature of the free will:

The will contains (a) the element of *pure indeterminacy* or the I's pure reflection into itself, in which every limitation, every content, whether present immediately through nature, through needs, desires, and drives, or given and determined in some other way,

---

[4] There are a number of influential works on Hegel's practical philosophy, such as Avineri (1972), Hardimon (1994), Wood (1990), but it is Neuhouser (2000), Patten (2002), and Pippin (2008) who have emphasized Hegel's conception of freedom. More recently Moyar (2011) and Yeomans (2011) have reinvigorated this question of freedom in their interpretations of agency and practical rationality.

is dissolved; this is the limitless infinity of *absolute abstraction* or *universality*, the pure *thinking* of oneself. (PR §5)

At the same time, Hegel is worried about its exercise. In some contexts he suggests that it tends to lead astray, motivating abstract accounts of social life, accounts that distort the objective dimension of actualized freedom. In other contexts he suggests that excessive reliance on reflection indicates that your will is not yet subjectively free. He even argues that a free will is one that proceeds unreflectively. We have evidence of it already, for the passage cited earlier identifies actualized freedom as a world that has become "second nature." So why does Hegel identify actualized freedom with second nature, rather than with reflection? Why is this capacity for reflection nonetheless an essential feature of the free will? And when does its exercise prove productive, in Hegel's eyes?

This set of questions already indicates how my approach to the *Philosophy of Right* will differ from much of the contemporary scholarship on this text. In an effort to demonstrate that Hegel is not a conservative who advises that we stick to our "station and its duties" or an apologist of the status quo, many have valorized reflection and granted it a central place in Hegel's picture of ethical life.[5] For example, some have argued that the exercise of reflection is necessary for subjective freedom, for it is only once we have reflected that we are justified in endorsing our social roles and institutions.[6] As a consequence, Hegel's emphasis on the unreflective, specifically on the habitual, has received relatively little attention. These approaches have thus underplayed the ambiguity in Hegel's position. Hegel does not unequivocally favor reflection, nor does he grant it a central place in ethical life. And although he identifies the capacity for it as crucial for freedom, he is highly suspicious of its exercise. My reading seeks to make sense of the status of reflection in ethical life while taking its ambiguity and Hegel's own ambivalence seriously. I will explain why Hegel privileges the habitual over the reflective. And I will explore what forms of reflection remain compatible with Hegel's preferred relation to ethical life. As

---

[5] Wood (1990): "Sittlichkeit, as Hegel means it, is a special kind of critical reflection on social life, not a prohibition against reflection" (196). Pippin (2008): "for Hegel freedom consists in being in a certain reflective and deliberative relation to oneself (which he describes as being able to give my inclinations and incentives a 'rational form')" (4). Moland (2011): "Only finally through being a reflective member of a political community are the agent's desires fully her own; only when she is aware of political principles that best shape the life of a community can an individual be concretely free" (15). Moland even defines concrete freedom as "the individual's ability ... to mold her desires in such a way that she can reflectively endorse them" (17).

[6] Patten (2002) has argued that Hegel is advocating "*complete* reflective awareness with respect to one's determinations and the reasons underlying them, an awareness that does not stop at anything given" (44), and that "there is an important sense, for Hegel, in which freedom involves abstracting from one's contingently given desires and inclinations and acting on the basis of thought and reason alone" (47).

we will see, some forms of reflection are not just compatible, but even vital to ethical life. In fact, what makes this conception of the embedded standpoint especially peerless is not its emphasis on the unreflective per se, but precisely its incorporation of reflection in a variety of ways. A significant portion of my study is thus devoted to investigating those modes of reflection in which Hegel thinks we do – and should continue to – engage.

I will outline and defend my project in the following order: I will begin by clarifying what Hegel means by reflection and why it introduces the difficulties he thinks it does. Here my focus will be on the structure of reflection found in Hegel's *Science of Logic* and its relevance to his practical philosophy. I will address my methodology in this study, which is to supplement the *Philosophy of Right* with appeals to other texts from Hegel's corpus, especially to the *Phenomenology of Spirit*. This raises questions about the scholarly claim that I am making, whether the position I go on to elaborate can be ascribed to Hegel himself or whether it is better described as Hegelian in spirit. Finally, I will offer an overview of the chapters and explain why I proceed in the order in which I do.

I.1 Reflection

The first order of business is to clarify what Hegel means by reflection, specifically in the practical context, so in the context of ethical life. The sense of reflection relevant to this context seems to be in fact quite similar to what we ordinarily mean by reflection. Although Hegel is not thinking of reflection along the lines of introspection, so as a surveying of the contents of one's own mind, he does think of it as essentially self-reflective in structure. When I reflect, I step away from an aspect of myself, usually with a critical eye. I am trying to decide whether to affirm or reject this aspect of myself, which Hegel calls my "determination." This is why Hegel characterizes reflection as an activity of abstraction – I am abstracting away from a given feature and in this way establishing a distance between myself and it. It is an act of dis-identification. And it is usually thought of as a conscious and deliberate activity.

The reason that this activity might be considered so essential to subjective freedom is that one could think that dis-identification is a necessary step in the process of rational identification. In other words, the thought is that I would have to distance myself from something in order to be in a position to affirm it on rational grounds, rather than simply because it is already my determination. It is only once I have reflected that I can proceed in a knowing fashion, rather than merely "blindly." And habit and custom tend to be identified with such blindness. This book will reject this picture on Hegel's behalf because it will challenge the assumption that we are only subjectively free in our social engagement when we have explicitly reflected on that engagement and asked ourselves whether we should continue as we habitually or customarily do. This is not, however, incompatible with Hegel's simultaneous insistence that the free will contains a moment of (reflective) abstraction. One reason has to do with the ways in which the moment of abstraction is already present, even in unreflective forms of participation. Hegel is thinking of reflection as a more fundamental self-relation that can take covert and mundane forms and that does not require what we ordinarily think of as an act of stepping back, let alone asking whether I have good reasons for doing what I do. So the structure of reflection is already present in what looks to be unreflective, such as habitual action and customary participation. I will return to this in a moment. Another reason has to do with the dependence of reflection on objective circumstances. It is Hegel's view that reflection of the critical variety is appropriate only when the institutions in which we habitually or customary participate have proven deficient. Such reflection is a response to an insufficiency in objective freedom, rather than a requirement of subjective freedom, even when the social world does not call for it. When reflection swings free of these objective circumstances, it is liable to create confusion that compromises our subjective freedom precisely because it obscures the rationality of ethical life, of which we are otherwise already aware.

These aspects of reflection – its basic structure as well as its perils – can be found in his general account of reflection in the *Science of Logic*. There is a big question looming over the scholarship on Hegel's practical philosophy about the relevance of the *Logic* to his *Philosophy of Right*. I will address it more directly in my final chapter, where I investigate Hegel's philosophical method and its reliance on other parts of his system. But it is a question that cannot be avoided, even at the outset, since it is in the *Logic* that Hegel delineates the structure of reflection. Here a word of caution is in order: although the kind of reflection that is at issue in ethical life will share features with reflection in the *Logic*, it is not to be conflated with it. What Hegel has in mind is a movement that need not be conscious at all. It is a movement that can be discerned in any object that is capable of transforming into something else while remaining what it is, so retaining its identity in the face of differentiation. Even a tree undergoes reflection when it grows from a seed but remains the same plant. So it is not an activity that is characteristic of human beings and is not limited to their self-critical capacity for abstraction.

Reflection in the *Logic* appears in the context of his "logic of essence" because it is in the service of capturing this elusive "essence." This is a highly technical problem in Hegel's *Logic* that emerges in the transition from "being" to "essence," so in the effort to give determinacy to "being." In this context Hegel defines reflection as a *movement* – by which he means a transformative process – that involves creating differences (through negation) and overcoming them (by negating the negation). It is a fundamentally negative transformation, one that consists in positing a "seeming"[7] (*Schein*) that is *not* identical with one's "essence" (*Wesen*) and then overcoming this negative relation to one's own "seeming" by negating it and recognizing that I am indeed as I "seem" to be. Thus, according to Hegel, it is ultimately a "movement from nothing to nothing" (WL II, 24), since neither my essence nor my seeming can be independently defined. Each only makes sense when contrasted with the other (through reflection), though reflection at the same time reveals that the needed contrast cannot be maintained. It is a "movement from nothing to nothing, and thereby back to itself" (WL II, 24).[8]

Before I briefly summarize Hegel's argument, it is worth noting that this account of reflection has two practical applications that will become relevant for us.[9] First of all, Hegel's account is meant to show how reflection can be present in activities that appear unreflective, so how a similar structure can permeate a process even when it is not being thematized or foregrounded in a self-conscious manner. The movement of reflection is for Hegel far more basic than its self-conscious exercise.[10] In my first two chapters, but especially in the second, I will point it out in seemingly unreflective forms of social participation. Second, Hegel's account also investigates the problems that reflection can generate, thus shedding light on his own hesitations about its practical exercise. In other words, Hegel wants to demonstrate what makes reflection a potential source of distortion and instability. Thus this account of reflection gives us a clue as to how reflection can be both indispensable and pernicious.

The logical account exposes the essentially self-reflective nature of reflection. Hegel is here outlining an act of distancing oneself from oneself and then

---

[7] There is no obvious English equivalent of *Schein*. I have chosen to translate it as "seeming," though there are more skeptical ("illusory being") and less skeptical ("show") translations on the table. It is important to keep in mind that *Schein* is not as such meant to have negative connotations. Although it is distinct from essence, it would ideally allow essence to "shine through."

[8] "Das Werdem im Wesen, seine reflektierende Bewegung, ist daher die *Bewegung von Nichts zu Nichts and dadurch zu sich selbst zurück*" (WL II, 24).

[9] Yeomans (2011) makes Hegel's account of reflection in the *Science of Logic* central to the question of practical agency. As he puts it, "Self-determination seems to require not just that I am able to identify with my actions retrospectively, but that my reflection on my action plays some role in future actions" (15). But, unlike me, he reads the chapter on reflection specifically with an eye to its relevance to the problem of free will, so to Hegel's compatibilism: "Because the categories of essence come in these weighted pairs, we are always explicitly creating and interpreting at the same time. As a matter of everyday life of reflection, this seems unexceptionable. But as a matter of basic conceptual structures, it seems miraculous" (57).

[10] This could raise the question of why we would want to call both movements' instances of "reflection," since only one is self-conscious, while the other is not. They seem to be quite different in kind. I think the reason Hegel has for calling both instances of reflection is because they share a structure. Hegel is interested in this isomorphism of which any being that undergoes transformation while maintaining its identity is capable. Thanks to Karen Ng for raising this question.

overcoming this distance by recognizing that that from which one has distanced oneself is nothing other than oneself. So reflection is self-reflection, a relation one establishes to oneself, even when it is not conducted in a self-conscious manner. It can best be visualized through one's relation to one's own mirror image. When I look in the mirror, I see myself, but as another – an image that now stands over and against me. In this way I have established a distance between myself and my "seeming" (or "appearance," as the term is sometimes translated). This introduces the question: am I really identical with my mirror image, or not? Is my mirror image me, or is it something other than me? This dimension will become relevant to practical forms of reflection because they will also be essentially self-reflective in structure. When I engage in reflection in ethical life, I am distinguishing myself from an aspect of myself, standing apart from it, in an effort to determine whether it is something that I can affirm. This is another way of raising the question of whether it really is *me* or not, whether it expresses my essential nature.

What Hegel explores in the *Logic* is the instability that reflection generates through this movement of stepping away from one's own mirror image. As we have seen, reflection is responsible for establishing the basic distinction between "essence" and "seeming." Essence refers to what something really is, and seeming refers to how it seems to be, though it remains an open question whether the way it seems to be is as it really is. So seeming and essence could in principle coincide. Nevertheless, Hegel thinks that the mere act of drawing this distinction already introduces a kernel of skepticism, because to call the appearance of an object a mere "seeming" is to discredit this appearance as a manifestation of essence.[11] This means that to speak of an essence only makes sense so long as essence is being contrasted with seeming. At the same time, an essence cannot be completely disassociated from seeming either, for it must be visible in ("shine through") the way the object seems to be.[12] As Hegel puts it, "the seeming in the essence is not the seeming of another, rather it is the seeming in itself, the seeming of the essence itself" (WL II, 22). What Hegel concludes, to jump a few steps ahead, is that the skepticism introduced by the act of drawing such a distinction eventually collapses this very distinction, showing it to be insufficient for the task of determining an object.

Hegel suggests that the ultimate untenability of this distinction can be traced back to the instability at the core of this reflective movement. The essence of

---

[11] Hegel explicitly associates this talk of "seeming" with both skepticism and idealism. See WL II, 20.
[12] Pippin (1989) explains this identity of seeming and essence through the example of the essence of a person (his character): while a person's essence needs to be distinguished from his deeds, it must nevertheless animate his deeds and give unity to his conduct. So there is no "inner self" that can remain wholly inner and unexpressed (206).

an object, if it is to have one, cannot be something immediately given, but must first be determined through an activity of abstracting from what is immediately given and figuring out the essence on its basis. This, again, presupposes a connection between seeming and essence, because it assumes that seeming can be treated as an expression of essence, that the essence can be discovered in the seeming. At the same time, such an activity requires something to abstract *from*, so it demands a fixed starting point from which an essence can be determined in the first place, a starting point that is not itself the product of this activity. In this respect, reflection banks on the persistent contrast between something that is merely given, which can serve as its point of departure, and something that is eventually derived through reflection itself.

In characterizing this activity as a "movement of nothing to nothing, and so back to itself," Hegel means to suggest that, when we engage in reflection, neither essence nor seeming present us with a stable reference point, because each already presupposes the other and is only meaningful in relation to the other. In other words, neither can be taken independently for granted. In its three variations – positing, external, and determining – reflection falls prey to a perpetual effort to fix such a point of departure from which to proceed, while failing to recognize that every starting point is precisely already its own product.[13] In this light "external reflection" proves most paradigmatic,[14] because this reflecting activity takes something to be given – something from which it can then proceed to abstract an essence – without recognizing that the act of taking something as given is itself an act and the status of givenness is one that this activity itself bestows. What makes this form of reflection "external" is its conviction that this activity is not implicated in its starting point, but merely abstracts from what is already there, independently of it. This involves a failure to see that the seeming is itself only a seeming from the standpoint of reflection, so from a standpoint that assumes that there is an essence to be discerned in the first place, and that this essence better be distinguished from what is immediately

---

[13] In positing reflection, we think we can uncover the essence without taking anything for granted, but what we take for granted is that there is an essence to uncover. In external reflection, we accept that we must start with something, namely the way something seems, and then determine the essence of its basis. But here we likewise fail to see that seeming is also a product of reflection, because it only makes sense to describe a set of features as the way something seems to be once we have already drawn the distinction with essence. In determining reflection, we accept that seeming and essence are both products of reflective activity, but we then lean on the "determinations of reflection," i.e., the laws of thought, as the fixed, stable, and given reference point.

[14] As Hegel puts it, "External reflection was also what was meant, when reflection in general, as was the trend for a while in contemporary philosophy, was blamed for all evil and was regarded with its determination as the antipode and nemesis of the absolute perspective" (WL II, 31). In fact, his own use of the term "reflection" in his early publications, such as the *Differenzschrift*, could have served as an example of this "trend in contemporary philosophy."

given.¹⁵ It is the reflective stance that generates the contrast, and so pits the way something seems against the way it really is. Reflection can take neither for granted, because both – the status of being an essence as well as the status of being a seeming – are artifacts of this very activity.

As we can see, Hegel's official story about the perils of reflection is both highly abstract and wedded to a particular theoretical problem of lending determinacy to an object, making its relevance to the practical context not directly apparent. But I think there are several respects in which this story can help us see what Hegel means in characterizing reflection in the *Philosophy of Right* as a "restless activity," and one that tends to leave us empty-handed. The first has to do with the skeptical kernel that reflection introduces and ultimately dissipates far and wide. According to Hegel, to be skeptical about the way things seem, and to hunt for an essence concealed by appearance, is to invoke an unstable and destabilizing distinction that tends to erode our confidence in all seemings, robbing us of any resources with which to discern an essence in the first place. In the practical context, it would be to seek the authority, the "essence," of our ethical laws behind, beneath, or above those laws themselves, thus neglecting what he calls their "internal rationality," which is already exhibited (and so "appears") in our pre-reflective modes of engagement. We were already justified in heeding them, whereas reflection leads us to suspect that they need to be justified from scratch, so without recourse to the reasons we already had for doing what we do.

The second has to do with the specific lesson from "external reflection," which was unable to see *itself* in its object of investigation. The way Hegel puts it in the *Science of Logic* is perhaps less helpful here, since Hegel's point there is simply that, whatever we take to be given is something *we take* to be given. Its status of givenness is an artifact of our reflective activity. In the *Philosophy of Right*, I think, Hegel is worried about a deeper entanglement with our object of assessment. He thinks that, when we adopt a reflective stance toward ethical life, we are inclined to treat it as a burden with which our predecessors have saddled us. We fail to see that ethical life is itself a "spiritual" achievement and so expresses deliberate efforts to shape a rational social order.¹⁶ More importantly, we fail to see that ethical life is "spiritual" in a further sense, namely, that it is one with which we do already identify and are right to identify. This identification is one that reflection itself either obscures or discredits. So this

---

[15] "Reflection thus finds the immediate as given, which it moves beyond and from which it returns. But this return is first the presupposing of what is given. This given *becomes* only given in the act of being left behind; its immediacy is the sublated [*aufgehobene*] immediacy" (WL II, 27).

[16] This is one way to make sense of Hegel's complaint that we see the ethical world as "god-forsaken" [*gottverlassen*] (PR, 16).

second sense is connected to the first, since taking one's object of reflection to be something external, something that is merely hoisted upon one, is another way of approaching it with skepticism, with the suspicion that it is a mere seeming. It is akin to treating one's mirror image as a burden one must bear, one that conceals one's true nature, rather than one's own expression. In the context of ethical life, it would be to look upon ethical life as *merely* objective, without seeing that one's own "willing and knowing" is satisfied in it.

Even though Hegel shows appreciation for the modern demand for reflective acceptability, he does so with ambivalence, and nowhere is this ambivalence more pronounced than in his diagnosis of the moral point of view. In the *Philosophy of Right* Hegel defines "morality" (*Moralität*) as a standpoint achieved through "reflection of the will into itself" (*Reflexion des Willens in sich*) (PR §105), a standpoint that turns out to be lacking in objective orientation. Hegel is here identifying morality not so much with any specific moral theory, but rather with more basic efforts to derive an evaluative standard through exclusively subjective resources. Morality is tied to and emerges out of the activity of reflection precisely because it aspires to attain a standpoint that does not take anything "external" for granted, in this case any given social context and its corresponding norms. It is the application of the basic structure of reflection to the practical question of what I *really* ought to do, which is another version of the question of what I *really* or essentially am. This is admittedly at best a mere sketch and I will return to Hegel's critique of morality in the proceeding chapters. At this point it is sufficient to note that even reflection in the context of ethical life exhibits tendencies akin to those in the logic of essence. Such reflection is also self-reflective and can destabilize, because it introduces unstable distinctions that parallel those between essence and seeming.

In ethical life, Hegel is particularly worried about the confusion that reflection generates, for he thinks that reflection can obscure the knowledge we as competent social participants have. It encourages us to discredit these unreflective modes of knowing and in this way makes us forget what we ordinarily know. This is why his own philosophical method will have the task of mending the rupture that reflection has created and of retrieving this knowledge while simultaneously showing it to be genuine knowledge. It can perhaps be described as reflection turned against itself, or reflection in the service of overcoming reflection. In a way it is nothing other than reflection completing its own mission of negating the negation or of restoring the "immediacy" that serves as our point of departure.[17] In the practical context this task has the upshot of bringing back into view that which reflection tends to abstract away

---

[17] This can be understood in terms of the Hegelian theme of "mediated immediacy" – an immediacy that is not naïve and untouched by mediation, but achieved through it.

from, namely, the objective rationality of ethical life – an objective rationality that is better reflected in our unreflective modes of engagement than in our reflective ones.

At the bottom of the demand for reflective acceptability seems to be a worry about conservatism. Although it is no longer fashionable to read Hegel as an advocate of "my station and its duties" or an apologist for the status quo, there is still an open question about how exactly to fortify Hegel against this damning verdict. One way has been to show that a social order must meet genuine normative requirements in order to count as objectively rational by his lights.[18] Another way has been to find room for *critical* reflection in this order, to show that Hegel does not mean to discourage us from critically interrogating the norms at work in ethical life. Since my focus will initially be on less reflective forms of social participation, the possibility of critique is a crucial question that I will have to address.

I.2 *Phenomenology of Spirit*

My interpretive approach is also in need of a defense. Since Hegel offers his account of a rational social order in the *Philosophy of Right*, it will provide the frame for this study. In other words, I am offering an interpretation first and foremost of his *Philosophy of Right*. But I want to show that this account benefits greatly from supplementation. I thus turn to other texts by Hegel, sometimes written at different times of his career, in order to complete this account. One prime example is precisely the role of habit in the *Philosophy of Right*. Although Hegel there insists that habit and second nature are central to ethical life, it is difficult to see how he can legitimately do so without first examining his definition of habit in "Subjective Spirit." Whenever one pulls from different texts, it is important to keep their systematic place in mind, since Hegel's system imposes constraints on any interpretation one wants to give of any part of it. His methodology makes it difficult to address a discrete set of problems without addressing them all. But it also makes it difficult to pull from different textual sources without making such an approach seem haphazard.

This issue arises especially for any effort to bring his *Phenomenology of Spirit* to bear on his system proper. The *Phenomenology* was Hegel's first published ambitious and unique systematic undertaking, but it was written at a relatively early point in his career, a point at which he had not yet developed in detail what later became his system. Hegel himself characterized this text

---

[18] Neuhouser (2000), for example, states that his book will raise "the more fundamental question concerning the nature of the normative criteria Hegel uses in judging that a particular set of institutions constitute[s] a rational social world" (3).

as serving an initiating role: because it tracks the "becoming of Science" it is meant to prepare his readership for the "scientific" point of view. It tells the story of the *Bildung* of consciousness (PR ¶78) and in this way contributes to our own *Bildung* achieved in the reading of it. After its publication, however, Hegel seems to have changed his mind about its exact place in what was to become his system. He ended up incorporating the first few chapters into his *Encyclopedia* under the heading of "Consciousness," demoting it from its status as a preamble to the system as a whole. And when in 1831 Hegel was asked to prepare a second edition of the *Phenomenology*, he soon gave up the task of rewriting it, noting "Peculiar work, not to be reworked" (GW 9:448). All of this makes it difficult to ascertain its relevance to later texts like the *Philosophy of Right*, which is articulated from what Hegel then took to be the properly "scientific" standpoint.

I will frequently turn to the *Phenomenology* in order to clarify aspects of the *Philosophy of Right*. I will do so in order to investigate Hegel's conception of culture and cultural participation, but also in order to examine Hegel's unique philosophical methodology. Even more controversially, I will turn to the *Phenomenology* in order to challenge certain verdicts that Hegel gives in the *Philosophy of Right*, in particular his conclusion that ethical life is contradiction-free and so invulnerable to critical contestation. In some cases I will stick to the letter of Hegel's text and demonstrate that the connections I am drawing reflect Hegel's official position. In other cases, specifically when dealing with critical reflection, I will admit that I am elaborating Hegel's position in a way that he might have been reluctant to endorse. But my aim here is not simply to clarify his own position on ethical life, so to present a view that the historical Hegel in fact espoused. Instead I hope to expose some tensions within his view that lead in a direction perhaps unanticipated by him, but one that is both warranted by his writings and worth exploring, even on independent grounds. In short, I am trying to reconstruct Hegel's view in a coherent and compelling way, but to do so by thinking through his project as he himself conceived of it.

One way to make Hegel's view attractive would be to show that it accords with intuitions that we bring to the table, or with philosophical positions that we find in current debates, in this way making him fit a contemporary mold. The worry with such approaches is that they do not take Hegel on his own terms, terms that have the potential to challenge our pre-philosophical and philosophically informed intuitions. Given Hegel's innovative framework, this would be a real shame. In this study I aim to tread the line between on one hand domesticating Hegel by finding analogs, drawing comparisons, and enlisting examples, and on the other hand "exoticizing" him by taking his peculiar vocabulary and alien ambitions on board. To paraphrase Hans-Georg Gadamer, genuine understanding can anyway only take place in the space between the familiar and the strange.

The relationship between the *Phenomenology of Spirit* and the *Philosophy of Right* presents a particular hermeneutic challenge. I will have to justify the connections I draw between the two texts at every step. But it is possible to cite a few general reasons in support of drawing such connections. Although the *Phenomenology* speaks to a wide range of issues, Hegel frames it as an investigation into knowledge, or "the actual cognition of what truly is" (PR¶73), as he tells us in the very first paragraph of the "Introduction." It is moreover an investigation into "appearances" of knowing. This means that Hegel is interested in the way in which knowledge has manifested or expressed itself, in claims to knowledge that have been (historically) made. But it also means that these manifestations and expressions are going to be revealed to be "mere" appearances because they will prove incapable of doing justice to that which they claim to manifest and express. Hegel calls these various conceptions of what it means to know "configurations," first of consciousness, and eventually of spirit. In the *Phenomenology* we are observing the self-undermining efforts of each configuration and noting its necessary progression to the next.

This might strike us as a very different endeavor from the *Philosophy of Right*, since the latter deals with actualized freedom, specifically with a rational social order. Thus it does not seem to be concerned with mere appearance of anything. Plus, its specific subject matter is the domain of right, so the norms governing relations among participants in such an order. But the two projects are not as disconnected as they seem. First, the question of knowledge is not absent from the latter text. As we have seen, subjective freedom is marked by *insight* into the good. And even though the *Phenomenology* tells a story about failures of knowledge, and so is concerned with frameworks that prove irreparably deficient, it sheds light on the function of experience in the attainment of genuine insight. Moreover, its final chapter is meant to offer a positive account of what it means to know. So the conclusions reached within the *Phenomenology* have at least the potential to bear on those reached within the *Philosophy of Right*. Second, the *Phenomenology* is tracking a developmental process, which can be described as the "actualization" of knowledge. Similarly, the *Philosophy of Right* is tracking the actualization of freedom, so the necessary development that conceptions of freedom must undergo in order to become "actual" in Hegel's technical sense. So the procedures of the two texts are not going to be as different as they seem.

Third, and perhaps most importantly, the *Phenomenology* foregrounds the role of reflection, specifically of self-reflection, in this process, and so can illuminate its relation to objective failure. What the *Phenomenology* reveals is the ways in which reflection is tacitly present in each configuration, even though its self-critical stance emerges as a response to contradictions between a commitment and its enactment. We might be inclined to think that the normative framework under scrutiny in the *Philosophy of Right* is going to differ radically from those found in the *Phenomenology*, since Hegel does not consider the former similarly contradictory. But, even though Hegel does not characterize it as a "configuration," ethical life shares the same structure as those found in the *Phenomenology*, especially in its "Spirit" chapter. It also includes a commitment to a measure (or *Maßstab*) that informs how we conduct ourselves and can thus be weighed against its own enactment. And as a configuration of *spirit*, its measure is already more complex and cannot be reduced to a single principle by which to evaluate all others. The particular difficulty that the *Philosophy of Right* faces is that the pertinent measure is not readily available for evaluation. So the very configuration that is embodied in ethical life requires philosophical excavation.

These points of comparison are simply meant to suggest that my interpretive approach has promise. In what follows I will have more to say about the object and strategy of the *Phenomenology* and its resemblance to those found in the *Philosophy of Right*. As I admitted, I will have to vindicate the connections I go on to make. I should also add that this study is only one piece in the much larger question about the relationship of the *Phenomenology* to Hegel's mature system. Given that readers tend to arrive at divergent pictures of Hegel's philosophical project depending on which text they privilege, it is a question that continues to loom large over Hegel scholarship and remains unexhausted.

I.3 Overview

I framed my study as an effort to understand the two ends of the spectrum of reflection, so to clarify what kind of relation to ethical life each of them involves. This study is divided into four chapters, each addressing an increasingly more demanding, and thus less inconspicuous form of reflection.

My first challenge will be to explain why Hegel privileges an unreflective relation to ethical life, in particular, why he wants to rehabilitate a habit of the ethical. Even if we accept that reflection is perilous in the way Hegel describes, we might nevertheless worry that habit can hardly present a preferable alternative. The question I need to address is whether habit is indeed in tension with the seeming benefits of reflection, specifically whether it is "blind," incapable of expressing a conviction in or insight into the goodness of social norms. Habit represents the thoroughly embedded perspective, one that Hegel describes as "simple identification" with ethical life. Those who inhabit ethical life, especially when they do so fully, typically do not reflect about the principles governing what they do. These principles have become their second nature. But Hegel is not merely making a sociological observation. He emphasizes habit, not because it is generally true of us that we as a matter of fact act habitually, rather than reflectively, but because he regards this as a positive ethical achievement, the attainment of subjective freedom. The first chapter will examine how Hegel arrives at this conclusion.

This chapter will address two central questions plaguing ethical habits: 1. How can habits ever be ethical? And 2. Why are we only fully virtuous when we have developed ethical habits? Answering these two questions will require going beyond the *Philosophy of Right* and taking a look at his "Anthropology," where he offers an explicit definition of habit. It will also require situating Hegel between the two alternatives with which he is clearly engaged. One is Kant, who disparages habit and dismisses its prospect to generate morally worthy actions. The other is Aristotle, who makes habituation integral to the cultivation of virtue. What I argue is that Hegel retains core elements from both positions. He wants to offer a conception of intelligent and insightful ethical habits that is suitable to a rational social order, whose complexity requires occasional recourse to principles of action. So even though habits are not "blind" for him, there are circumstances in which they are not sufficient either.

It would thus be a mistake to think that the embedded point of view that Hegel wants to grasp through philosophical comprehension is free from reflection altogether. One way to motivate Hegel's thought that some forms of reflection are an integral part of ordinary life in a rational social order is by considering what it takes for a rational social order to remain "alive." The English translation of *Sittlichkeit* is especially apt because it captures Hegel's concern with the *vitality* of ethical life. So a question worth raising is what kinds of relations to ethical life sustain its vitality and ensure its longevity. Part of the answer is habit, for Hegel thinks that a form of life comes to life, so to speak, precisely when its ethical laws have "struck root" in us, when they are incorporated into our second nature. But what we find is that habit can also usher in the death of ethical life. Hegel frequently characterizes a dead society in terms of "positivity," which suggests that its ethical laws have ossified and their adherents have grown indifferent to them, both of which seem to be potential side effects of successful habituation.

In the second chapter I turn to one form of reflection that is vital to ethical life, namely, that which is a part of cultural participation. Although cultural participation is largely habitual, it also introduces a reflective structure that opens a space for evaluation, though usually of an affirmative kind. In other words, by participating in a culture, we are perpetually affirming its customs and in this way sustaining our identification with them. But this affirmation is possible only because our participation in a culture both constitutes and reflects this culture. This means that cultural participation is more demanding than mere *immersion* in ethical life, though it does not conflict with it either. I investigate this reflective structure through Hegel's conception of *Bildung* in the *Phenomenology*, which illustrates the connection between individual cultivation and the formation of a shared culture and emphasizes that the cultural world is a *work*, one on which we continue to work.

The aim of this second chapter is to answer two sets of questions: 1. What is the proper relation to custom, on Hegel's view? And 2. Does his account of ethical life leave room for a plurality of customs? Both of these questions stem from divergent ways of reading Hegel's *Philosophy of Right*. His emphasis on custom has made him an inspiration to traditionalism, communitarianism, and pluralism. But he has also been read as someone who does not accommodate cultural diversity because he is delineating institutions that any rational order would have to contain, irrespective of cultural context. Although these are largely contemporary questions, they were not far from Hegel's own concerns. What I offer is a reconstruction of Hegel's conception of *Bildung* and its role in ethical life that shows how Hegel can accommodate multiple cultural identities without making them immune to challenge and change. This conception further elaborates the embedded point of view, since *Bildung* is a process of cultural participation that already takes place in ethical life, whenever we engage in productive activities within it.

The third chapter investigates another vital form of reflection in ethical life – namely, social critique. It addresses the extent to which critical reflection is possible or legitimate, even within a rational social order. What could occasion criticism and what resources are there for engaging in it? What I argue is that Hegel does not regard critical reflection as such to be impossible or illegitimate, although he also does not take it to be of unqualified value, worth undertaking even when we have no basis for suspecting that our social norms are ethically problematic. I suggest that we look to Hegel's conception of "immanent critique" in the *Phenomenology of Spirit* as a revisionary enterprise that is motivated by contradictions internal to a given practice and that evaluates this practice in light of its own standards, thereby leaving neither practice nor standard unscathed. It can thus be described as the process by which social participants are themselves reflectively responding to objective problems within the society they inhabit. And this form of reflection is not affirmative, serving to sustain identification with a given practices. It is critical, calling for a revision of the principles that have generated the contradiction in the first place. It is thus in fundamental tension with habit, since we cannot habitually perpetuate given practices and criticize them at the same time. If criticism is indeed warranted, then habit is no longer a viable option for us – not until the principles themselves have changed.

So my way of investigating the possibility of critique is indirect. Instead of looking for traces of critique in the *Philosophy of Right* itself, I focus on certain points of connection between this text and the *Phenomenology of Spirit*. Since the *Phenomenology*, specifically the "Spirit" chapter, explores the structure of social change, it sheds light on the connection between critical reflection and practical contradiction. Although Hegel famously concludes that modern ethical life does not generate the same kinds of contradictions as its predecessors, I show that occasions for critical reflection remain, even in a society that is on the whole rational. The prime example of a contradiction in ethical life is poverty, for poverty exposes a systematic impossibility of living up to the standards to which participation in the institution of civil society commits us.

I frame this study in terms of a contrast between the ordinary and the philosophical standpoint, indicating that they are not to be conflated, though they bear an important relation to each other. One significant difference between them has to do with this issue of critique. Even if it turns out that Hegel does think that we can and should criticize ethical life, he definitely does not think that philosophy ought to engage in this business in any direct way. The question that lingers is what philosophy has to offer those living inside ethical life and coping with its internal challenges at various reflective levels.

So the fourth and final chapter explores a form of reflection that cannot be described as *vital* to ethical life, though it has a valuable task – philosophical reflection. Arriving at an understanding of Hegel's conception of philosophical reflection is central to this study because it speaks to his entire project in the *Philosophy of Right* and so bears on each of the preceding chapters. Moreover, it represents the other end of the reflective spectrum, which Hegel characterizes as a conceptual grasp of the embedded point of view. I say that it is not a vital form of reflection in Hegel's eyes because he insists that he is not teaching social participants anything they do not already know. Its aim is limited to making the implicit explicit. So a question worth raising is why this project is worth undertaking, if Hegel is not offering any "new and unheard-of truths." What I propose is that Hegel's method in the *Phenomenology of Spirit*, which he identifies with "recollection," provides a helpful model because it shows how philosophical reflection can make a valuable contribution to ethical life merely by recalling knowledge that its participants already have. This clarifies the relation between the philosophical and the ordinary points of view and shows how the former is uniquely suitable to capturing the latter.

Giving an account of Hegel's methodology requires answering a number of pressing questions surrounding his project: 1. What does he mean by a "science of right" and in what ways is a "scientific" approach superior to a "theoretical" one? 2. Can Hegel's "science of right" be detached from his broader systematic ambitions? 3. What are Hegel's methodological constraints? In particular, why does he claim that conceptual comprehension sticks to the tenet that "what is rational is actual; and what is actual is rational"? And how does this conceptual comprehension of the rationality/actuality of ethical life manage to stay true to the embedded point of view, even though it does not necessarily coincide with the *opinions* of social participants? In order to answer these questions, it is important to keep in mind that Hegel is not simply assuming that the ordinary perspective must be authoritative. His method is instead meant to vindicate this perspective by showing that it does indeed do justice to the rationality of ethical life.

1   Habit

Among all of Hegel's purportedly necessary transitions, there seems to be something especially disconcerting about the one from "Morality" to "Ethical Life" in his *Philosophy of Right*. Although in this transition we first enter into an objectively rational social order (what Hegel calls *Sittlichkeit*), it seems to come at the expense of our previous subjective attitudes. Hegel defines the perspective distinctive of morality as the "reflection of the will into itself" (PR §105), and he traces the damaging consequences of such an ever more reflective withdrawal from the world of practices and institutions. Once we discover that it leaves us empty-handed, we are supposed to realize that we require objective criteria for determining principles of action, criteria that only a social order can provide. But we are also supposed to realize that we need a correspondingly new outlook as well. Hegel describes it in the following passage:

> But in the simple identification of individuals with actuality (*Wirklichkeit*), the ethical (*das Sittliche*) appears as their general manner of conduct (*allgemeine Handlungsweise*), as custom (*Sitte*) – the habit (*Gewohnheit*) of the ethical appears as a *second nature*, which is put in place of the first, purely natural will and which is the soul, meaning, and reality permeating its existence, spirit as a living and present world. (PR §151)

Strikingly enough, this outlook seems to retain little of the "moral" point of view, for it replaces reflection with something that is thought to be its antithesis: *habit*.

It is thus no surprise that this transition has given rise to a host of concerns. If Hegel is indeed privileging habit, does it mean he wants us to refrain from engaging in reflection altogether? And if so, how can this avoid amounting to a thoroughgoing immersion in social life? Such an immersion would not just be politically pernicious, cementing an unquestioning acceptance of the status quo. It would also seemingly represent regression to an earlier stage in history, perhaps to that of the Greeks, at least in the way Hegel himself characterized them. As Allen Wood remarks, "[the] ethical attitude seems primitive or immature by comparison with the reflective moral attitude with which Hegel often favorably contrasts it."[1] Though the Greek polis is admittedly one

---

[1] Wood (1993), 217.

of Hegel's inspirations for modern ethical life, Hegel would thereby be asking us to renounce one of our central values. Reflection is, after all, crucial to the modern self-understanding, as Hegel himself is well aware. In fact, he even praises his contemporaries for this "great obstinacy, an obstinacy that does honor to the human being, to refuse to acknowledge in attitude anything that has not been justified by thought – and this obstinacy is the characteristic of the modern age" (PR, 27).

As worrisome as these implications might seem, we would first need to get a clearer sense of what Hegel means by habit and of what contribution it is meant to make to ethical life before we are in a position to assess their depth and scope. My main aim in this chapter is to delineate Hegel's conception of habit with these questions in mind. I hope that it will dispel at least some worries, for I suspect that many of them derive from an assumed conception of habit, a conception I believe Hegel seeks to challenge. According to this conception, habit, even though it comprises our *second* nature, is nevertheless thought to make animals of us, for it replaces instinct with a new set of dispositions that are no less automatic and involuntary than those provided by our *first*. Human habits are thought to be similarly determined by mere behavioral dispositions without engaging the thought or will of the agent. When we act out of habit, we might be aware of what we are doing, for it is not as if we are sleepwalking. But we are not aware of why we are doing it, nor (more importantly) whether doing it is the right thing to do. Full-fledged insight, so the story goes, is won only through reflection. It is only when I pause to deliberate and consider that I am able to proceed in a "sighted" – namely, deliberate and considered – manner. To put this slightly differently, it is only when I have explicitly thought about what I ought to do that I am acting on norms I take to be good ones to uphold. Of course it is not a problem if some of our behavior becomes a matter of habit for us, like brushing one's teeth. It would, however, be a problem if ethically relevant actions were to become habitual and correspondingly "blind."

I am aware that challenging this picture will not dispel all worries, for some of them have more to do with reflection than with habit. Though reflection is often treated as if it were a single activity, it can take numerous forms that are, at least in this context, better kept apart. It might be right to say that all reflection is generally speaking an exercise in "abstraction," of distancing oneself from a given object in order to put oneself in a position to evaluate it. But this abstraction can take place on different levels. On one end of the spectrum is something like *deliberation* about what to do in a specific situation, namely, which principles to invoke and how to apply them in action. On the other end of the spectrum is something like *critique*, namely, a critical interrogation of those very principles or a questioning of their validity. The viability of critical reflection is clearly an important question that any reading of Hegel's *Philosophy of Right* will have to address. I will return to it in the third chapter.

But habit seems to be most overtly in tension with reflection as deliberation, for it looks like I cannot simultaneously act out of habit and pause to deliberate about how to proceed.

Although Hegel does not speak in terms of blindness, there is an analog within his own vocabulary, for "immediacy" seems similar and similarly worrisome. One could say that something is immediate for Hegel if it is given in a brute way. This can mean that it simply has not yet been reflectively endorsed by me and so remains immediate so long as it does not yet express my thought or will. For example, I might acquire many characteristics long before I am in a position to evaluate them, and these would remain immediate until I do. And this condition would be overcome as soon as I do evaluate and endorse them. But there seems to be another level of immediacy that speaks to the problem of habit more directly. Something is immediate, even if I can (and do) reflectively endorse it, if it does not actively engage my thought or will. So even habits of which I do approve would continue to count as immediate in this second sense. What makes them immediate is the absence of the needed distinction between them and me when enacting them. The thought here is that I cannot adequately distance myself from what determines how I behave, at least not in the moment of action, even if it is retrospectively possible for me to adopt a reflective perspective on what I did, even reflectively to endorse it.

One might suppose that Hegel has this latter sense of immediacy in mind when he describes habit as a "simple identification" with ethical life, where simplicity suggests an absence of distinction or "mediation." To identify with ethical life is to identify with my particular social role in it. And to say that my identification with my social role is simple is to say that I do not draw a line between it and myself and conceive of myself without it. Most importantly, this identification is kept simple by habit, since those who act out of habit cannot help but enact the demands of their social roles, whatever these happen to be, because such demands have become entrenched in tendencies to meet them. Here a comparison with animals might be instructive because we tend to think of their behavior as paradigmatically blind when we assume that they are not following norms at all, but acting out of natural instinct. Their behavior could count as blind at the most elementary level, since animals do not seem to be aware of why they are doing what they do. Even when animal behavior displays regularities, it is not because animals are deliberately adhering to laws. But animal behavior would certainly count as blind at a higher level, given that animals do not conceive of what they are doing as the right (or the wrong) thing to do. Another way to put this would be to say that animal behavior is not guided by any kind of "insight" at all, let alone insight into the good.

It is, however, far from clear whether Hegel could be alluding to immediacy of this kind when he characterizes habit as a "simple identification." The problem is that, if habit proves to be so immediate, Hegel would be in deep trouble, because he would have to deny that participation in ethical life could ever count as relevantly *ethical*. Such participatory behavior would in that case not be norm-governed at all, let alone governed by norms that we take to be good ones to uphold. This seems to me to be a bullet that Hegel would clearly never bite. Even though he abandons a strictly moral standpoint on action, he claims that his account of ethical life can accommodate a notion of *virtue*, which he sometimes refers to as the "ethical disposition" (*sittliche Gesinnung*). He moreover suggests that this disposition must incorporate true conscience, which is characterized by insight into the good, without which it would fall short of subjective freedom. So he needs to be able to square these two claims, namely, to show that the habitual comportment he so privileges could be regarded as a manifestation, not just of trained patterns of behavior, but also of a specifically ethical "frame of mind."[2]

Hegel goes one step further when he suggests an even bolder thesis: not just that virtue could take the form of habit, though it could take other forms as well, but that virtue *is* habit. I take this to be implied by the previously cited passage (PR §151), in which Hegel identifies the ethical and the habitual. Hegel goes beyond conceding that what we do out of habit can, under certain circumstances, count as ethical conduct. His claim is rather that we cannot be ethical without habit, that we cannot be regarded as virtuous unless acting ethically is something we habitually do. Virtue for him seems positively to require a habit of the ethical as its fullest expression.

So this habit of the ethical presents us with two puzzles. First, how is it possible for the ethical ever to appear in the form of habit, or how can our habitual conduct ever count as an expression of virtue? Second, why must the ethical appear in the form of habit, or why is it only our habitual conduct that counts as an adequate expression of virtue? Both of these puzzles have to my knowledge remained undetected.[3] The common strategy for defending Hegel on this front is to point out that he ascribes a habit of the ethical only to those who already inhabit ethical life, which he thinks is an objectively rational social order.[4] For

---

[2] This is the translation of *Gesinnung* that Neuhouser recommends. See Neuhouser (2000), 85 (2n).

[3] One exception is Goldstein (2004), though I do not see how he resolves the puzzle. He does state that "despite the appearance of unreflective obedience, Hegel's conception of habit [involves] ... a robust self-awareness that integrates modes of knowing from Kantian duty to ancient virtue to modern rectitude" (483). But all he can show is how habit preserves the content of duty, virtue, and rectitude, not how habit itself can be regarded as an expression of knowledge.

[4] Some commentators have tried to argue that §151 describes agents who have not yet reached maturity. For example, Lewis (2008) calls this "pre-reflective ethical life," arguing that the "individual begins in immediate identification with ethical life as an existing system of customs and values," before moving on to reflect on them (38). Similarly, Wood (1993) interprets Hegel's claim that in habit spirit becomes present in the world as implying "that spirit also exists in other, later, more developed forms" (198). But as Franco (1999) has pointed out, "there is little evidence ... to suggest that Hegel means this passage to be understood in this

example, as Ido Geiger qualifies, "Hegel holds that such immediate action is moral, if its agent has been acculturated within a just society."[5] But this does not yet explain why Hegel thinks it is better, even if only for those inside a just society, to act in this immediate way. Nor does it explain how Hegel can hold this view without conceiving of "immediate" action in a significantly different way. The best it can do is to point out that Hegel is not recommending that we make a habit out of heeding unjust laws.

There has been a more promising strategy for making sense of Hegel's position, according to which habit is supposed to address the issue of motivation. To be more exact, habituation has the central function, not of making our conduct habitual per se, but of reforming our inclinations to accord with our duties. In this way it provides us with additional motives for doing what we know we ought to do. As Fred Neuhouser puts this, "The force of Hegel's emphasis on habit is to make a point about how socially free individuals are motivationally constituted – that their desires, dispositions, and values are formed by their upbringing such that their social participation is largely spontaneous, or 'comes naturally' to them."[6] This interpretive approach has significant advantages, for it does not require that we think of ethical conduct itself as a matter of habit. In other words, our activity could still be preceded by deliberation and in this way directed by our thought and will. What habit adds is a new set of desires to do our duty and so allows us to find sensuous satisfaction in acting ethically.

Such a reading would also fit quite well into a tradition to which Hegel is evidently alluding. Hegel clearly means to channel Aristotle, who likewise grants habit a significant place in his account of virtue.[7] According to Aristotle, we learn what we ought to do through instruction, whereas habituation targets the non-rational part of the soul and makes it receptive to the dictates of the rational part[8] by instilling what are usually translated as "virtues of character."[9]

---

developmental way" (230). I agree with Franco that Hegel gives us every reason to believe that he is here talking about fully formed ethical agents. What we find within the chapter of "Ethical Life" is not a kind of development in which the earlier characterizations of the free will are fundamentally challenged and substantially revised. It is a characterization that Hegel subsequently elaborates, not abandons. The clearest example of this is what Hegel calls patriotism or the political disposition, which he defines in §268 as a "a willing that has become a habit."

[5] Geiger (2007), 3.

[6] Neuhouser (2000), 112. Alznauer has more recently (and more strongly) argued that ethical actions are, for Hegel, evaluated according to whether they are motivated by a "habitual disposition to act in accord with [one's] role" (2015, 111). This would mean that Hegel is, like Kant, evaluating actions according to their corresponding motive. But, unlike Kant, for him, the right motive would be a habitual disposition: "An action is only truly ethical when it immediately and habitually conforms to the rational customs of ethical life: when the individual takes his own will to be inseparable from the duties that flow from his station in the social whole" (112/113).

[7] For studies of Aristotle's influence on Hegel, see Ferrarin (2001) and Ilting (1963–1964).

[8] Aristotle describes it as the non-rational part's capacity to "listen" to reason "as if to one's father" (*Nicomachean Ethics* 1103a4).

[9] *Ethike arete*, in Greek.

In this way habit cultivates the right kinds of desires and allows us to take pleasure in the right sorts of things. And even though we would also need to cultivate "intellectual virtues" to become virtuous in the full sense, habituation is nevertheless assigned an indispensable task from the perspective of ethical upbringing because it instills in us the basic dispositions that can then be intelligently enacted. Thus Aristotle concludes that "it does not make a small difference whether people are habituated to behave in one way or in another way from childhood on, but a very great one; or rather, it makes all the difference in the world."[10]

There are good grounds for thinking that Hegel wants to appropriate these elements of Aristotle's theory, for he clearly disparages the austerity of the Kantian picture, according to which we ought to act solely out of a sense of duty, irrespective of whether our desires are thereby satisfied. It is worth noting that Kant objects to habituation in part because he thinks it generates inclinations so conducive to morality that they could usurp the motive of duty. This suggests that Kant also regards habit as giving shape to the so-called nonrational part of us. At the same time, I am not persuaded that Hegel appeals to habit in order to rehabilitate inclination as an appropriate source of motivation. Even if reforming our inclinations is one benefit of habit, I do not think that in Hegel's estimation this comprises its primary contribution. Habituation possesses for Hegel a far more rational task, so to speak, for it bears directly on our claims to ethical knowledge in the first place. In short, Hegel holds that we cannot be said to know our duty unless we demonstrate a commitment to doing it, and we only demonstrate such a commitment through the habit of the ethical. So it is habituation that brings about the frame of mind Hegel associates with the ethical disposition, and it is habituation that brings about the kind of insight we are after, so the very insight we thought habit was doomed to exclude.

Because there is another appropriation of Aristotle that shares numerous features with the view I am ascribing to Hegel, it will be important to keep Hegel's enduring Kantian commitments in mind. In his paper "Virtue and Reason," John McDowell puts forward a highly compelling variation of virtue ethics that casts habit in a similarly rational role. According to McDowell, virtue is best thought of, not as a collection of blind dispositions, but as a perceptiveness in the face of situational requirements that provide us with reasons for action. This perceptiveness (a *sensitivity*, as he calls it) is moreover manifest, not in explicit deliberation about what to do, but in one's immediate responsiveness to those requirements. Even when I act unreflectively, I can be acting in an intelligent manner, so long as I have a clear vision of the situation in which I find myself. And it is my upbringing that is largely responsible for the

---

[10] Aristotle, *Nicomachean Ethics* 1103b24–26.

clarity of my vision. Although this conception of virtue overlaps with Hegel's in significant respects, it diverges from his as well, for Hegel insists that the relevant insight must be explicable in terms of principles, which is something McDowell overtly denies. I will eventually turn to Hegel's reasons for this insistence.

I begin, however, with the more interpretive task of explicating the habit of the ethical in Hegel's own work. It is especially surprising, I think, that Hegel's official account of habit in his "Anthropology"[11] has not been brought to bear on his rather elliptical remarks in the *Philosophy of Right*.[12] As we will see, this "anthropological" account does introduce difficulties of its own, for it seems on the face of it to confirm the picture of habit as essentially blind. So I admit that we might not see its connection to the habit of the ethical at first sight, and that drawing such a connection can even make matters worse, for here Hegel explicitly characterizes habit as "immediate" in the problematic sense. But a closer look at this account does reveal habit to be capable of a more complicated structure. In his "Anthropology" we discover a form of habit that is sighted in a way that the habit of the ethical would have to be in order to be ethical in the first place.

In the following my aim will be to resolve both puzzles and so disambiguate the habit of the ethical and clarify the basis of its centrality in modern ethical life. I will begin by motivating the kind of difficulty that habit seems to pose for Hegel, especially in light of his anthropological account. I will do this by bringing his account in dialog with Kant's, which is explicitly developed from a "pragmatic point of view," and so with a view to the ethical contribution of habit as such. I will then offer a reconstruction of Hegel's critique of morality in order to set the stage for his introduction of the ethical disposition. As this critique will show, Hegel means to honor what he calls the right of the subjective will and he holds that the ethical disposition can satisfy this right. I will then explain what Hegel means by the ethical disposition and why he thinks that only habit can adequately express such a disposition. Finally, I will return

---

[11] This text is not self-standing, but comprises a subsection of "Subjective Spirit" in his *Encyclopedia of the Philosophical Sciences*. The *Encyclopedia* is meant to serve as the comprehensive exposition of Hegel's "system," and so incorporates the subject matter of the *Philosophy of Right* as well, in the later division called "Objective Spirit," albeit in abbreviated form.

[12] Two papers draw this connection. Lewis (2008) relates Hegel's discussion of habit in the "Anthropology" to the role of habit in ethical life, but he nevertheless associates it with "pre-reflective ethical life" that requires a further transition from habit to freedom. Forman in "Second Nature and Spirit" notes a possible comparison between habits of skill discussed in the "Anthropology" and ethical habits. But he also concludes by suggesting that the habit of the ethical is likewise a stage that needs to be surpassed. This is precisely what I want to deny. So in the end they both read the "Anthropology" rather differently than I will, and do not draw my lessons from it for habit in the *Philosophy of Right*.

to habit in the "Anthropology" in order to question whether the account he gives in that context really poses the kind of difficulty it seemed to on a first reading. Although I hope to show that the difficulty can be resolved and that the habit of the ethical can assume its central place in the modern social order, I will conclude by returning to some of the dangers that we might think even the habit of the ethical so conceived could never completely shed. Despite his optimism, Hegel seems to be well aware of them and traces them back to the proximity between habit and death.

1.1 Pragmatic Point of View

The habit of the ethical has encountered few harsher critics than Kant, who denies in no uncertain terms that habit could ever become ethical. As he puts it in his *Anthropology from a Pragmatic Point of View*, "as a rule all habits are reprehensible"[13] and so unsuitable to the ends of ethical living. Given the central tenets of his moral theory, especially the significance he places on autonomy, this verdict is not all that surprising. As Kant sees it, habit is "a physical inner necessitation to proceed in the same manner that one has proceeded until now,"[14] and so introduces a compulsion inimical to free activity. When a certain activity becomes habitual, it falls outside our immediate control and so ceases to be relevantly up to us. In other words, we are no longer choosing our own course of action and so are no longer fully in charge of what we do. As this preliminary characterization already shows, one need not subscribe to Kant's robust conception of autonomy in order to see the problem, for habit would appear to be incompatible with freedom in a fairly ordinary sense. When I act out of habit, I seem to no longer be following norms at all, irrespective of whether or not these norms stem from my rational nature. To put this in Kantian terms, I am no longer acting on a conception of the law, even though to an observer my behavior is likely to look exceptionally law-abiding.[15]

Although Kant speaks critically about habit as such, he is particularly concerned to deny that virtue can stand in any relation to habit, let alone require it. As he puts it in the *Anthropology*, "virtue is moral strength in adherence to one's duty, which never should become habit but should always emerge entirely new and original from one's way of thinking,"[16] adding that habit

---

[13] Kant, *Anthropology from a Pragmatic Point of View*, 7:149.
[14] Ibid., 7:147 and 7:149.
[15] I have the following passage in mind: "Everything in nature works according to laws. Only a rational being has the capacity to act in accordance with the representation of laws, that is, in accordance with principles" (Kant, *Groundwork of the Metaphysics of Morals*, 4:412).
[16] Kant, *Anthropology*, 7:147.

"deprives even good actions of their moral worth before it impairs the freedom of the mind."[17] His unyielding stance is clearly intended to be a response to Aristotle, who regards habit as integral to a virtuous life. Though some have attempted to stress its significance,[18] virtue does not seem to occupy a central place in Kant's official theory, mainly because he does not think it provides a criterion by which to evaluate the moral worth of an action. Each action is to be evaluated on the basis of its corresponding motive, and not on the basis of one's overall character. But Kant does think he can give an account of virtue that fits his theory: virtue would have to be moral *strength* in adherence to one's duty, a strength that persists from one action to another and lends consistency to the series of discrete deeds. Although Kant does not put it in quite these terms, one could say that for him one attains the requisite strength by becoming "principled." Virtue for him would then amount to nothing more and nothing less than consistent adherence to principles.[19]

As I mentioned, Kant's objection to habit on this score is frequently tied to his rather ascetic picture of moral motivation, according to which duty alone ought to motivate action. If habituation is meant to incline us to act morally, it can never supplant the motive of duty without robbing our dutiful actions of moral worth. Admittedly, this does not yet mean that we should instead do nothing to rid ourselves of inclinations to act immorally, inclinations that directly conflict with duty and compete with its influence on our will. In that case, habituation could plausibly play a negative role of eradicating wayward desires, or at least lessening their power over us, without cultivating better desires in their stead.[20] But even if we concede that habituation can contribute to the ends of ethics by disciplining our inclinations and so moderating the friction they impose, it is still clear that habit could never issue in actions of moral worth. Given Kant's conception of habit as a physical inner necessitation to proceed in the same manner as before, any attempt to turn principles into habits would amount to giving

---

[17] Ibid., 7:149.
[18] See, for example, Herman (2007).
[19] It might be confusing to talk of a plurality of principles in Kant's case, for he seems to be interested only in one principle: the moral law. At the same time, he suggests that all action, even action that is morally impermissible, is guided by rules that can be articulated as *maxims*. As Patricia Kitcher (2003) has shown, maxims for Kant must possess a certain rule-like form already if they are to be measured by the master principle of the categorical imperative, which asks whether the rule they contain could become a law.
[20] As Robert Stern (2012) provocatively argues, Kant seems to think that the very concept of duty hinges on a friction with inclination that is responsible for the experience of necessitation distinctive of morality. We are not and should not aspire to be holy wills, wills that face no temptation to do anything other than what is right and good. Since holy wills are not subject to imperatives in the first place, the categorical imperative so central to morality has no grip on them. See especially his responses to Baxley and Korsgaard (230–235).

up on principles altogether by stripping them of their role as conscious and deliberate guides of our conduct.[21]

While Hegel clearly wants to shed numerous dualisms at the basis of Kant's theory, including the dualism between the motives of duty and inclination, he cannot easily escape the problem Kant believes confronts the habit of the ethical. Whatever inspiration he may have found in Aristotle's theory, Hegel remains concerned with the possibility of freedom and regards it as central for ethical life. Freedom for Hegel is a multifaceted ideal that involves a twofold structure, for it contains an objective as well as a subjective component. We are objectively free when we inhabit a rational social order, one whose instituted norms are as a matter of fact good, and he argues that inside this order we do not need to apply the categorical imperative (or any other inward measure) in order to figure out what to do. But even if we are lucky enough to inhabit such an order, we must also be subjectively free, namely, we must *grasp* these instituted norms *as* good.[22] As we will see in more detail, this is an aspect of the "moral" perspective that Hegel clearly does not want to abandon.

Although subjective freedom in this sense is not exclusively a matter of motivation, it does bear on why I am doing what I do. One might say that Hegel rejects the dualism of duty and inclination not because he denies that they can be conceptually distinguished or that they can practically conflict. Rather, he rejects this dualism because he deems it a product of excessive abstraction.[23] As an agent acting within a rational social order, I am moved *neither* by considerations of duty *nor* by those of inclination, but by the rational social order itself, specifically by the demands of my roles with in. Granted, I probably do not have the social order as a whole in mind whenever I act, and sustaining it is rarely my conscious reason for enacting my role within it. But because the survival of this order is at stake in each of its official institutions, even in many of its informal practices, I am faced with it in the largely mundane situations in which I find myself.[24] It is the universal manifested concretely. So someone

---

[21] Interestingly enough, the problem is not that habit would make *holy* wills of ours. In fact, it is quite the opposite. As he puts it, "the reason why the habits of another stimulate the arousal of disgust in us is that here the animal in the human being jumps out far too much, and that here one is led *instinctively* by the rule of habituation, exactly like another (non-human) nature, and so runs the risk of falling into one and the same class with the beast" (Kant, *Anthropology from a Pragmatic Point of View*, 7:149).

[22] Hegel identifies this as the "right of subjectivity," which he defines as the requirement "that whatever [the subjective will] should recognize as valid, be seen [*eingesehen*] by it as good" (PR §132). I will say more about this requirement in the discussion of the Morality chapter.

[23] As we will see, Hegel does not abandon talk of duty, but he characterizes duty as "a liberation ... from the burden [one] labors under as a particular subject in moral reflections on ought and can" (PR §149).

[24] If I believe that the survival of my institution (say, the university) *depends* on *my* participation, am I not wrong about this? Is it not the case that this institution would survive, even if I ceased to participate in it? But what I am describing here is not meant to be a piece of consequentialist

who is subjectively free "does not have the self-consciousness of [her] own particularity, but has it only in the universal. This must be done, so I want to do it – for the sake of the thing (*die Sache*), not for my own sake, must the thing be done" (VRP, 291). According to Hegel, it is *die Sache* that moves me to act, and not any representation I might have about what duty demands or what I wish I could do instead. If my attitude is appropriately outward-directed, this tension simply does not show up for me. And *die Sache* refers to that which is at stake in the specific situations that confront me day in and day out. It is both particular and universal: particular because it involves the specifics of the situation in which I find myself (including the specifics of my own ends circumscribed by my institutional roles), and universal because in those specifics I am able to discern requirements imposed by the rational social order as a whole. In doing my part, I implicitly affirm the goodness of the society in which I participate. *Die Sache* incorporates both dimensions because it is something that is at stake for me as well as for the social order I am thereby helping sustain.[25]

Even this mere sketch provides clues to Hegel's alternative proposal. It shows that Hegel is critical of the kind of "mediation" that both considerations of inclination and duty introduce, for choosing either requires that we step back from the situation that is calling us to act and preoccupy ourselves with our inner lives. But it also shows that Hegel cannot be recommending that acting ethically becomes so automatic that we are no longer acting for the sake of anything, let alone *die Sache*.[26] For Hegel, ethical action requires that we grasp what we are doing as good. So Hegel inherits the problem that the habit of the ethical presents, even if he does not want to take Kant's moral theory, especially its conception of motivation, on board. It is thus especially striking that Hegel also defines habit along the lines of a physical inner necessitation, calling it a "mechanism."[27] This is for Hegel the lowest form of natural necessity, one that is even lower than the necessity determining the behavior of mere organisms, and must be most distant from the requirements of freedom.

Hegel's account of habit is a part of his version of an "Anthropology." There are some notable differences between the purposes of the two texts, since

---

reasoning, since such reasoning (especially when motivated by a desire to exempt myself from participation) is already the product of abstraction. If these are the sorts of questions that I am asking myself – whether I should continue doing what I am doing – then I have ceased to identify fully with my social role. Hegel thinks that I participate in certain institutions so long as I take them to be good ones to uphold, even if reflection might reveal to me that my *individual* participation is not necessary for their continuation.

[25] It is worth noting that this topic of *die Sache* is already to be found in the *Phenomenology* in the chapter titled "The Spiritual Animal Kingdom and Deceit, or the 'Matter in Hand' Itself."

[26] This attention to (and knowledge of) *die Sache* is also a feature of conscience in the *Phenomenology* (¶642), which goes to underscore that conscience is preserved in habit.

[27] Hegel claims that "habit is a determination of feeling, as well as intelligence and will, that has been made natural and mechanical" (Enz. III §410).

Hegel's "Anthropology" is meant to play a much more systematic role than Kant's.[28] But there are some less conspicuous similarities as well. One peculiar feature of Kant's *Anthropology from a Pragmatic Point of View* is that it is written from a "pragmatic point of view," so with a view to the ethical advantages and disadvantages of human nature. Kant defines pragmatic knowledge of the human being as "the investigation of what *he* as a free-acting being makes of himself, or can and should make of himself."[29] In short, his Anthropology is not inspired by a neutral interest in natural facts about us, but investigates the extent to which those facts can positively assist the ends of ethics.[30] Although Hegel's "Anthropology" has the official task of explaining the transition from nature to spirit, specifically the emergence of a conscious relationship to the world, it is also guided by a similar question, for Hegel is focusing on those human capacities that, even if they enable the initial stages of our subjective development, are only fully realized in ethical life – the province of "Objective Spirit" in his *Encyclopedia*. He insists repeatedly that the relevant forms of subjectivity remain mere forms until they are filled with an objective content, which only ethical life can provide. The question then becomes which forms are more suitable to this content than others.[31]

Moreover, Hegel points out that the placement of the Anthropology (or of Subjective Spirit as a whole) cannot avoid seeming one-sided, for Subjective Spirit and Objective Spirit are two sides of the same coin. In his words, "One could say just as well that spirit is at first objective and should become subjective, as that spirit is at first subjective and has to make itself objective. Consequently the difference of subjective and objective spirit is not to be seen as rigid" (PS: §387A).[32] Part of Hegel's argument is that "Subjective Spirit" anticipates what he calls "Objective Spirit" and so can only become fully realized within the social context it provides. This suggests that his Anthropology has the additional task, not only of clarifying how we develop the subjective

---

[28] "If the Kantian Anthropology had been lost or never written, the Kantian metaphysic of knowledge would remain essentially unimpaired. If Hegel's Anthropology had been lost, the foundation would be missing in the logical structure of Subjective Spirit, which is an important part of Hegel's metaphysic of knowledge" (Greene 1972, IX).

[29] Kant, *Anthropology*, 3.

[30] Kant differentiates between practical and pragmatic knowledge. Practical knowledge is knowledge about what is constitutive of ethics, so knowledge of what our duties are and our motives ought to be. Pragmatic knowledge is knowledge about what can be useful to ethics, even if it is not constitutive of it.

[31] Here the distinction between pragmatic and practical is not as relevant, for Hegel does not think that these forms are only instrumentally valuable for the end of ethics.

[32] As I will discuss at greater length in Chapter 4, this comment is consistent with Hegel's broader methodological commitments to the circularity of his system. Because the story he is telling is not only a developmental one, but also reveals ever-deeper conditions for what comes before, it could also have been rewritten by starting with the conclusion and working backward to the beginning.

capacities necessary for a conscious relation to the objective world, but also how we can succeed in turning this objective world into something *subjective* in turn, something with which we identify, which we have incorporated, and to which we are committed.

Despite these broad similarities to Kant's Anthropology, the particular place of the "Anthropology" chapter in Hegel's *Encyclopedia* as a whole must be kept in mind, for this chapter is supposed to contribute to a larger story tracking the development of a self-conscious I out of the shortcomings of the feeling soul, a developmental stage that we share with other animals. This means that habit is here viewed from a specific systematic vantage point, one that could potentially limit its ethical relevance. To be more precise, Hegel is interested in the contribution habit makes to our emergence out of mere nature. Indeed, most of his examples are of habits that help us cope with our natural surroundings, rather than those that might help us navigate our social world. He also uses examples of habits that even animals develop, suggesting that habituation is not a distinctly human transformation. In fact, habit is already introduced at the end of his preceding "Philosophy of Nature." This has led some, such as Catherine Malabou, to challenge the very distinction between first and second nature, arguing that "the account developed here shows that, for Hegel, nature is always *second nature*." She goes on to raise the question, "If all animals are habituated animals, how do we distinguish the boundaries of that exemplary living being called man?"[33] Such concerns raise doubts about whether this anthropological account is going to be able to shed light on what Hegel means by the habit of the ethical. Nevertheless, I do not think that its placement within the *Encyclopedia* makes it irrelevant for our purposes, since Hegel does claim to be delineating the very form of habit, one that is ultimately independent of its initially natural content and can eventually come to bear an ethical content as well.

1.2 Habit in the "Anthropology"

Hegel's anthropological account of habit is being introduced at a crucial juncture, namely, as a solution to the madness accompanying "self-feeling." According to Hegel's narrative, self-feeling develops out of the feeling soul, which was completely passive with respect to its sensations, by engaging in the activity of taking up some of its feelings at the expense of others. The way that Hegel characterizes it is that, as self-feeling, I am identifying myself wholly with one feeling (or a handful of feelings) in particular, and so ignore the fact that it or they are particular. This exclusive identification with some particular

---

[33] Malabou (2005), 57.

feelings can have pathological consequences, because it can lead to fixation and delusion. The self-feeling soul is thus prone to fixate on one emotional attachment in an exaggerated and damaging way, or on one perception without putting it in an objective context and allowing it to be judged against other perceptions. For Hegel, this amounts to madness, or "sleeping while awake" [*wachend träumen*] (Enz. III §408A). Hegel goes so far as to call madness a "contradiction" at the heart of self-feeling (Enz. III §408), a contradiction between the particularity of the feeling and the exclusivity of my identification. If this feeling I am having is just one feeling among others, it does not merit this kind of single-minded devotion, and it is contradictory to treat it as if it were absolutely authoritative and exhaustive.

Habit emerges as a cure for madness because it achieves the two goals that are driving this developmental process: it introduces stability into my feelings and thus paves the way for perceptual consciousness[34] and allows me to become individuated, to gain a sense of self. The way it achieves these aims is by significantly changing our relationship to our feelings, and by extension to the body as a whole. He defines habit in the following way:

Habit is the soul making itself into an abstract universal being and reducing the particularity of feeling to a mere determination of it. In this way the soul has the content in its possession and preserves [this content] in it, so that it is not sensitive [*empfindend*] in its determinations, not indistinguishable in its relation to them nor immersed in them, but has them in it in an insensitive [*empfindungslos*] and unconscious [*bewusstlos*] manner and moves within them. [The soul] is free from them to the extent to which it is not interested in them or preoccupied with them; by existing in these forms as its possession, [the soul] is simultaneously open for further activity and occupation – of sensation as well as of spiritual consciousness in general. (Enz. III §410)

Habit represents an advance because it permits a different kind of self-relation, for it is habit that first introduces the distinction between my self and my feelings, and so reduces them to the level of "determinations." They are now no longer *me*, but *mine*.[35] Whatever this self-relation ultimately amounts to, Hegel is very clear that it is first achieved through the process of habituation.

In fact, Hegel seems to be far more interested in this process itself than in its result. And it is not difficult to see why he might be, for habituation is unequivocally a kind of activity, an active molding through repetition and practice, and so a deliberate effort to take possession of my own body and make it conform more effectively to my will. Although habituation is not always intentionally undertaken, habituating myself does require the exercise of my intellect and the conscious control of my movements and limbs. Through

---

[34] For an excellent account of the role of habit in perceptual consciousness, see Forman (2010).
[35] McCumber (1990), 158.

practice and repetition, I alter some of my natural determinations (by learning to stand upright) as well as give myself new determinations, produced by me (by learning, say, to fashion a spear). This makes habituation a "spiritual" process, which means that it is mediated by my thought and my will. Hegel even announces at this rather early stage that "the form of habit encompasses all sorts and stages of the activity of spirit" (E §410), suggesting that habituation is the paradigmatic spiritual activity and that all others will eventually emulate its basic structure.[36]

The result of this process is, however, a more ambiguous matter. So let me begin with one of its benefits that Hegel singles out as being of lasting value. Hegel states that, at the most basic level at least, "habit possesses the greatness to be freed from that to which one is habituated" (Enz III, §410). He is thinking of habituation as a process of liberation, of emancipation from our prior imprisonment in first nature, and so understands its enduring contribution in primarily negative terms. In particular, habits free us from the overwhelming and maddening imposition of sensations, from the distracting effects of drives and desires, and even from the mental exertion involved in acquiring skills like learning how to carve and throw a spear.[37] In this respect, habit can even contribute to activities of a higher sort, though only indirectly. By eliminating these extraneous sources of imposition, distraction, and exertion, it clears our attention for more cerebral matters, like philosophy.[38]

There is a further benefit, which might be even more valuable, though also more difficult to capture. As Hegel's very definition indicates, habituation introduces a new self-relation made possible through a laborious effort to differentiate myself from my determinations. In this way it seems to establish a potentially *reflective* relation that I might adopt toward that which determines me. Unfortunately, we are at most actively reflecting while we are in the process of forming habits. Once these are fully formed, we no longer need to

---

[36] As I read this remark, spirit is characterized by the activity of self-determination, and this activity is presumably most vivid when I am compelled to abstract away from what was given to me in order to earn my identification with it. Habituation positively requires both of these acts – of abstraction and of identification – from me, and is for this reason paradigmatic.

[37] Hegel distinguishes between three types of habits – habits of hardening (*Abhärtung*), specifically to sensations; habits of indifference (*Gleichgültigkeit*), specifically toward the satisfaction of desires; and habits of skill (*Geschicklichkeit*). I will return to this taxonomy later.

[38] For example: "[Habit] is free from them [sensations, etc.] insofar as it is not interested in and preoccupied with them; by existing in these forms as its possession, it is likewise open to further activity and occupation – of sensation as well as of the consciousness of spirit" (Enz. III §410). Hegel explicitly mentions the dependence of philosophy on habit in his Addition to §151 of the *Philosophy of Right*, when he writes that "habit belongs to the ethical just as it belongs to philosophical thinking, since the latter demands that spirit be cultivated against arbitrary ideas and that these be eliminated and overcome so that rational thinking can have free reign."

reflect about what we are doing, even if it were true that we remain no less capable of doing so. In fact Hegel's main point is that habit makes us capable of reflection to the extent that it creates a difference between me and my determinations, making them mine (rather than *me*). One way to think about this is that we become responsible for our habits in a way that we were not for our feelings prior to habituation. In discovering that our nature is malleable and that we can shape it in active ways – that our nature is not our fate – we now must take credit for who we have become, for better or for worse.

But habitual behavior does not seem to be Hegel's primary concern in this chapter. His taxonomy divides habits into three categories – those that strengthen us against sensations, those that make us indifferent to our desires, and skills – of which only the last contains habits that manifest themselves in anything like activity. One of the reasons why Hegel is especially concerned with these "negative" habits (as I call those of the first two categories) has to do with their unequivocally liberating function, since it is they that free up our consciousness without impinging on it in turn. As Hegel puts it, the soul is "free from [its determinations] insofar as it is not interested and occupied with them" (Enz. III §410). This is especially true of those habits that fortify our bodies, like the hardening of the skin to cold temperatures, but also of those that lessen the force of our natural desires like thirst or hunger. In both cases, we become so accustomed to something that we cease to notice it, thus banishing it from our minds.[39] And Hegel's point is that such habits are able to free up our consciousness precisely because they are themselves "unconscious" (*bewusstlos*).

As far as "negative" habits go, this strikes me as a relatively unproblematic claim, but is this true of habitual activities, so of "positive" habits, as well? Hegel argues that even skills must be partly unconscious in order to fulfill their own liberating function. In learning a skill, we initially need to pay a great deal of attention to what we are doing, but we truly possess a skill only when we can go on (nearly) automatically. For example, someone who is first learning how to play the piano is conscious of the position and motion of every finger, but a virtuoso has mastered the art to such an extent that she is no longer aware of each discrete step she is taking while playing. It is as if her hands now have a mind of their own. Being skilled in this way is liberating because it makes my body into a more effective instrument, which it becomes once I no longer need to attend to its every movement.

---

[39] For Hegel, habituation is a more effective measure than efforts to eradicate sensations and desires altogether. He criticizes the ascetic solution, since ascetics are completely preoccupied with the very determinations they are trying to negate. According to Hegel, someone who has grown so accustomed to them that she learns to ignore them is freer than someone who wants to get rid of them altogether.

In this respect, skills do resemble the activity of standing upright, even when they are consciously cultivated and directed at higher ends. When it comes to standing upright, Hegel even notes that reflection can be practically incompatible with habitual behavior. For example, "Adopted *directly, without thinking*, his upright stance continues through the persistent involvement of his will. The human being stands upright only because and insofar as he wants to stand, and only as long as he wills to do so without consciousness of this" (Enz. III §410). In claiming that I can will this posture only as long as I am not conscious of it, he is pointing out that, for some habits at least, I cannot think about what I am doing while I am doing it. It is only because I am not attending to my posture that I can stand upright, for turning my attention to it could destabilize it in a similar way in which attention has on occasion made me forget the code to my apartment building, which I otherwise enter unthinkingly every day.[40]

But such liberation from excessive attention to detail seems to come at a significant cost. Even though all habit has an invaluable function of liberating us from aspects of our given nature, it can fulfill this function only by putting another nature in its place, a nature from which we would seemingly need to be liberated. This is why Hegel claims that there is a tension at the bottom of habit, a tension that is aptly captured in the phrase "second nature":

Habit is rightly called a "second nature" – *nature*, for it is an immediate being of the soul – a *second*, for it is an immediacy posited by the soul, an impressing and moulding of corporeality, which enters into the determinations of feeling as such and into the representational and volitional determinations made corporeal. (Enz. III §410)

Insofar as it is a *second* nature, it is a product of free activity. But what we are dealing with remains *nature* and thus a form of blind immediacy determined by mechanical necessity.

It is one thing to admit that some habits are bad because of their content, because of the kinds of behaviors they produce. And such habits would presumably strike us as compulsory, because we would be unable to see our own volition reflected in them. Consider, for example, exemplary instances of implicit biases, such as the habit of addressing oneself automatically to the members of one social group rather than those of another while conversing

---

[40] This is reminiscent of Hubert Dreyfus's concept of expertise he calls "embodied coping." Dreyfus argues that this expertise requires that it be and remain unreflective and it is fundamentally threatened by the intrusion of reflection. He provides the following example to illustrate this point: "As second baseman for the New York Yankees, Knoblauch was ... voted best infielder of the year, but one day, rather than simply fielding a hit and throwing the ball to first base, it seems he stepped back and took up a 'free, distanced orientation' towards the ball and how he was throwing it – the mechanics of it, as he put it. After that, he couldn't recover his former absorption and often – though not always – threw the ball to first base erratically – once into the face of a spectator" (Dreyfus 2007, 354).

at a philosophy department reception. I may wish this habit away, may wish that I made equal eye contact with all of my interlocutors, irrespective of whether they are, say, men or women. So when in these contexts I direct or avert my attention in habitual ways, I would be acting unfreely. But is this due to the particular habits I have developed, or is it part and parcel of habit as such? In other words, am I always unfree whenever I act habitually, even if my habits seem to me to be good ones, like that of recycling?

As we have seen, if unfreedom were true of the very form of habit, habit as such would prove to be unsuitable to ethical action. The standard reading of Hegel's account has argued that, yes, habit as such must be unfree. While cultivating habits comprises a significant stage in our ethical development, it is a stage that needs to be surpassed in order to attain an even higher form of subjective freedom. At best habit is preserved as a background to our free activity, because certain habits need to remain in place in order for us to be able to engage in more demanding projects. To use Hegel's own example, we would be unable to do philosophy unless we were used to sitting hunched over, reading for long periods of time, ignoring the arbitrary ideas that might strike our fancy, and unless we had grown immune to certain sources of temptation and distraction. A popular Internet blocking software meant to compensate for the failure of habit is even appropriately named "Freedom." But it is indisputable, according to this reading, that Hegel thinks freedom itself could never become habitual without ceasing to be freedom at all. Although he is by no means alone,[41] John McCumber provides an especially lucid articulation of such a reading. According to McCumber, habit has no more than the instrumental value of liberating us from our first nature, and to this end it does not matter which habits we develop. Even bad ones will do. But all habits reintroduce a form of compulsion that ultimately needs to be transcended. Thus McCumber concludes that Hegel "views habit as, like falsity, a phenomenon of transition which, though not good in itself, can help bring about a better state of affairs. This, its liberating role, is its 'essential determination.' "[42]

While there is admittedly some textual support for such a reading, it cannot reflect Hegel's final word on the matter, especially within the *Encyclopedia* at large. It is worth recalling the systematic context of the anthropological account. Since its particular purpose is to explain the transition from mere nature into "spiritual" territory, Hegel is here considering habit first and foremost with this transition in mind. But this is not its only systematic place. In fact, habit returns in "Objective Spirit," where Hegel investigates ethical life.

---

[41] Another example of this is Lewis (2008), who writes that "the more internalized or natural a habit is to us, the more it is something given, necessary, and not fully free" (56).
[42] McCumber (1990), 157.

And as we have seen in the companion text, *The Philosophy of Right*, Hegel grants habit in ethical life what may look to be a puzzling centrality, if we accept these formal shortcomings, namely, that the form of habit is incompatible with freedom. His concern in this social context is, however, no longer the transition out of first nature, but rather a return back to nature, so to speak. As he puts it, in ethical life "self-conscious freedom has become nature" (E §513) once again. So even if McCumber is right to read the anthropological account as he does, he is in any case too quick to conclude that any resemblance our second nature bears to our first makes it fundamentally at odds with freedom.

1.3 True Conscience

Hegel introduces subjective freedom in his chapter on "Morality" in the *Philosophy of Right*. In this context, subjective freedom appears as the "right of the subjective will," which he associates very closely with the standpoint of morality in general[43] and with "conscience" in particular: "The *right of the subjective will* is that whatever it should recognize as valid be *seen by it as good*, and that it be held accountable for an action – as its end entering external objectivity – as right or wrong, good or evil, legal or illegal, according to its *knowledge* of the value which that action has in this objectivity" (PR §132). In other words, it is the right of subjects to have insight into the value of what is required of them (and, less relevantly for our purposes, to be held responsible only to the extent to which they acted in knowledge of this value).[44] This right to insight appears to represent the subjective freedom that our actions would have to express in order to count as genuinely ethical, even in an objectively free social order. At the same time, these are only its initial formulations. And Hegel is a notoriously harsh critic of the moral standpoint, arguing that it lacks the resources to accomplish its aims outside of the confines of ethical life.

It is well known that Hegel is launching a critique of "Morality" while seeking to preserve what is true about it.[45] What makes Hegel's chapter on Morality

---

[43] "The moral point of view therefore takes the shape of the right of the subjective will. In accordance with this right, the will can *recognize* something or *be* something only in so far as that thing is *its own*, and in so far as the will is present to itself in it as subjectivity" (PR §107).

[44] Since I am not concerned with the question of responsibility, I will put this second aspect of the right of subjectivity aside. For an illuminating study of Hegel's theory of responsibility, see Alznauer (2015), especially 137–146.

[45] See, for example, Siep (1983), who speaks about the *Aufhebung* of Morality in Ethical Life. According to Siep, Morality becomes integrated into Ethical Life because Ethical Life itself undergoes a process of development, beginning with an immediate identification, embodied in custom and habit, and then progresses through stages of trust, insight due to reasons, and finally to the level of adequate knowledge. This is an excellent example of exactly the kind of reading that I am disputing, because I do not think the stage of custom and habit is being surpassed in a subsequent development.

such an interpretive challenge is that its standpoint is one that Hegel both affirms and rejects, thus raising the question about which aspects exactly he wants to affirm, and which he wants to reject. One way that this challenge has been met is to say that Hegel wants to find a place for moral reflection in ethical life, but that he rejects its overly individualistic exercise, its unwillingness to let itself be challenged by others. Hegel clearly criticizes the unyieldingness of conscience, as he does in the *Phenomenology of Spirit*. In that context he mocks conscience conceived of as "the moral genius which knows the inner voice of its immediate knowledge to be a divine voice" (PG ¶655), thus insulating itself from external criticism. The solution to these shortcomings of conscience is recognition, which in the *Phenomenology* is preceded by confession and forgiveness. So Hegel rejects an individualistic conception of conscience that takes its own verdict to be beyond reproach. What I want to suggest, however, is that this individualism (or subjectivism as Hegel here calls it) is an artifact of the idea that moral reflection can serve as a source of ethical knowledge. This makes moral reflection, and not just its individualist exercise, the true target of Hegel's criticism.

But Hegel's objections to moral reflection in the Morality chapter are not yet sufficient to make a case for the habit of the ethical. What Hegel wants to show is that moral reflection cannot accomplish its very specific aim of discovering objective standards of evaluation by means of subjective resources. These standards are sought through reflection in the sense that I am looking within myself in order to discover what I ought to do, how I ought to conduct myself. This is not a matter of introspection or self-observation,[46] but it does involve a withdrawal from what I take to be merely foisted upon me by the external world. I am no longer content to orient my behavior around standards that are already publicly recognized because I do not find my own subjectivity mirrored in them. And from the moral standpoint, I have no reason to acknowledge them *as truly objective* and so as legitimate requirements unless my "will is present to itself in [them] as subjectivity" (PR §107). Hegel stresses that, within the framework of morality, I make "positive reference" to the wills of others, whereas I did not do so within the framework of abstract right. What this means, I take it, is that in my capacity as rights-bearer others appeared to me to be mere limitations on my pursuit of my own interests. But as a moral subject, I am committed to the legitimacy of what I am pursuing, so I am hoping that others will recognize my actions as good, even though these have their source in my own purpose, intention, or conscience.

---

[46] Moyar (2011) has convincingly shown that conscience for Hegel is not exercised through "an internal hunt for the feeling of certainty that would allow me to *infer* that a certain course of action is right" (19). It involves forming beliefs that take a certain course to be the right one. So convictions involve a commitment to truth.

Hegel characterizes conscience as the most developed form of the moral standpoint because it is the most reflective: "Subjectivity, which is in its universality reflected into itself the absolute inward certainty of itself, that which posits particularity, and the determining and decisive factor" (PR §136). Conscience represents the height of self-consciousness because it is here that I have withdrawn entirely into myself, seeking orientation solely within myself, namely, among my commitments as a particular subject. By taking my particular commitments to be absolutely authoritative, I am positing my particularity as the "decisive factor." This makes my relationship to social norms an essentially critical one. According to Hegel, conscience relates to social norms by "evaporating them" [*verflüchtigt*] (PR §138), by denying their legitimacy *until* they have been tested by the measure of its own convictions. Since conscience is meant to represent moral knowledge, it contains two poles: a conception of what counts as objectively valid and a conception of what it would take to know it.[47] Objectivity is here understood to be duty, something I truly ought to do. Since it is my particularity that is the decisive factor, it is not going to be duty in the abstract, but my duty as a particular individual. I accept that my duty might not be the same as yours, since our commitments may differ. But I still seek your recognition of my action as dutiful, as an adherence to my particular duty. And the way that I know my duty is through conviction. The basic tenet of conscience is that I will recognize as my duty only that of which I am convinced, because it is conviction, rather than mere conformity with social expectations, that yields genuine objectivity.

Hegel already makes this association between conscience and conviction in his Preface, where he speaks harshly against Fries for promoting a form of conscience that "identifies right with subjective conviction" (PR, p. 17). This sets the tone for his general criticism of conscience. According to Hegel, because conscience is committed to the truth of its own conviction, it opens itself up to the question of whether its convictions are indeed true, or whether they are mere opinion. Whenever I enact my own convictions, I am doing what I do because I take it to be required of me. I am not enacting my own convictions simply *because* they are my convictions, since my convictions do not *make* something into a duty – they are meant to track the truth of the matter about what my duties are. But this means that simply pointing to my own convictions and insisting that I acted conscientiously is not going to settle the question of their objective goodness.[48] As Hegel puts it, "Conscience is therefore subject

---

[47] In the *Phenomenology of Spirit*, Hegel characterizes conscience as a "configuration of consciousness" because it contains these two poles. This makes conscience a particular conception of knowledge that involves a conception of the corresponding object of knowledge.

[48] Moyar (2011) has analyzed conscience in terms of the relationship between "motivating" and "justifying" reasons. He has likewise emphasized that conscience, even though it is acting out its own particular commitments, is making a claim to universality in the sense that it is

to the judgment about whether it is *true* [*wahrhaft*] or not, and its appeal solely *to itself* is immediately opposed to what it wants to be – the rule for a rational and universal mode of conduct that is valid in and for itself" (PR §137R). Since conviction cannot serve as a criterion of goodness, conscience proves to be without resources to justify its own claim to objectivity.[49]

Hegel thinks that it is no surprise that such appeals to conviction become more pronounced during times when the social world is "unable to satisfy the better will." Hegel takes Socrates as an example, because he "evaporated the existing world and retreated into himself in search of the right and the good" (PR §138A). Socrates' requests that his compatriots reflect about the nature of virtue, knowledge, etc. were thus a response to a social order that had devolved into a "hollow, spiritless, and unsettled existence." But if conscience stands out when it opposes itself to the world and is itself a symptom of an inadequate world, can it retain a place in a rational social order? Hegel is quite explicit that this form of conscience, the one that makes itself known through evaporation, is merely "formal." It retreats into its own convictions even though these on their own cannot determine objectively valid content.[50] This retreat might be a last resort when all orientation has been lost, but conscience in its formal capacity cannot provide orientation either.

Hegel, however, contrasts formal conscience with what he calls "true conscience," which marries conscientious form with an objectively valid content. And he suggests that true conscience is preserved in the transition from morality to ethical life. As Hegel concludes, "the identity – which is therefore *concrete* – of the good and the subjective will, the truth of them both, is *ethical life*" (PR §141). True conscience is true in at least two respects. What makes true conscience "true" is that it is committed to a true content, namely, to that which is objectively good. This means that conscience respects the "right of objectivity," which is determined within a rational social order. So true conscience is no longer engaged in deriving objective content through its own resources or testing what is publicly recognized against the measure of its

---

committed to its justifiability to others. "Conscience both embodies particularity and is above particularity in that it expresses the unity of the two abstract sides of the rational will" (67).

[49] Hegel also entertains a more radical version of conscience, according to which conviction is regarded as the criterion of goodness. "My good intention in my action and my conviction of its goodness *make it good*" (PR §140R). According to this version, my action is good (or at least excusable) as long as I am convinced that what I am doing is good. But Hegel notes that this criterion is completely vacuous, because every action can be re-described as an expression of conviction. If I am doing it, I must be convinced that it is worth doing. So conscientiousness so conceived is simply a feature of all action, not a criterion that can set the good ones apart.

[50] "Here, within the formal point of view of morality, conscience is without this objective content, and is thus for itself the infinite formal certainty of itself, which for this very reason is at the same time the certainty of *this* subject" (PR §137).

subjective convictions.[51] Its particular duties are prescribed by its specific position within the social order and it is committed to the requirements internal to its roles. So in an objectively rational social order the basic tension between social expectations and particular commitment is (for the most part) overcome, since I form my commitments within the context of institutional roles.

At the same time Hegel takes himself to be honoring the right of the subjective will and the "sanctity of conscience" by showing how it is satisfied in a rational social order, without requiring the exercise of moral reflection. True conscience is thus also "true" in a second sense, namely, because it has a valid, even *vital* function in ethical life. Ethical life would not be genuinely ethical, would not embody a "living good," if it did not satisfy the requirements of conscience. In other words, ethical life would not be a source of practical orientation for us if we were not committed to sustaining it through our participation. This makes conviction vital for ethical life. So the Morality chapter demonstrates that it is indeed important that we be committed to that which is expected of us. Our activities should issue from and express our convictions. But Hegel wants to show that, in a rational social order, they already do.

The best evidence for this claim appears in his handwritten marginalia to §132. I include the relevant passage in full:

> The right of the subjective will, that it knows, knew – can have known – that something is good or not good – is lawful or not right etc. – Here is left completely indeterminate, of which form and kind this knowing is to be – If I demand – from the standpoint of reflection – that I be convinced on the basis of reasons (*aus Gründen*), that I have insight – then this is my business, which is left up to me – for in this way I put myself on the particular standpoint. It is possible to wish that human beings are familiar with the reasons, with the deeper sources of right – but this is not objectively necessary. Trust, faith, healthy reason, custom is the universal objective mode of justification (*Begründung*).

Hegel is here making a number of interesting points. He is pointing out that there are different ways of knowing that something is good and that the right of the subjective will on its own does not specify which of these is to be preferred. He is also pointing out that it is possible to adopt a reflective standpoint and demand the same of others, but this is not necessary from the universal and objective point of view. Finally, he is making the additional and especially striking point that ordinarily "trust, faith, healthy common sense, custom" – so the whole range of unreflective ways of relating to social requirements – should count as an adequate mode of justification. The German word he uses

---

[51] I should note that true conscience can only be true in this sense, if the order it happens to inhabit is objectively rational. If this order is inadequate, then true conscience cannot be true, because it cannot become convinced of a true content, through no fault of its own.

is *Begründung* and it is meant to stand in contrast to this demand that reasons (*Gründe*) be given.

Thus true conscience can appear to be fundamentally unlike formal conscience. Whereas the latter stands out through its activity of "evaporation," true conscience is nearly invisible because it is already satisfied: "The right of individuals to their subjective determination to freedom is fulfilled in so far as they belong to ethical actuality; for their certainty of their own freedom has its truth in such objectivity, and it is in the ethical realm that they actually possess their own essence and their inner universality" (PR §153R). But this satisfaction does not happen automatically, as soon as I enter a rational social order. What Hegel suggests is that "true conscience is contained in the ethical disposition" (PR §137R), because it is "the disposition [*Gesinnung*] to will what is good *in and for itself*; it therefore has fixed principles [*feste Grundsätze*] and these have for it the character of determinacy and duties which are objective for themselves" (PR §137). As we will see, cultivating this disposition is no easy feat, since it involves a change in attitude, orienting itself around fixed principles that have the character of determinacy. And as we will see, cultivating this disposition is achieved through habituation. Here a comparison with the political disposition is especially fruitful, for Hegel defines the political disposition as a "certainty based on *truth* (merely subjective certainty does not originate in *truth*, but is only opinion) and a willing which has become *habitual*" (PR §268). In other words, true conscience is realized in the ethical disposition, which we achieved when willing has become habitual.

Thus, Hegel clearly wants to preserve what he takes to be valuable features of the moral standpoint. He is not denying that it is important that we have insight into the goodness of the standards to which we are being held, so that our actions express our genuine convictions. In fact, Hegel considers conscience so conceived an essential dimension of ethical life, a dimension without which ethical life would wither and perish. What he rejects in the moral standpoint is its privileging of reflection as a source of objectivity. Reflection cannot yield objectivity if it involves measuring my socially prescribed obligations against my subjective convictions. It cannot yield objectivity because I need some way of distinguishing those convictions that are worth taking seriously from mere opinion, of which I might be equally staunchly convinced. For Hegel, the right of subjectivity thus needs to be complemented by the "right of objectivity," which it cannot derive.

Hegel's engagement with the standpoint of morality is relevant to understanding his introduction of the habit of the ethical because it clarifies the burden that it will have to bear. Habitual comportment will have to prove itself capable of expressing the convictions of true conscience, namely, insight into the good. Hegel even holds that habitual comportment is not just capable of this, but is in fact the full realization of subjective freedom in a rational social order. But the Morality chapter on its own is not yet an argument in favor of this conclusion. In fact, Hegel even seems to speak disparagingly of habit in the conclusion of the Morality chapter, remarking that "[it] is of course not irrelevant whether I do something from habit or custom or from persuasion of its truth" (PR §140A). This could lead one to conclude that Hegel wants to maintain a strict divide between conscientious and habitual actions. At the same time, Hegel emphasizes that the transition from morality to ethical life involves a significantly different understanding of what subjective freedom looks like. One striking feature of the ethical disposition is that it looks to be far less reflective than formal conscience, because it is no longer making the effort to determine what it ought to do through withdrawal or evaporation.[52] Conscience is only true when its content is true, and this it is unable to determine through reflection. But conscience is also true when it ceases to engage in reflection in the first place, so when it turns into an ethical disposition.

1.4 Ethical Disposition

Although the Morality chapter engages aspects of Kant's moral theory,[53] it does not directly confront Kant's conception of virtue, which turns out to be the inspiration for the ethical disposition. By suggesting that the ethical disposition is achieved when "self-conscious freedom has become nature" once again, I take Hegel to be offering an alternative to Kant's conception of virtue. As we have seen, virtue for Kant can never become habitual without losing its basis in principles, for as soon as we make them our habit, we stop following them in a free manner, which means that we stop, strictly speaking, following them at all. Hegel's proposal challenges this line of thought, for it suggests that such a self-conscious relation to principles indicates precisely the opposite – that we are *not yet* following them freely. According to Hegel, freedom is only fully realized when it appears in seemingly natural guise, as a second nature.

---

[52] Patten (2002) has defended the opposite view, arguing that Hegel is advocating "*complete* reflective awareness with respect to one's determinations and the reasons underlying them, an awareness that does not stop at anything given" (44), and that "there is an important sense, for Hegel, in which freedom involves abstracting from one's contingently given desires and inclinations and acting on the basis of thought and reason alone" (p. 47). I think it is beyond doubt that Hegel does not share Patten's view. Subjective freedom for Hegel is not to be confused with "complete reflective awareness."

[53] Although the Morality chapter contains Hegel's famous "emptiness charge" against Kant's moral law, Kant is not his sole or even primary target. Especially the "conscience" section seems to be directed at representatives of an "ethics of conviction" such as his former colleague Fries.

This is another way of saying that virtue is fully realized only in the habit of the ethical.

It bears mentioning that Hegel was not fond of the term "virtue" or *Tugend*. He speaks of it every once in a while, and not always unfavorably, but virtue for him remains too closely wedded to virtuosity and to the moral genius of exceptional individuals.[54] He thinks that, in a rational social order, virtuosity and genius are no longer needed and virtue becomes, even if not thoroughly commonplace, nevertheless largely mundane. Whereas for the Greeks, for example, ethical action required heroic personal qualities, this is no longer the case in modern ethical life, in which virtue need not stand out against the backdrop of an objectively inadequate social world. Virtue in his own time has become almost invisible because it rarely requires anything above rectitude, or the "ethical order reflected [*reflektiert*] in the individual character" (PR §150). This is for Hegel an indication, not of lowered expectations on our part, but of the rationality of modern ethical life, which does not demand the same level of personal sacrifice. This mirrors Hegel's suggestion that true conscience, too, is almost invisible in a rational social order and that retreats into formal conscience become more common when the objective context has proven dissatisfactory.

Despite Hegel's reluctance to speak in terms of virtue, his conception of the ethical disposition shares many of its features. He characterizes it as a "simple, undeviating, fixed orientation" (LNR, 132), adding that

[a]n ethical disposition on the part of the subject involves setting aside reflection, which is always ready to pass over from universal substance to the particular. It involves knowing and recognizing the universal element of substance, the laws, as an eternal mode of being subsisting in and for itself and as the distinctive essence of self-consciousness; and it involves acting in, and being simply oriented toward, its substantive vocation. (LNR, 132)

This definition is meant to echo the truth of conscience, since the ethical disposition "involves knowing and recognizing the universal element of substance," which suggests that it is supposed to exhibit insight into the goodness of social requirements and in this way satisfy the right of the subjective will. But it is also clear that the ethical disposition goes beyond the truth of conscience, for it is not expressed in discrete actions (some of which might be conscientious, others not), but in a "simple, undeviating, and fixed orientation," presumably manifest in stable patterns of activity.

---

[54] As Hegel puts it, "Virtue consists rather in ethical virtuosity, and if we speak less about virtue nowadays than before, the reason is that the ethical is no longer so much the form of a particular individual" (PR §150A).

Though Hegel opens with a contrast between the ethical disposition and a reflective stance, there are at least three respects in which the ethical disposition overlaps with Kantian virtue. First, the ethical disposition is meant to be intelligent, expressive of a "knowing and recognizing," which makes it akin to the kind of "moral strength" that Kant has in mind. In both cases, it is that which ensures dependability and consistency in one's conduct, though not through behavioral dispositions, but through a correspondingly firm frame of mind. Second, Hegel is also committed to the unity of virtue, which means that he thinks that either one is virtuous, or one isn't. Although his account admits of gradation, he is a harsh critic of a conception of *character* as comprised of disparate traits. He makes this explicit in his "Anthropology," where he dismisses the idea that people can possess different character. According to Hegel, people do differ in their character, but only because some have character, and others do not (Enz. III, §395A). Third, what the ethical disposition knows and recognizes is the "universal element of substance," which Hegel specifies as its *laws*. This means that the content of this knowledge is a law, or set of laws. Since laws and principles share a rule-like form,[55] one could go so far as to say that, for both Kant and Hegel, being virtuous amounts to being principled, dependably and consistently so.

This is not an uncontroversial characterization of Hegel's position. According to Dean Moyar, "Hegel insists that abstract ethical principles rarely determine action in a straightforward way. They find application only within a determine context, and are usually only one kind of reason in a complex whole of considerations. Hegel has a dynamic view of normativity rather than a static model of fixed rules and mechanical application."[56] Although it is true that Hegel is not thinking of rule-following along the lines of "mechanical application" – especially because he is not thinking of rules that are sufficiently integrated as something we *apply* – he does emphasize that principles are what we know when we possess ethical knowledge. I will return to Hegel's reasons for insisting on this. In any case, Hegelian principles would have to differ in significant respects from the Kantian variety. They could not, first of all, be nearly as abstract, and certainly neither reducible to nor derivable from anything as formal as the categorical imperative. He explicitly rejects this strategy in the Morality chapter. Rather, they would have to attach to the specific social roles we inhabit, roles through which we partake in ethical life. For example, it is in my position as a doctor that I am bound by a certain code of conduct, captured

---

[55] One difference between them is that laws possess objective authority, whether or not we recognize it, whereas principles involve an additional element of subjective identification. I will use the two terms somewhat interchangeably, because laws should become principles, too, while principles should also possess an objectively valid content.

[56] Moyar (2011), 38.

in the Hippocratic Oath, and this code is not the same as the one pertaining to a teacher. Since we occupy numerous roles without access to a "master principle" like Kant's moral law, these could come into genuine conflict, in which case I might find it difficult to figure out which one to privilege. But as long as my social order remains sufficiently rational, I am not regularly torn between them and so they do ensure that I am reliable and dependable in what I do.

In fact, Hegel emphasizes that virtue cannot be discerned in particular actions, but in the way I lead my life as a whole: "When the human being performs this or that ethical action, he is not immediately virtuous, but indeed then, when the manner of conduct is a steadiness of character" (PR §150A). In other words, it is not enough that I muster moral strength every once in a while, or even most of the time. I am only virtuous if and when all of my actions cohere in a certain way. So the steadiness of my character must span over the manner of my conduct. As Hegel states rather ruthlessly, "What the subject *is*, *is the series of his actions*. If these are a series of worthless productions, then the subjectivity of willing is just as worthless; but if the series of his deeds is of a substantive nature, then the same is true also of the inner will of the individual" (PR §124).[57] Since my life is presumably still in progress, what matters is not the sum total of my actions, but the broader patterns they display. It is these patterns that betray my frame of mind and expose it as virtuous – or not. And if my actions displayed no pattern and the series were disjointed, this would show that I am definitely not virtuous, because I lack a firm frame of mind.

Hegel's definition of the ethical disposition suggests that he holds a version of the "intellectualist" thesis that virtue is knowledge (and vice ignorance), but with a significant qualification.[58] Although Hegel is clearly not interested in reducing the ethical disposition to a collection of character traits, he does not think that it can consist in the mere acknowledgment that certain principles

---

[57] It is worth noting that Hegel here switches from "*Handlung*" to "*Tat*": he begins by saying that the subject is a series of his *actions* and then repeats the same formulation, but this time referring to the series of his *deeds*. Although much has been made of Hegel's technical distinction between the two, this passage suggests that it is perhaps not as central to his view as it is believed to be.

[58] There is one important piece of textual evidence in favor of my suggestion that Hegel is best read as an intellectualist. In a note to §140, Hegel discusses Pascal's take on Aristotle's conception of involuntary action. Aristotle draws a distinction between two forms of ignorance – ignorance of the external circumstances, which can absolve us of responsibility, and ignorance of the wrongness of our actions, which cannot. Hegel quotes Aristotle approvingly as saying that the latter ignorance is the source of evil, remarking that "Aristotle, of course, had a deeper insight into the connection between cognition and volition than has become usual in that superficial philosophy which teaches that emotion and enthusiasm, not cognition, are the true principles of ethical action" (PR §140n). Hegel is here explicitly making the intellectualist point that wrongdoing is evidence of ignorance (though not one that absolves us of responsibility), because someone could not both know that an action is wrong and do it. I am grateful to Mark Alznauer for directing me to this passage.

are good ones to uphold – the kind of acknowledgment I might voice if someone were to provide a very compelling argument in their favor. For Hegel, the ethical disposition has to involve a commitment to live in a principled manner. What makes this nonetheless a version of the intellectualist thesis is that such a commitment turns out to be an integral part of what it takes to know that certain principles are good ones to uphold. I cannot be said to truly know it, to be *convinced* of it, unless I am committed to it. A failure to commit to them indicates a failure to believe that they are indeed good, worthy of being upheld. It indicates a failure of insight. One reason Hegel holds this view has do with his insistence that it is what we actually do that displays what we as a matter of fact believe – not whatever we claim to believe. Another reason has to do with the requirement of unity. Unless I am genuinely committed to living in accordance with principles, they will not inform my conduct as a whole, but at best sporadically.

The importance of commitment is not wholly missing from Kant's own conception of virtue. In his *Religion within the Bounds of Reason*, Kant even emphasizes that virtue is founded on what he calls a "revolution of the heart" – and "heart" here in the sense of *Gesinnung*.[59] According to Kant, my character must be grounded in a deliberate decision to lead a principled life. Kant's reason for making this decision a requirement seems to be that it is the only way I can become responsible for my virtue or vice, because it is the only way I can be said to have chosen the principles I live by, aligning myself either with that of morality or that of self-love.[60] If virtue were acquired in any other way, then it would not be grounded in a free act. But in the absence of such a commitment to the moral law, I might still recognize that the moral law is the one I *ought* to heed, but do so without aligning myself with it and so without making it authoritative over me. So even for Kant, it looks like mere acknowledgment is not enough, unless it is accompanied by a wholesale transformation in attitude.

Although Hegel never engages Kant directly on this front, this seems to be the point where their respective conceptions of virtue most radically diverge. This divergence sets the stage for the habit of the ethical. It is worth considering whether Hegel would agree that commitment requires a deliberate decision of a revolutionary sort, namely, whether we must commit ourselves in a self-conscious manner to the principles to which we end up being committed. It does not seem that Hegel would want to make this a requirement, since he thinks that our commitments far outstrip what we deliberately choose or even

---

[59] Kant, *Religion within the Bounds of Reason*, 6:47.
[60] The principle of self-love does not count as a proper principle, because its content is too contingent on the whim of desire. This means that Kant does not acknowledge two kinds of character – the virtuous and the un-virtuous kind – but that for him only those who are virtuous have character at all.

reflectively affirm.[61] It is clear, however, that he would consider a decision in any case insufficient in achieving its end. Hegel thinks that what proves a genuine commitment, irrespective of the manner in which it is made, is a corresponding *decisiveness* in demeanor. He takes this to be a crucial aspect of virtue that the Kantian account not only lacks, but also cannot adequately accommodate. On Kant's conception, it makes no ethical difference whether the right thing is something I do with reluctance, or whether it is something I am already ready to do, whenever the situation should call for it. I must in a sense be ready to do it – that is true. But I can be ready to do it, even if it remains difficult to do. All that matters is that I do the right thing and for the right reason, regardless of whether doing so does or does not come easily to me.

There are moments in which it sounds as if Kant thinks it is somehow better if performing my duty does not come easily to me. He says this not because such an inner struggle raises the moral worth of my action, but because it demonstrates the strength of virtue, which stands out most vividly when it perseveres in the face of sensuous opposition. Other times it sounds as if Kant thinks it is simply impossible for us to make duty an easy matter, given our fallen condition. In a revealing passage from the *Metaphysics of Morals*, Kant even suggests that we can never eradicate this reluctance on our part:

The moral imperative makes this constraint known through the categorical nature of its pronouncement (the unconditional ought). Such constraint, therefore, does not apply to rational beings as such (there could also be *holy* ones) but rather to *human beings*, rational *natural* beings, who are unholy enough that pleasure can induce them to break the moral law, even though they recognize its authority; and even when they do obey the law, they do it *reluctantly* [*ungern*] ... and it is in this that such *constraint* properly consists.[62]

But I do not think we need to emphasize these moments in order to understand Hegel's dissatisfaction with Kant's view. Though Kant could in principle admit that we should do our best to remove this reluctance by overcoming those inclinations that induce us to break the moral law, what he could not say is that it is better, from an ethical point of view, that we do, namely, that we prove virtuous only when we do the right thing, not just for the right reason, but without strain or restraint.

---

[61] At times he indicates that good upbringing is all that is needed in order to cultivate an ethical disposition. He was fond of citing the story of the father who asked a Pythagorean for advice on how to raise a virtuous son, a question to which Pythagorean replied: by making him the citizen of a state with good laws (PR §153). He even describes good upbringing as a process as gradual as habituation itself (VPR, 89). Such passages do suggest that Hegel would probably consider a deliberate decision superfluous, called for at most in cases of paralyzing conflict, when circumstances force us to pick between competing principles.

[62] Kant, *Metaphysics of Morals*, 6:378.

This kind of criticism has something in common with the familiar objection raised against Kant's moral theory, namely, that he lacks the resources for distinguishing virtue from mere continence.[63] This distinction is to be found in Aristotle, who claims that continence is not yet virtue, because the continent person lacks the right sorts of desires and fails to take pleasure in the right sorts of things, whereas in the virtuous person the rational and the non-rational parts of the soul "speak in the same voice." But Hegel's point is not simply that virtue positively requires that we overcome conflicting inclinations and cultivate inclinations that agree with the requirements of duty. Rather, he is denying the very intelligibility of continence as a way of life. According to Hegel, the rational part does not truly govern until it can do so without perpetual effort and exertion. Such a person is not genuinely reliable in her conduct precisely because she has to struggle to do the right thing again and again, on each and every occasion. Although Hegel cannot possibly be denying that doing the right thing can sometimes be demanding, what he contests is that someone can be called virtuous for whom every principled action is a struggle.

It is for this reason that Hegel lauds the attitude that Antigone exhibits. What he emphasizes is that her action – albeit requiring personal sacrifice – was performed with great decisiveness. Hegel even stresses that her decisiveness was not an artifact of any deliberate decision on her part. According to his characterization in the *Phenomenology of Spirit*, Antigone never chose to obey the divine law at the expense of its human counterpart. Though she was simply assigned to the former, her obedience displayed an unwavering commitment to its execution.[64] But this is not the element of Antigone's attitude that Hegel lauds. He even suggests that Antigone was to a large extent in denial about her own implication in the divine law precisely because she assumed that nature was responsible for her commitment to it and in this way failed to see that it was a commitment she herself had made.

What is so great about Antigone, despite all of her limitations, is that she did not hesitate. Interestingly enough, Hegel takes this, not as evidence that she was not plagued by competing inclinations, but simply as a testament to

---

[63] This objection can be traced back to Schiller, though Schiller formulated the relevant distinction as that between dignity and grace. For a helpful discussion of the Schiller–Kant debate on this front, see Baxley (2010), 98–114.

[64] "But the ethical consciousness knows, what it has to do, and it is decided [*entschieden*] whether to belong to the divine or to the human law. This immediacy of its decision [*Entscheidung*] is an being-in-itself [*Ansichsein*] and has therefore also the significance of a natural being, as we have seen; nature, and not the contingency or circumstances or choice [*Wahl*] assigns the one sex to the one, and the other to the other law" (PG ¶465). It is worth noting that Hegel describes this consciousness as *entschieden*, so decided, even though it never (takes itself) to have come to an *Entscheidung* or decision. Even if it did in some sense decide, there was nothing to deliberate about, and so the decision appears as an "immediate" one.

the depth of her commitment to the law. At the end of the preceding chapter ("Reason as Law-Tester," one of his more scathing criticisms of the standpoint of morality), Hegel contrasts the perspective involved in looking to test particular laws with what he there also calls the ethical disposition, which "consists in sticking steadfastly to what is right, and abstaining from all attempts to move or shake it, or derive it" (PG ¶347). Antigone enters the scene as the embodiment of Hegel's preferred frame of mind. From her perspective, laws simply *are*. This means that she does not need first to inquire into the basis of their authority in order to know them to be valid. But it is not as if they simply are, out there, independently of her. Rather, she has integrated them to such an extent that they have become the "essence" of her self-consciousness. She and the law have grown inseparable, for not only is her sense of self bound up with it, but also that the law continue to *be* is what is at stake in her action.

While it is clear that Hegel does not want us to blame nature for our commitment to the laws of modern ethical life, Hegel hopes to retain significant aspects of Antigone's relation to those of her own social order.[65] Like she, we should not regard our laws as awaiting reflective validation, though we should know them to be valid. Moreover, only someone who is convinced that a law is legitimately authoritative over her conduct can be said to know it to be so.[66] And the more decisively we enact them, the more convincingly we demonstrate that we are convinced in them. It is this element of decisiveness that Antigone introduces and that Hegel finds missing in Kant. To return to this contrast with Kantian virtue, Hegel's point, I take it, is not that such decisiveness would embellish or enrich our dependability and consistency. It is rather that without it we cannot be said to be truly dependable and consistent in the first place. Even in cases in which our ethical disposition is grounded in a deliberate decision to lead a principled life, such a disposition cannot be acquired overnight, and this precisely because, as Hegel puts it, "what one has to do, one must do straight away without further hesitation" (LNR, 132). In other words, my commitment to ethical principles remains flimsy and unstable so long as heeding them does not come naturally to me, but remains labored and forced.

---

[65] Hegel alludes to her in an opening paragraph of "Ethical Life" in his *Philosophy of Right*, arguing that modern laws should possess "being in and for themselves" for us, as the divine law did for Antigone.

[66] This connection between conviction on one hand and knowledge on the other can seem rather tenuous. Is it not possible for me to be convinced of principles that are as a matter of fact bad? And would this not mean that I do not genuinely *know* them to be good? Hegel is worried about a disconnection between conviction and knowledge in contexts where our convictions stray from social requirements and in this way lose their objective orientation. But one could also worry that we inhabit a social order that is so ideological that our conviction in the goodness of its laws is a result of delusion or indoctrination. I will return to this issue in the third chapter and argue that this is for Hegel not possible, at least not in a permanent way.

In light of these considerations, I want to suggest that the ethical disposition is best understood as a form of *whole-hearted* identification.[67] As Hegel puts it in an already quoted passage, "[Ethical laws] are not something alien to the subject, rather the subject bears *a witness of spirit* to them as to its own essence, in which it has its *self-feeling* and wherein it lives as in an element indistinguishable from itself – a relation that is more identical than even *belief* and *trust*" (PR §147). Hegel's point, I should note, is not that the virtuous agent cannot distance herself from the laws in question, should the need for such distancing arise. It is that she has integrated these laws into her sense of who she is – into her very nature – so that she ceases to look upon them as imperatives or limitations on her will. This is for Hegel to be fully free in her adherence to them.

If we think of the ethical disposition in terms of whole-heartedness, we can get a better sense of why habit becomes indispensable to virtue on this account. The view I am ascribing to Hegel is the following: my commitment to a principle proves whole-hearted only when I no longer need to remind myself of what it is in order to live it out. To put this slightly differently: if I have to call to mind my duty whenever I am called upon to act, then the "revolution of my heart" was half-hearted at best, arrested at the level of wishful thinking. In Hegel's own formulation, to identify with my duty is to cease to see it as a duty. At that point, doing what I ought to do will have become second nature to me, and my conduct will exhibit a principled consistency and committed stability precisely in being decisive, unhesitating, and seemingly natural. While habit is admittedly not always a sign of a whole-hearted commitment, a commitment without it is not yet a genuine commitment, for it has not yet become internalized, incorporated, and made one's own.[68]

I think Hegel's argument is quite intuitive from a first-person perspective, for making a commitment to a certain practice is often aimed at removing it

---

[67] Here I am deliberately alluding to Harry Frankfurt's well-known use of this term, though Frankfurt makes somewhat different use of it. For example, Frankfurt (1998) argues that the objects of whole-hearted commitment are some among our first-order desires, which we reflectively permit to motivate our will. First, Hegel is not concerned with our commitments to desires, but to ethical principles. Second, Hegel does not think it is essential that this commitment be made at a reflective, or "second-order" level. So even though I am drawing on this term, I admit that the analogy with Frankfurt is not seamless. I should also mention that I am not the first to draw a comparison between Hegel and Frankfurt, although others have drawn it at different points. See, for example, Quante (1997) and Honneth (2010), 26.

[68] Nietzsche suggests a similar conception of incorporated knowledge: "the strength of knowledge does not depend on its degree of truth but on its age, on the degree to which it has been incorporated, on its character as a condition of life ... knowledge became a piece of life itself. ... To what extent can truth endure incorporation? That is the question; that is the experiment" (*Gay Science*, §110). Though Hegel would deny that knowledge has only little to do with truth, he would agree that knowledge is only true knowledge once it has become a "piece of life itself."

from the domain of deliberation. For example, I do not see myself as truly committed to the practice of yoga unless I make this practice so habitual that I do not have to make a daily decision to do it. I realize that my commitment is rather flimsy, liable to be overturned, so long as it requires that I decide again and again to make the trek to the studio. I only feel firm in my commitment when I cease to think about it, when there is no longer an open question in my mind. Another example might be a commitment to vegetarianism. I can make the decision to become a vegetarian, perhaps persuaded by an ethical argument against industrialized farming. But I know full well that I have not succeeded in becoming a vegetarian until I no longer have to decide perpetually against eating meat. During the period of re-habituation, when I still have to pause to deliberate whenever faced with a menu, I am not yet fully committed. My own goal is to eradicate meat-eating from my way of life so thoroughly that it no longer even occurs to me to consider meat something I *could* eat, but choose not to.

Although Hegel's line of thought raises a challenge to Kant, it becomes all the clearer why virtue might require a commitment of a whole-hearted kind as soon as we distance ourselves even further from Kant's starting point. Because Kantian principles are authored by me and so have their origin in my will, the issue of my identification with them does not arise in quite the same way as it does for Hegel, who believes that I initially discover them as the laws of the social order into which I am born and eventually socialized. This means that Hegel must explain how I am ever able to identify with these laws to such an extent that they look to me no different than if I myself had authored them, though I (strictly speaking) did not. So the "simple identification" to which Hegel's contentious passage refers is from his point of view not in any tension with freedom, but articulates a difficult, though essential requirement for its realization. We don't identify with these laws simply from the start. Such identification is won through considerable effort. As Hegel states, "education (*Erziehung*) consists only in becoming suitable to the world, but in such a way that one grasps it internally. One becomes accustomed (*gewöhnt*) to this or that, one only receives it. Thus his transformation (*Umbildung*) towards the customs (*Sitten*) is not a limitation on the individual. It is his liberation. It would be a limitation only if I wanted something else" (VPR, 89). So becoming virtuous must for Hegel involve a transformative process in which I go from merely *receiving* the laws of the social world to *grasping* them internally.[69]

---

[69] This view is also similar to the conception of moral authorship that Sabina Lovibond (2004) proposes. She tries to defend Socrates' claim that akrasia is a form of ignorance by distinguishing between knowing something and merely believing that you know it. The weak-willed agent might say, "I know that smoking is bad, but I can't help myself." But in failing to act on the belief she is avowing, she reveals that she does not really know it, that she is merely being a mouthpiece for public opinion. Lovibond argues that someone is an author of her

In light of this challenge that we internalize what is initially outer to us, it is less surprising that Hegel thinks habituation might be up to the task of bridging the initial gap between the objective and the subjective and thus shedding the external guise in which laws at first appear. Habituation is after all a process of appropriation, of giving myself determinations that I can consequently regard as posited by my will, and so paradigmatically a process of "inheriting, earning, and owning."[70] Hegel makes a similar point in the "Anthropology," when he states in rather strong terms that "habit is what is most essential to the existence of everything spiritual in the individual subject ... so that the content, religious, moral, etc. can belong to him as *this* self, *this* soul, and no other" (Enz. III, §410). He means, conversely, that without habit this content would never belong to me, but would remain from my vantage point something imposed from without. Thus it is habit that expresses true conscience because habit indicates that I have succeeded in turning objective requirements into subjective convictions, that I am now thoroughly persuaded of what I am doing. And it is habit that expresses the ethical disposition, because it demonstrates a stable and enduring commitment to principles of action.[71]

Hegel's discussion of the distinctly "political" disposition in the *Philosophy of Right* brings this broader argument into clearest focus. According to Hegel, the political disposition (which he also identifies as *patriotism*) is best expressed in unreflective ways of living within the state. He criticizes those who think that this disposition can be cashed out as a willingness to make extraordinary sacrifices. Although life in the state might occasionally require such sacrifices, these express patriotism only when they are grounded in a deeper awareness of the unity between our interests and those of the state, an awareness that is largely unreflective. Hegel's example of a patriotic action is walking around at night without fear, but also without thinking about the conditions that make this possible:

> moral judgments only when what she claims to know has become part of her nature and she is immediately motivated by her judgments, whereas the akratic person is a mere "actor" who mimics what she has heard others say. Lovibond concludes that the aim of ethical formation is to cultivate such authorship.

[70] A phrase borrowed from Moland (2003, 2011), which is meant to echo a famous passage from Goethe's *Faust*: "Was du ererbt von deinen Vätern hast, erwirb es, um es zu besitzen." Moland, however, has a fundamentally different understanding of how this ownership is achieved. According to her reading (2011), "[w]e become ourselves ... by making the characteristics we inherit our own through reflection and endorsement" (24).

[71] Although Moyar (2011) does not emphasize the role of habit, he speaks about autonomy as "practical incorporation," which seems to refer to the same process I have outlined: "Hegel's claim is not that you reflect on what is given and put a stamp of approval on it through your belief. Rather, the model is that you make the objective your own through action – not a single action, and not action in isolation, but by developing patterns of action as one matures in one's family, career, and citizenship" (110).

Human beings have the trust that the state has to persist and that private interests can only be achieved within it, but habit makes that, upon which our entire existence rests, invisible. When someone goes at nighttime securely across the street, he doesn't notice that this could also be different, for this habit of security has become another nature and one does not even think about how this is just the effect of particular institutions. (PR §268A)

Through this example Hegel is first and foremost trying to emphasize the codependence between patriotism so conceived and the institution of the state. They both enable and uphold each other. If the state were badly organized, people would be unable to make life within it into a second nature. They would not be able to pursue their individual projects in the trust that these will not be thwarted or wrecked. But if people did not inhabit the state in this trusting way, then it could not persist as an ordered institution. Thus political order likewise depends on the political disposition – it could never be achieved through mere force and the threat of it.

What makes Hegel's characterization of the political disposition so illuminating is that Hegel clearly thinks that it *does* express knowledge of the state as a condition for the possibility of our habitual way of life. It is a consciousness (*Bewußtsein*) that my particular interests will be preserved within the universal interests of the state. According to Hegel, "[Patriotism] is essentially the disposition, which in the ordinary states of affairs [*gewöhnlichen Zustande*] and living conditions is in habit of knowing [*zu wissen gewohnt*] the community as the substantial basis and purpose" (PR §268R). Hegel's choice of words is of importance. He is etymologically connecting ordinary conditions and a habitual (or familiar) way of knowing. But he is also explicitly calling this a way of "knowing," despite its implicit, covert, *unreflective* form. And what I know in this way is that the community I inhabit is both my basis (what enables me to pursue my individual projects) and my purpose (what I aim to uphold by performing my role within it).[72]

---

[72] Hegel in this context also distinguishes "disposition" and "opinion": "If furthermore *disposition* is considered to be that, which can originate independently [*für sich*] and arise out of subjective representations and thoughts, it is being confused with opinion, for from this perspective it is being deprived of its true ground, i.e. objective reality" (PR §268R). This distinction will be especially relevant for us when we get to Hegel's critique of opinion, which will be a topic of the fourth chapter. At this point, I want to flag that Hegel thinks opinions can indeed swing free of, and even conflict with, the content of this disposition. In other words, it is possible for someone to be of the opinion that their private wealth has no social conditions, that he is a "self-made man," though this would be at odds with the disposition he expresses as an integrated member of ethical life (assuming that he is an integrated member of ethical life).

1.5 Principled Habits

Although passages of this kind leave little room to doubt that Hegel takes habit to be absolutely vital to ethical life and that he considers habit an expression of knowledge about ethical life, it is still unclear how this conception of ethical habits is compatible with his anthropological account. Habit after all poses a difficulty that Hegel must acknowledge, given that he seems to share Kant's picture of habit. So the next task is to reconsider whether Hegel's anthropological account really does compel him to dismiss fully formed habit as essentially unfree. Here a second look at the "Anthropology" reveals a richer understanding of the range of habits of which we are capable. While Hegel focuses on those habits that are not fundamentally different in kind from those we share with nonhuman animals, he does indicate that at least some human habits do exhibit a more complex structure that sets them apart from fixed behavioral dispositions. What is important about them is that exercising them requires intelligence and so makes them normatively guided.

Although Hegel emphasizes that habit frees up our minds for other matters, he also challenges any stark antithesis between habit and attention that such a conception presupposes. This antithesis is once again especially pronounced in Kant's *Anthropology*, in which Kant writes that attention is only enlivened "through the *new … Everyday life* or the *familiar* extinguishes it."[73] The idea seems to be that habituation employs repetition in order to familiarize us with our environment, making us inattentive to our surroundings, and that it is only an encounter with something unfamiliar that ruptures our habituated expectations and thus enlivens our attention. Without denying that habit can produce inattentiveness,[74] Hegel nevertheless suggests that the exercise of at least certain habits seems to require that we be attentive and inattentive both at once, and not one at the expense of the other. "Thus we see that in habit our consciousness is at the same time present in the thing, is interested in it and conversely nevertheless is absent from it, is indifferent to it" (Enz. III §410A).

Such a structure is already visible in many of our skills. While it is true that, when I become skilled in a certain activity, I no longer need to think about every movement I make, this does not mean that I am unaware of what I am doing or why I am doing it. The difference is that I now conceive of my own action as a single process, rather than as a sequence of discrete steps.[75] The steps themselves have become "mechanical" in the sense of fluidly automatic.

---

[73] Kant, *Anthropology from a Pragmatic Point of View*, 7:163.
[74] This is a feature of habit that Hegel takes quite seriously, and that he associates with its potentially "deadening" side effect. I will return to this topic.
[75] "This [general manner of conduct] is one which is integrated into a simplicity to such an extent that in it I am no longer conscious of the particular differences among my individual activities" (E §410A).

Moreover, my awareness of my own action is mediated in a further way. An agent puts her skills to use in pursuit of certain ends that direct her activity as a whole, including those movements to which she is no longer attending. We have already seen that the skilled body becomes an instrument for the attainment of these ends. But skills are rarely mere means to extrinsic ends, for they become part of one's self-conception. When I learn how to play the piano, I not only make my body into a better tool for producing melodies, I also come to conceive of myself as a piano player. It is in virtue of this self-conception that I care to play *well*, and not merely "efficiently," and thus to subject my activity to musical norms. In this way skilled actions can be guided by a determinate self-conception that is formed through habituation and in turn manifested in habitual conduct.[76] As unconscious or mechanical as various aspects of my activity may become, this activity as a whole remains nonetheless expressive of a self-conception, moreover of a self-conception to which only habit entitles me.

What really complicates the standard reading, however, is the role Hegel ultimately reserves for the presence of consciousness *in* habitual conduct itself. I take this to be the true lesson of his anthropological account, one that is initially obscured by a rather generic characterization of habit and that for this reason seems to have remained relatively unnoticed. The crowning illustration is, according to Hegel, the habit of writing. Learning how to write is at face value the acquisition of a skill like any other. I have to practice it in order to be able to do it. But the ensuing activity is not simply unconscious or mechanical. As we learn how to write, we admittedly grow oblivious of the particular features that distinguish one instance from another. But through this very same training we likewise learn to attend to what these diverse instances share. In a highly rich and revealing passage, Hegel claims that

> If the activity of writing has become a habit, then our self has so completely mastered all of the relevant details, has so infected them with its universality, that they are no longer present to us as peculiarities and we only have the universal before our eyes. Consequently we see that in habit our consciousness is simultaneously present in the subject matter, interested in it, and yet conversely absent from it, indifferent to it. (Enz. III §410A)

What Hegel suggests is that, in the exercise of writing, the mind is *both* present and absent, interested and indifferent. I am paying attention to what Hegel calls the "universal" aspect of my activity – to the content I am trying to

---

[76] As Hegel puts it, "In habit the human being relates himself not to contingent and singular emotions, representations, desires, etc., but to himself, to a general manner of acting (*allgemeine Weise des Tuns*) that is posited through himself and that has become his own, and this is why he appears as free" (Enz. III §410A).

communicate, but also to the means (words, sentences, paragraphs) available to me for doing so. At the same time, I have learned to disregard many irrelevant peculiarities, such as the idiosyncrasy of my handwriting, the individual letters that compose the words that I am now so used to seeing written down. One could say that such behavior expresses a grasp of how to proceed from one instance to the next in a consistent manner.

Hegel explains this double aspect through the concept of a "rule," since following rules requires simultaneous attention to commonalities and disregard for difference in precisely this way. But the term "rule" may strike us as misleading, for when an agent has acquired the relevant habit, the rule itself becomes disposable. In fact, habit indicates that the agent has internalized the rule to such an extent that she has no further use for it. Rules may be useful during the process of habituation. For example, I may need to think about the rules for placing commas before I am successful at putting them in the right places. But even when rules serve such an educational purpose, habituation is complete only when we know how to go on without their aid. So when writing has become second nature to us, we no longer need continually to rehearse the *Chicago Manual of Style*. It is for this reason that Hegel describes habit as possessing "the form of recollection" (Enz. III §410A) – once we acquire the habit, the rule itself recedes into memory and formulating it would require calling it back to mind.

Hegel's point, however, is that rules have not thereby ceased to guide our behavior. It is similar to the point Gilbert Ryle makes about the skilled arithmetician: "In a certain sense of 'think' he never thinks of the rules. In another sense of the word, however, he is thinking of the rules all the time; for he is continually applying them currently and skillfully. The rules are now *habits* of operating."[77] Both the skilled arithmetician and the habitual writer are keeping the rules in mind precisely because they need no further reminders. So in one sense, a habitual writer does not think about them, but in another sense, she is thinking of them, for her gaze is now directed away from the particular and solely toward the universal aspects of what lies before her. As we can see, when it comes to habits of meeting normative requirements, Hegel admits that these are guided by insight into how to proceed, though this insight is an implicit one.[78] Rather than applying the universal to the particular, she recognizes the universal *in* the particular, even while her attention remains fully absorbed by the specific situation at hand.[79]

---

[77] Ryle (2009), 36–37.
[78] Ryle (2000) actually draws a distinction between habits and intelligent capacities, characterizing the former as merely automatic (42–44).
[79] I just want to flag that this conception of habitual action differs from that proposed by Pollard (2003), who has argued that it is an intellectualist prejudice to expect that habitual actions are

At this point, it is worth recalling how Hegel characterizes the content of ethical insight. He objects to the motive of duty and to that of inclination on similar grounds, because he regards them both as products of abstraction, of turning our attention away from the situation in which we find ourselves and toward our inner lives. So the thought of what I ought to do as such is for him no less an artifact of excessive abstraction than the thought of what I want to do. Rather, what should move us to act is *die Sache*, which I spelled out as the universal made concrete in the specific situation confronting me. Now we see that it is precisely habit that directs our attention toward *die Sache* in the right way, for habit crowds out abstract considerations about the law as a law and its tentative applicability by fixing our gaze on its concrete manifestation. In other words, habit overcomes the abstract form of the law without sacrificing its universality. But Hegel understands this universality differently from Kant. A law is universal, not because it is binding on all rational beings, nor because it conforms to sheer lawfulness as such, but because its enactment bears on the survival of the rational social order. It need not be anything grander than, say, a professional code.

In order to illustrate how this might work, let us return to an earlier example, a physician committed to the Hippocratic Oath. As a first-year medical student, she participates in something called the "white coat ceremony," during which she is asked to recite this oath, to call to mind its explicit formulations, and to note which types of actions it commands and which it prohibits. But even though the oath outlines the code of conduct to which her profession commits her, it would be very odd if she needed to run through its provisions whenever faced with a patient. Once she becomes a doctor, her conduct itself becomes an expression of the code. One might say that the rules it contains have become her second nature. And this seems to be true even in professions that lack a ceremonious oath of this kind. In my capacity as an educator, I make a habit of showing up for my office hours and for responding to student emails in a timely manner. These habits are grounded in a commitment to making myself available to students when they need academic help. I take this to be a pedagogical principle inscribed into my role, though it is not one I need to invoke very often. When I interact with students, I simply am a teacher, and not just playing the part.

It is nonetheless crucial for Hegel that internalizing rules in this way does not amount to disposing of them for good, for it must at least remain possible for us to translate our habits back into rule-like form, even if we as a matter of fact rarely do so. So despite the privileged status he accords the habit of

---

only rational if they involve consciousness (rather than absentmindedness) at the moment of action. See especially 423–424.

the ethical, it is this translatability that limits the extent to which Hegel would agree with more recent efforts to rehabilitate Aristotelian virtue ethics. There is an obvious way in which the conception of virtue I have been ascribing to Hegel deliberately overlaps with that of Aristotle. Both hold that habituation must comprise a significant component of moral education and both would probably accuse Kantian virtue of being mere continence, namely self-control in the face of contrary inclinations. But Hegel does retain Kantian elements worth highlighting, specifically the continued significance of principles, even once these have become submerged into our habitual conduct. This is something that seems to be absent from Aristotle's account, since virtue for Aristotle consists in knowledge of particulars and so possesses a content that cannot be captured "under any set of rules."[80]

This difference becomes better visible when comparing Hegel's picture of virtue with that put forward by John McDowell. Like Hegel, McDowell foregrounds the significance of second nature and insists on its indispensable role in ethical action. The virtuous agent, according to McDowell, simply knows how to respond to a particular situation without needing first to call general rules of conduct to mind. Her behavior is largely unreflective, though the mind remains at work in it. Once we have acquired the right second nature, "the practical intellect does not dictate to one's formed character – one's nature as it has become – from the outside. One's formed practical intellect – which is operative in one's character-revealing behavior – just is an aspect of one's nature as it has become."[81] But unlike Hegel, McDowell insists that the insight constitutive of virtue is irreducibly "uncodifiable," by which he means that it resists being translated into a code.[82] The virtuous agent knows what to do, not just without needing to invoke rules prospectively, but also without being retrospectively able to explicate what she knows in rule-like form. According to McDowell, to think otherwise is to fall prey to a prejudice about the nature of reason – "the idea that acting in the light of a specific conception of rationality must be explicable in terms of being guided by a formulable universal principle."[83] This insistence on uncodifiability is McDowell's debt to the Aristotelian tradition and to its skepticism about the capacity of rules to determine ethical judgment.[84]

---

[80] Aristotle, *Nicomachean Ethics*, 1104a7.

[81] McDowell (1998a), 186.

[82] To be more precise, McDowell means that the virtuous person cannot capture what she knows as a major premise of a practical syllogism, so as a principle that could dictate a particular action when combined with a minor premise. While it might be true that she cannot capture *all* she knows in terms of principles, this does not yet indicate that principles would be idle in practical reasoning.

[83] McDowell (1998b), 58.

[84] McDowell also enlists Wittgenstein's rule-following skepticism in order to argue for the uncodifiability of ethical knowledge. But he seems to overestimate the reach of this skepticism.

Principled Habits 61

Hegel clearly does not subscribe to uncodifiability. That this is his position could not be any clearer, given his polemical writings against the uncodifiability of German law. Those opposed to codification, such as his colleague Savigny, argued that the richness of the German way of life would be lost, if customs were translated into an explicit code. These arguments rested on a sharp divide between a customary way of proceeding and formulated rules of conduct. Hegel addresses these arguments directly in his *Philosophy of Right* and objects to the assumption that law and habit are fundamentally opposed. Codification is not attempting to introduce a new content, so to revise our habits, but merely to capture the very content they already contain. And codification would not prevent us from following laws habitually. As he puts it, "That [such customary rights] [*Gewohnheitsrechte*] should have, through their form of being habits [*Gewohnheiten*], the advantage of becoming a piece of life ... is an illusion, since the valid laws of a nation do not cease to be its habits merely because they have been written down and collected" (PR §211R). In calling for an explicitly formulated legal code, Hegel recognizes full well that laws underdetermine their application and that good judgment is and always will be needed.[85] So a legal code does not make judicial courts obsolete. But Hegel thinks that there are a number of grave dangers in dispensing with laws altogether and encouraging that judgment swing free from rule-like constraints. The first has to do with objectivity, the second with consistency, and the third with critique.

Hegel worries that, without the constraints that only explicit rules are capable of imposing, socially cultivated habits could evolve into something arbitrary and contingent and thus lose their objective orientation.

Customary rights themselves – since only animals have their law as instinct, whereas only human beings have theirs as habit – contain the moment of being thoughts and being known. Their difference from laws consists only in the fact that the former are known in a subjective and contingent manner, so that they are less determinate for themselves and the universality of thought is more obscure. (PR §211R)

As this passage suggests, Hegel is not retracting his view that ethical habits express insight into the good. He is merely reminding us that they express genuine insight, and not mere subjective conviction, only when they remain

---

Just because rules do not interpret themselves and depend on perception and judgment does not mean that they are impotent in guiding conduct at all. Wittgenstein is contesting only a certain philosophical conception of rules. And he certainly does not advocate that we stop thinking of mathematics – his primary example – as a rule-governed practice. This criticism of McDowell can be found in Wallace (2006).

[85] As Hegel admits, "That collisions arise in the application of the laws, where the understanding of the judge has its place, is completely necessary, for otherwise implementation would be a completely mechanical process" (PR §211A).

tethered to the "right of objectivity." It is only when habits concord with shared codes of conduct that they can be said to be properly "sighted," rather than merely contingent and arbitrary. Left to my own devices, I can develop all sorts of ways of behaving like an educator, not all of which are properly circumscribed by my role. An explicit code of conduct is needed to prevent such wayward subjective developments, to help me keep myself in line with institutional requirements.

Hegel's second worry, which concerns consistency, is closely related to this first. Even if we do not need to lean on principles very often in our lives, Hegel suggests that we might need them, should we stumble upon an unfamiliar situation, one in which we are unable to proceed naturally. I might find myself in a situation that is sufficiently unfamiliar that I cannot simply react as I otherwise would, but need first to pause and to deliberate about how to approach it. Hegel suggests that this process of deliberation would in large part involve determining how to stay true to the principle that has been at work in my previous responses. And even if I discover that the principle is irrelevant to the next step, I will still need to be able to articulate what it is in order to decide whether it can continue to provide adequate guidance. These kinds of cases are especially pronounced in legal judgments. In fact, Hegel speaks against the idea that a "collections of verdicts" could take the place of a code of law in ensuring consistency in future deliberation.[86]

Hegel's third worry about critique goes one step further. Even when we are enacting shared habits and when we enact them consistently, we might stumble upon situations that put into question the ways in which we would otherwise naturally proceed. I will have more to say about these kinds of situations in Chapter 3. At this point, it's worth noting that Hegel is especially concerned to anticipate situations that do not only challenge what it takes to remain true to the principle to which I am committed, but that challenge whether I should seek to remain true to it in the first place. And he suggests that we need to be able to revert to principles when our way of life is shown to be in need of reevaluation, perhaps even revision. As he remarks in his discussion of codification, it is mistake to think that habits are more tied to "life" than explicitly formulated laws, for behind this insistence on "life" is actually a hidden desire to ossify the customs and insulate them from critical scrutiny. This suggests that the primary function of principles is to ensure, not so much

---

[86] "It has likewise been held that collections of verdicts, such as are found in the *corpus juris*, are preferable to a legal code worked out in the most general way, because such verdicts always retain some particularity and historical memory [*geschichtliche Erinnerung*], which one is reluctant to let go. The practice of English law shows clearly enough how pernicious such collections are" (PR §211A).

Principled Habits   63

stability in our conduct, but openness to normative change.[87] Perhaps we only need to invoke them in those moments in which they fail. But, for Hegel, this still means that there must be a translatability between habits and principles, that it must be possible for us to move from one form that the ethical can take, to the other.

I read these remarks about codification and uncodifiability as extending beyond the narrowly legal framework. Although Hegel is certainly not recommending that we turn every institutional principle into an enforceable *law*, he is making a deeper point about the relationship between ethical habits and their implicit rule-like form, a form that might only occasionally require explication. This makes Hegel's position diametrically opposed to McDowell's. For McDowell, the best evidence against codifiability comes precisely from considering unfamiliar situations, in the face of which any given principle will come up short. But it is also no surprise that, even though McDowell officially insists that we are capable of criticizing components of our second nature, he has strikingly little to say about this process.[88] Given the way he conceives of our second nature, it looks like it can at best change behind our backs, so to speak, rather than becoming an object of critical reflection. Though Hegel does not deny that habits can also change gradually and covertly, he thinks that it must be possible for us actively to challenge aspects of our subjectively incorporated social world. And his position is that principles are needed in contexts of critique, for they lend themselves better to reevaluation than implicit, tacit, merely customary ways of life.[89]

Hegel concludes, "To deny a cultured nation, or the legal profession in it, the ability to draw up a legal code – since this does not involve that a system

---

[87] Barbara Herman (2007) cites a similar reason in favor of Kant's view of character against Aristotle's, suggesting that principles have the advantage of keeping the Kantian agent open to new moral phenomena.

[88] Here I have in mind McDowell's recurring image of Neurath's ship, which is supposed to reassure us that we are able to revise our norms without needing a stable standpoint outside of our normative framework. See, for example, McDowell (1996), 81.

[89] I think that there is a further reason that Hegel would not accept the uncodifiability of ethical knowledge. For Hegel, it is important that ethical knowledge not be esoteric, limited to those who are already virtuous. We must be able to communicate what it is that we know when we want to explain or justify our actions to others. It would not be satisfactory if all we could say were, "you have to see things the way I see them." Sometimes it sounds as if this is all that McDowell's virtuous agent can ultimately say, given that the relevant insight is a matter of perception, and given that its content is inextricably wedded to the particular context at hand. But, for Hegel, this would be to conflate virtue and virtuosity, even if the virtuosity in question is not a natural talent, but a skill cultivated through good upbringing. As crucial as good upbringing may be in first enabling us to make ethical judgments, it cannot be a condition for understanding these judgments, even when made by someone else. This means that as a virtuous agent, I must be capable of formulating my insight in terms sufficiently general to become intelligible to others, especially to those affected by my deeds.

of laws with a new content should be made, but only that the present law-like content should be recognized in its determinate universality, i.e. to grasp it in thought – would be one of the greatest insults one could offer to either" (PR §211R). It is an insult because it represents an effort to inhibit a nation's rational activity, which *under certain circumstances* requires an appeal to a system of laws. But this is not to deny that it is better for social participants to heed those laws habitually, rather than experiencing them as external constraints. Hegel does not take habits to be compromised by codification. As a translation, the code still retains the same content as "customary rights," so it is not meant to impoverish, distort, or even revise our habits. And it is anyway not a code that we have to keep perpetually in mind, whenever we adhere to it. As he puts it, "When the ethical is actual in individuals, then it is the soul in general, the general manner of their activity. On the one hand, it can be expressed as a law, but what the law is, is the manner of actuality; it is second nature" (VPR, 88).

1.6 Death by Habit

My aim has been to show that habit is, in Hegel's estimation, not a provisional form that the ethical may or may not take, but that the habit of the ethical is the only adequate realization of subjective freedom in an objectively rational social order. He esteems it so highly because, when the ethical has become habitual to me, it means that I have incorporated certain principles to such an extent that I am now thoroughly convinced of them precisely because I no longer have to think about them as principles. Due to this incorporation, insight into the good turns out to be a piece of self-knowledge, for it is then that "the human being knows the law, but not as something foreign, but instead as his own. It is not even a relation of belief, for in it we are already positing a kind of reflection, but rather it is that in which individuals have their self-feeling, in which they know themselves" (VPR, 87). Hegel hopes to clarify this unreflective relation through a telling analogy with first nature: "The subjective knows [the ethical] as the objective, but it is its own, wherein it lives (fish in the water – lung and air)" (VPR, 85). We are not, unlike fish in the water, "blindly" immersed in ethical life. The similarity between us has rather to do with our willingness to take part in it, shown by our ability to move around it with ease, without reluctance.

Even if one admits that this is a plausible and appealing interpretation of Hegel, one might nevertheless worry that it casts habit in too "affirmative" a light, thus neglecting Hegel's continued ambivalence toward it, an ambivalence that persists well beyond the "Anthropology." In the *Philosophy of Right*, for instance, Hegel (in the Addition) concludes his identification of the ethical and the habitual with the following warning:

The human being also dies out of habit, that is, if he has become completely habituated [*eingewohnt*] to life and has become spiritually and physically blunted, and the opposition between subjective consciousness and spiritual activity has disappeared, for the human being is active only insofar as he has not yet attained something and wants to exert and prove himself in relation to it. When this has been achieved, the activity and vitality disappear, and the indifference [*Interesselosigkeit*] that ensues is spiritual or physical death. (PR §151A)

If Hegel indeed holds that habit is a harbinger of death – that the human being "dies out of habit" – then his assessment of it could not be as unequivocally positive as I have suggested. It might even serve as further evidence in favor of the standard reading, according to which habit is unable to shake the specter of unfreedom that haunts it from the start. In what follows, I will explain why I do not think that Hegel is hesitant about the value of habit, in spite of statements such as that cited above.

Christoph Menke has advanced an interpretation that is more sophisticated than those I have previously discussed, because he holds that habit for Hegel is an irreducibly paradoxical concept, one that is simultaneously "affirmative" and "critical." In one context, Menke describes it as the punch line of an antinomy meant to show that freedom necessarily results in unfreedom, but that this cannot be avoided or overcome.[90] As Menke puts it, "the concept of second nature marks, to Hegel's mind, both spirit's highest peak and its deepest lapse."[91] It is spirit's highest peak, and thus an achievement to be affirmed, because it enables liberation from mere nature and so allows for the development of a will with aims in the first place. Menke even calls habituation an "ontological transformation" that "turns the body, a given or predefined being that determines who I am and what I do, into a site of possibilities."[92] But Menke denies that this is the whole picture. To insists on it would be to assimilate Hegel to the ancient (or, more specifically, Aristotelian) conception of habit, according to which habit comprises the successful completion of an educational process. My reading would be an example of such an assimilation. According to Menke, in contrast, Hegel's concept of habit is meant to challenge and resist precisely this.

Thus he argues that habit must also be seen as a "critical concept" in Hegel's framework, by which he means that it "denotes a manifestation of spirit that is in contradiction with its own concept."[93] The contradiction in question is captured in the phrase "spiritual mechanism." While habit develops our capacities and thereby opens up new possibilities for action, genuinely spiritual activity is

---

[90] See Menke (2010), 687–688.
[91] Menke (2013), 31.
[92] Ibid., 36.
[93] Ibid., 41.

conducted *knowingly* – with what Menke calls "practical knowledge" – while habitual activity is not. This practical knowledge involves both universal and particular elements: "it is knowledge *of* the universal *in* the particular; it is knowledge of what it is good to do in a situation that has a variety of aspects and determinations."[94] Habit, in contrast, has nothing but a universal content. It can be fully captured in a rule that is applied in the same way every time. Not only does it not require a perceptiveness toward the particular features of the situation at hand – it is even incompatible with it. To act habitually is to act mechanically, ignorant of what sets this situation apart from others. Menke argues that this makes habit an example of "abstract universality," which is clearly a term of criticism in Hegel's vocabulary.

The fact that habit represents a "lapse" or even "contradiction," however, does not mean that it is merely a transitional stage, which is to give way to something higher, freer, more reflective. This is what makes Menke's interpretation more sophisticated than the standard reading. But I nonetheless think that it is no less off the mark. In order to see this, let us consider an example of a habitual action, such as brushing one's teeth. Although this activity surely has mechanical aspects, since I am capable of the motions involved without needing to think about each and every one of them, it is clearly exercised with an eye to the particular situation at hand. It is not as if I brush my teeth at 10 PM every day, irrespective of context. When I travel, I would ordinarily wait until I have reached my destination before brushing my teeth. I would not begin to brush them at the airport, simply because it is 10 PM and I brush my teeth at this hour every day. But under certain circumstances, I might brush them at the airport because I realize that I will be arriving at my destination late and exhausted and I want to be able to go to sleep straightaway. The crucial point is that, were I to practice teeth-brushing in this purely mechanical way, I would have developed a kind of tic or obsessive-compulsive behavior which is at best a perversion of habit, not its paradigmatic case. In other words, habits are not in principle a case of abstract universality, if "abstract" is meant to suggest context-insensitivity and lack of perceptiveness toward the particularities of the situation at hand. Habits can turn abstractly universal, but then they have declined into tics or obsessions. It is perhaps a terminological question whether it makes sense to continue to call such purely mechanical behavior "habitual" at all. In any case, while habits can decline into tics or obsessions, Menke makes the mistake of taking their features to be essential features of habit in general.

So my disagreement with Menke is the following: I would deny that habits are purely mechanical for Hegel, since Hegel himself admits that the rule

---

[94] Ibid., 38.

they express is one that cannot be applied without the assistance of attention, perception, and judgment. And while I admit that habits can turn into tics or obsessions that swing free of context, I would also deny that this process of decline is necessary. Menke strongly suggests that habits cannot help becoming thoroughly mechanical, that this is their fate. But I see no reason to think of this lapse of habit as its inevitable evolution. It is, however, a familiar one, and this explains why Hegel warns against excessive habituation and why he tends to associate habit and death. I conclude by showing how my reading can accommodate these warnings and associations.

Though Hegel does not state this explicitly, it would be reasonable to assume that the deadening effects of excessive habituation have something to do with habit's mechanical side. Mechanisms after all display an inflexibility in the face of unanticipated changes in their environment and so could present a hindrance to the end of living beings, which is to survive in the face of such changes. And this would be true of the habit of the ethical as well, even though as we have seen its exercise can never be purely mechanical. Let us consider another example – politically correct speech. I can develop the habit of speaking in ways that count as sensitive and considerate in my present environment and yet not in another, or no longer once my own environment has sufficiently changed. Since the rules of speech are themselves mutable, the habits of applying them must be as well. So if I want to stay true to a principle as general as "speak sensitively or considerately," my habits of speaking have to be adjusted to new circumstances. These objective changes might be cultural in an informal way, but they might also be institutional, even political. What this implies, I take it, is that sometimes an adjustment of habit is required, an adjustment that is beckoned by the circumstances themselves. The problem with habit, then, is that it could resist its own adjustment, even though it would be false to conclude that it makes adjustment principally impossible. The very fact that we have acquired habits should rather serve as evidence of the opposite – of our flexibility and capacity for adaptation. Nevertheless in the face of changing circumstances, circumstances in which new rules are in order, old habits can stand in the way.

But there might be a more pervasive problem facing the habit of the ethical, a problem that is not limited to occasions of social change, for any habit that is repeated often enough can turn into an empty ritual, sapped of its ethical significance. This would be another version of the decline of habit, its disintegration into something else. In other words, I could become so accustomed to doing the right thing that I cease to do it because I am convinced of its goodness. I would still be doing it in a context-sensitive way, and yet I would be merely going through the motions, alienated from my own activity. This detachment of habit from insight can be understood as a form of death. While it need not threaten my own individual survival, for I might very well remain perfectly adept at responding appropriately to my circumstances, it would threaten the survival of the social order as a form of ethical *life*, and so an embodiment of the "living good" (PR §142) that we are committed to sustaining. That said, I do not think that for Hegel this deadening effect of excessive habituation comprises the inevitable fate of the habit of the ethical. His warnings and associations appear, after all, in the Additions. They are meant to show the ways in which habits can degenerate, not challenge his main argument. And even though he takes this possibility seriously, it only goes to show that participating in a living form of ethical life is a more complicated matter than simple immersion in it. What I have in mind are forms of cultural participation that are as mundane as habits themselves, and yet represent a feat of reflection beyond that involved in mere habituation. These forms of cultural participation are partly habitual, but also partly reflective. They are the subject matter of the next chapter.[95]

---

[95] A part of this chapter has appeared in German in Novakovic (2015).

2 Culture

Even though Hegel privileges a habitual comportment within ethical life, this is not all that social participation amounts to for him. Being an active participant turns out to involve a higher degree of reflection than habit on its own incorporates. It involves, for one, a critical engagement with our practices, should they call for criticism. I will address this topic in the next chapter. But even when reflection is not critical in spirit, it remains a crucial, though largely inconspicuous aspect of social participation. This is in part why the dangers that habit introduces are not so worrisome after all. According to Hegel, we are (in this case *unlike* fish in the water) never merely immersed in ethical life. The major difference between us has to do, not just with the knowing way we conduct ourselves, but also with our role in shaping the very environment in which we immerse ourselves. This process of forming one's world – making this world a *work* – is one he associates with culture. Just like the process of habituation, it contains a moment of reflection. But unlike habituation, it establishes a relation to our practices that is itself more reflective than the one introduced by habit, in which reflection is initially employed but eventually overcome. So the habit of the ethical, even when reconceived, needs to be supplemented and complemented by cultural participation, which is nonetheless no less pervasive and mundane.

Although I want to show that cultural participation is for Hegel an integral aspect of what it means to be a member of ethical life and of what it takes to keep ethical life "alive," it bears mentioning that Hegel does not on the face of it appear especially concerned with it. In the *Philosophy of Right*, Hegel's task is to delineate the structure of a rational social order – a structure that any order would have to embody in order to count as rational, irrespective of its distinct cultural backdrop – so his focus is not on this cultural backdrop. In other contexts, too, Hegel does not seem to provide a unified conception of what can be classified as "culture." One obvious place to look for such a conception is in the domain of "Absolute Spirit," which refers to art, religion, and philosophy. But even though these could be regarded as a culture's highest articulation, they cannot represent the whole of culture, which extends to the backdrop from which art, religion, and philosophy emerge. In other words, a culture seems to exceed its own art, religion, and philosophy. And we participate in a culture, even when we do not make or view art, attend religious ceremonies, or practice philosophical reflection.[1] Indeed, it is the connection between ethical life [*Sittlichkeit*] and custom [*Sitte*] that raises questions about the status of culture in Hegel's account. We think of customs as culturally diverse and particular, but also as inherited and entrenched. And we think of them as comparatively commonplace, encompassing such things as culinary traditions, conversational norms, and modes of dress that determine in large part how we as a matter of fact conduct ourselves in daily life.[2]

My aim in this chapter is to show that Hegel does have an account of culture relevant to his practical philosophy and that it comes in the form of *Bildung*. Interestingly enough, Hegel never uses its more obvious synonym, *Kultur*.[3] He nearly always prefers to speak in terms of *Bildung* instead. *Bildung* is one of those German terms that can be translated in so many different ways that it is probably better to just leave it untranslated. It is relevant for my purposes here because it can be translated as "culture," but it has a different set of connotations from *Kultur*, which help explain Hegel's preference for it. First, *Kultur* tends to be associated with the particular customs that distinguish one cultural community from another, and *Bildung* isn't. This means that, unlike *Kultur*, it doesn't have connotations of provinciality. Second, *Bildung* encompasses not only the notion of culture as an end product, which is the domain of *Kultur*, but also the processes involved in forming a culture. Since the term refers to a process, it suggests that perhaps culture should be understood as an ongoing endeavor, rather than something that is at some point in time finished and fixed. Third, *Bildung* refers to the formation of a shared culture as well as to individual cultivation, which is why it is sometimes translated as "education." As we will come to see in the course of this discussion, these three aspect of *Bildung* are for Hegel equally essential and inextricably interlinked.

By focusing on Hegel's conception of *Bildung*, I want to foreground that culture, even though it can take a variety of forms, exhibits a consistently reflective structure throughout. Culture is not discontinuous with habit, but it is not reducible to it either. One can certainly participate in a culture in a habitual

---

[1] The relationship between "Objective Spirit" and "Absolute Spirit" will be the topic of the next chapter.

[2] As Eagleton (2016) has pointed out in his study of the concept, the scope of what is included under "culture" or "cultural" practice is significantly ambiguous: "'Lappish culture' can mean the poetry, music and dance of the Lapps; or it can include the food they eat, the sorts of sport they play and the type of religion they practice; or it can stretch even further to cover Lappish society as a whole, taking in its transport network, system of voting and methods of garbage disposal" (1).

[3] For a historical study of the concept "Kultur" and its relation to "Bildung," see Niedermann (1941).

way, and the foods we cook, the ways we converse, and the clothes we wear are in large part a matter of second nature. At the same time, as cultural practices, they generate a reflective relation between ourselves and what we produce. To recall Hegel's conception of reflection from the *Science of Logic*, I am making something that becomes my mirror image. Work is the prime example of this kind of production, since its products tend to be distinguishable from their producers and so can serve this mirroring function. When we paint a mural, for example, this mural partly constitutes the culture of which we are a part by becoming a piece of our cultural landscape. At the same time, this mural also has the power to reflect this culture back to us, say, by depicting a certain event or person that is of significance to us. In short, culture is for Hegel the site at which everyday forms of reflection take place.

Questions about the role of culture in Hegel's account of ethical life have fallen out of fashion in recent years. This can be explained, I think, by considering the way in which these questions were previously framed, namely, in terms of communitarianism, traditionalism, and sometimes even relativism. To insist that culture plays a role in ethical life was taken to be another way of making Hegel into a traditionalist, someone who privileges entrenched ways of life simply because they are entrenched or someone who wants to insulate these ways from external criticism. Hegel's famous dictum that the rational is actual and the actual rational was sometimes mistakenly taken to be evidence of this.[4] Traditionalists usually claim that customs ought to be preserved because they are customary, and sometimes they argue that they ought to be preserved because they are part of a culture, namely, one's own. This attitude toward culture has implications for reflection, since traditionalists seek to shield given customs from reflective scrutiny and to treat them as immune to reevaluation.

Although the application of these concepts to Hegel's texts may seem somewhat anachronistic, similar questions were not far from Hegel's mind. We should recall that Hegel had a stake in debates about "customary rights" that concerned exactly the proper attitude toward culture, custom, and tradition. Given his position in these debates, it may come as a surprise that Hegel was until relatively recently often cited as a forerunner to communitarianism. Communitarians tend to be especially accommodating to traditionalism, for

---

[4] Walsh (1969) argues that "[Hegel's] attitude is rather that, because [a principle] succeeded in getting itself accepted, it must have been right" (54). Although Walsh does not use this term, Hegel so construed would turn out to be traditionalist, someone who holds that we ought to adhere to whatever principles happen to be accepted simply because they have been accepted. Walsh thus calls Hegel a relativist who denies that there is an impartial perspective from which to evaluate the customs of a particular community. But for Walsh this means that Hegel is engaging in a purely descriptive endeavor. This reading is drawing heavily on Hegel's philosophical methodology and his dismissive attitude toward efforts to "prescribe" how the social world ought to be.

72   Culture

they defend the requests made by particular communities to maintain their local customs, even when these customs look objectionable from the outside, so to speak. Communitarianism is primarily a school of political thought because it emphasizes the role that the state ought to play in protecting the cultures of immigrant and other minority groups. Thus communitarians tend to speak in favor of cultural or group rights. But this school also introduces broader issues regarding the ethical role of culture. Alasdair MacIntyre, for example, argues in *After Virtue* that virtues can only be defined relative to a particular community with a shared way of life and that individual agents can only come to embody these virtues as members of such communities. Given what MacIntyre identifies as the social fragmentation pervasive in modern political and economic institutions, he calls for "the construction of local forms of community within which civility and the intellectual and moral life can be sustained through the dark ages which are already upon us."[5] For MacIntyre, it is the preservation of particular traditions that promises to save us from moral decline.[6]

But it was Charles Taylor who was most explicit in proposing a communitarian reading of Hegel himself. While his interpretation was important in reviving interest in Hegel's work, its influence has since waned. This is partly justified, since Taylor is clearly burdening Hegel with his own political commitments, reading these back into the text. At the same time, some of Taylor's interpretive claims have been dismissed too quickly, I think. Taylor stresses the role of culture in Hegel's account of ethical life, arguing that Hegel recognizes membership in a particular culture to be a necessary condition for any meaningful human activity, for "what we are as human beings we are only in a cultural community."[7] In saying this, Taylor is not merely noting the fact that all human beings inhabit some culture or another, for he wants to make the more contentious claim that cultural membership provides us with the most important basis for identification. Taylor finds evidence for his reading in Hegel's views about internal differentiation.[8] According to Taylor, Hegel thinks that the

---

[5] MacIntyre (1984), 261.
[6] Although MacIntyre is frequently read as a traditionalist, I do not think this is entirely fair. For example, he advocates what he calls "living traditions," which are not monolithic and which do incorporate a variety of voices about the ends and values of the tradition in question. In this respect, I think MacIntyre comes quite close to Hegel.
[7] Taylor (1979), 87.
[8] The lesson he takes from Hegel is that "differentiations of some fairly essential kinds are ineradicable. ... Moreover, they are recognized in our post-Romantic climate as essential to human identity. Men cannot simply identify themselves as men, but they define themselves more immediately by their partial community, cultural, linguistic, confessional and so on" (1979, 114). It is important for Taylor's argument that this differentiation cannot come merely at the institutional level (and so via our various *social* roles), but must come at the cultural level as well.

state as such is too thin and poor to serve as a source of identification and so needs to be internally differentiated into "estates" (*Stände*), which are smaller communities that are established around professional roles and that inevitably come to differ in "culture, values, and modes of life."[9] From this Taylor draws the overtly communitarian conclusion that such communities "in turn demand a certain measure of autonomous life within each state."[10] So Taylor's concern is perhaps less in defending traditionalism or ascribing traditionalism to Hegel, and more in making room for cultural pluralism. According to his reading, Hegel's account of ethical life must incorporate such pluralism in the form of diverse estates, which can be understood as relatively independent communities that coexist within a single state and that provide their members with a sufficiently thick and rich basis for identification.

So in thinking about the status of culture in ethical life, we are led to two sets of intersecting questions. One has to do with traditionalism and the extent to which our relation to custom is, can be, or ought to be a reflective one. The other has to do with pluralism about customs and the extent to which Hegel's conception of ethical life accommodates such internal diversity in ways of life. Taylor's communitarian reading seems to be more directly concerned with the second issue. At the same time, to insist on pluralism in the way he does is to insist that these plural communities should be permitted to perpetuate their customs without having to evaluate them. As a reading of Hegel, Taylor's is clearly exaggerated, for there is little evidence to suggest that Hegel thought of culture as the most important basis for identification, whatever that may even mean. If there is a candidate for such a basis in his *Philosophy of Right*, it would surely be the state, which is the most fundamental condition for living ethically.[11] Nonetheless, Taylor's recommendation that the role of culture be taken more seriously and his suggestion that it is estates that promise to introduce cultural diversity are not entirely misguided.

Let me briefly turn to two readings that have underplayed or even denied the role of culture altogether. One is Allen Wood's, who admits that "Hegel's conception of ethical life has often been interpreted as committing him to ethical relativism and traditionalism," but given that "customs and traditions often represent a culture's dead past (what Hegel calls 'positivity'), the ethical advice it yields would often be wrong and without any rational foundation."[12]

---

[9] Taylor (1979), 110.
[10] Ibid.
[11] Moland (2011) provides a helpful discussion of the distinction between *Volk* and *Staat* in Hegel's political philosophy. While a *Volk* is a culturally unified and distinct community that share inherited traditions, a *Staat* consists of a set of institutions that abstract from that inheritance and provide a reflective standpoint from which to evaluate those traditions. What Moland emphasizes is that the traditions of a *Volk* are not merely overcome, but reflectively, re-appropriated by a "*Volk als Staat*" (82–89).
[12] Wood (1990), 195.

As he states, "[if] we look closely at Hegel's detailed discussion of modern ethical life, it is striking how little he concedes to ethnic diversity, how little room he leaves for the impact of varying cultural traditions on the social and political structures of modern states."[13] In his words, Hegel is even "an apostle of a single modern world culture founded on universal principles of reason."[14] Although Wood is clearly right that Hegel is delineating the contours of a rational social order that is meant to transcend cultural divides, he draws some unwarranted conclusions on this basis.[15] For one, the fact that Hegel is delineating universal standards does not mean that he is promoting a single world culture. In fact, there is plenty of evidence to suggest that Hegel thought his philosophical project underdetermines many concrete customs, even many positive laws, operative in specific societies. To cite one example: although Hegel thinks he has shown that a rational form of social life must include a monogamous, nuclear family with the specific function of nurturing the individuality of its members, he admits that there is a wide range of ways of making family life happen. It can happen by encouraging that people who fall in love enter into marital unions. But it can also happen by letting the parents arrange the marriages of their children.[16] Although Hegel actually prefers the latter way (because it strikes him as less arbitrary), he admits that his philosophy has no real say in the matter.

Michael Hardimon is also someone who has stressed the differences between Hegel and communitarianism, but on slightly different (and more promising) grounds. Hardimon echoes Wood when he claims that Hegel is not interested in local forms of identification, but in our identification with broader structures that transcend cultural divides. His main disagreement, however, is with the communitarian conception of social identification. The communitarian thesis is that our social roles are so central to our self-conception that we cannot abandon them without losing a core part of ourselves. According to Hardimon, to assume that we have an explicit self-conception that takes social roles into account is to get things the wrong way around.[17] Hegel does not assume that

---

[13] Ibid., 207.

[14] Ibid., 208.

[15] For example: "Hegel's conception of the ethical is commonly understood to be an endorsement of cultural pluralism and relativism. But we have seen that on closer inspection it turns out to be just the opposite: a universal standard for ranking the rationality of different social orders" (Wood 1990, 205).

[16] In PR §162 and §162R, Hegel claims that it a duty to get married, and that marriage has to involve consent and an enduring connection (two becoming one), but that aside from these constraints, the customary practices can vary widely. In the case of arranged marriage, the decision precedes the affection. In the case of modern marriages, affection is what occasions the marriage. Hegel even suggests that the second is perhaps inferior from an objective standpoint, because it is less likely to result in a stable union.

[17] "One of Hegel's central aims in the Philosophy of Right is to help his readers recognize that they do in fact conceive of themselves as members of the family, civil society, and the state ...

we are self-conscious of our roles. Rather, our social identification must first be made explicit to us. Once it is made explicit, we face a moment of alienation – of distance from the roles we once thoroughly inhabited – but this also opens up the possibility of reflectively reconstituting this identification and so turning it into a self-conception for the very first time.

Many have noted that there is something paradoxical about the notion of a "cultural identity," because participating in a culture seems to be at least in tension with self-conscious identification. If I feel the need to insist on my cultural identity in an explicit way, I am only proving that my culture has already lost its hold over me and that I no longer inhabit my culture as I previously did, when I was a fully immersed and thus unreflective participant in it. As Anthony Appiah has observed, "you might wonder, in fact, whether there isn't a connection between the thinning of the cultural content of identities and the rising stridency of their claims."[18] In a similar vein, Samuel Scheffler remarks that "culture" is an ethnographic concept employed in describing, interpreting, or explaining the practices of a community from the standpoint of an outsider. It is not a concept employed by the members of that community in their own deliberations or justifications. According to Scheffler, "to describe something as being (merely) a cultural norm or value can sometimes be a way of debunking it: of denying that it has the kind of authority that its adherents take it to have."[19]

Hegel is indeed aware of this tension inherent in self-conscious identification, and he even suggests that highly reflective cultures inevitably come to erode their confidence in their own customs because they invite a skeptical attitude toward their justifiability.[20] At the same time, he also challenges this stark opposition between participating in a culture and adopting a reflective attitude toward it. In order to illustrate what Hegel takes their proper relationship to be, I will turn to his conception of *Bildung* as he outlines it in the *Phenomenology of Spirit*, specifically in the chapter titled "*Bildung*," but to a certain extent also in his chapter on "Lordship and Bondage." What I hope to show is that this conception of *Bildung* is relevant to the *Philosophy of Right* as well, for

---

from a Hegelian standpoint, the communitarian view that modern people start out explicitly conceiving of themselves in terms of their social roles gets things backwards. ... Coming to explicitly think of oneself as a family member, member of civil society, and citizen is, in Hegel's view, one of the crucial steps in the subjective process of reconciliation" (Hardimon 1994, 162).

[18] Appiah (2007), 117.

[19] Scheffler (2007), 120. For Scheffler, this makes the concept of "culture" significantly different from "tradition." Unlike the former, "tradition" is a normative concept that can be employed in deliberation and justification by those who perpetuate it.

[20] See the discussion of skeptical culture in Forster (1989). Wood (1990) even points this out: "Hegel even thinks that reflection inevitably exposes the limitations of every ethical order, and so tends, in the long run, to undermine both the ethical attitude and the ethical order" (218).

it outlines the underlying structure of all *Bildung*, even the sort discernible in ethical life. So once I have drawn this alternative picture, I will turn to the role that culture plays in the *Philosophy of Right*, specifically in his account of civil society. The interpretation I want to propose admits that culture is integral to Hegel's account of ethical life, but this requires that we first reconceive culture in such a way that we can see participation in it as a process of continued production of and reflection on culture.

So my aim in this chapter is to propose an account of culture that shows that Hegel takes our relation to custom to be far less unreflective than worries about traditionalism suggest, even when this relation remains strictly speaking uncritical. This means, first of all, that Hegel provides us with a way of distinguishing between being habitually immersed in a culture and actively participating in its constitution. These two relations are not discontinuous, since they emerge from one another and balance each other, thus preventing the death that habit on its own threatens. While cultural participation does not usually rupture our habitual perpetuation, it demands more from us than merely turning our social inheritance into our second nature. This also means that Hegel does not take culture to be something that is merely given, inherited from our predecessors, but rather something that we continue to shape. So what I argue is that the traditionalism charge rests on a misunderstanding of Hegel's conception of culture. He is instead suggesting that we are already reflecting, even when we perpetuate our customs, but in ways we often fail to notice because these forms of reflection are thoroughly pervasive and mundane and so do not draw attention to themselves in the way that critical reflection does.

2.1 *Bildung* in the *Phenomenology*

We can begin to explore Hegel's notion of culture by looking to the *Phenomenology of Spirit*, where *Bildung* plays a central role. There are at least three difficulties facing any effort to extract a conception of *Bildung* from the *Phenomenology*. The first has to do with the fact that Hegel identifies *Bildung* with his own philosophical project. In the Preface he claims that the *Phenomenology* as a whole is in the service of "educating" us to the scientific point of view. Hegel's invocation of the term has led some to describe the *Phenomenology* itself as a philosophical *Bildungsroman* whose subject is not a particular person, but rather the human spirit in general.[21] The basic idea is that we begin with what Hegel calls "natural consciousness," which represents the pre-philosophical point of view, and are then led through a series of failures to the properly philosophical standpoint, Hegel's own "science." This

---

[21] See Abrams (1973).

is an educational process for the reader, but the failures the reader is tracking are failures she is in a sense *re*living, for they are failures that the human spirit has already undergone in its historical development. Although there is clearly something correct about this description of Hegel's project, it does raise a difficulty for my interpretation: if *Bildung* is what is to be achieved in the reading of the *Phenomenology*, its relevance to the non-philosophical forms of culture seems less clear.

The second difficulty has to do with the relationship between this philosophical function of *Bildung* and the chapter within the *Phenomenology* that Hegel titles "*Bildung*,"[22] which represents a specific configuration of spirit, so not its historical development in its entirety. This configuration of spirit is moreover quite unique and distinct, raising questions about whether it can shed light on the nature of culture more generally. In other words, if Hegel is thinking of *Bildung* as something that occurs in a particular place and time – namely, early modern Europe – then it is unclear whether the picture of *Bildung* that we get will be applicable to other cultural contexts as well, whether it can illuminate the structure of all cultural participation, as I claim. The third difficulty arises specifically in connection with this chapter on *Bildung*. As with all configurations that Hegel there investigates, *Bildung* will prove deficient, incapable of meeting its own measure. So given this deficiency, it would seem that one cannot simply extract a conception of *Bildung* from this chapter that will be of enduring relevance for ethical life, at least not without accounting for its supposed shortcomings.

Putting these difficulties aside for now, let us begin by considering how Hegel introduces *Bildung* and what he says about its nature and aim in the Preface to the *Phenomenology*:

This past existence is already the earned possession of universal spirit, which constitutes the substance of the individual and so an inorganic nature that appears external to him. *Bildung* in this respect, regarded from the side of the individual, consists in [spirit's] acquiring that which lies at hand, devouring its inorganic nature, and taking possession of it for itself. But this is, regarded from the side of universal spirit as substance, nothing other than [substance's] acquiring self-consciousness and generating its own becoming and reflection into itself. (PG ¶28)

What is striking is that Hegel defines *Bildung* from two points of view, with respect to the individual and with respect to "spirit as substance," namely, the social order the individual inhabits. He is suggesting that one and the same

---

[22] A question worth flagging is why Hegel identifies *Bildung* as a specific configuration of spirit, given that in the Preface he claims that *Bildung* is both the content of the *Phenomenology* as a whole as well as the process that its reader is supposed to undergo. See Quentin Lauer (1983), 103.

process can be considered from two perspectives, from that of the individual member and from that of the social whole. Since the individual perspective is easier to assume, we can preliminarily say that Hegel has in mind something like a process of *ac*culturation into a way of life that precedes us, into which we are initially simply born. Hegel mentions the "pedagogical progress" during boyhood as the concrete context in which this process unfolds.

Why then does Hegel define *Bildung* as a process of "devouring one's inorganic nature" and "taking possession of it for oneself"? What is it that we need to take possession of, and why? What this formulation suggests is that "inorganic nature" refers to a past existence that has the appearance of something external, even though it is not, since it is already an earned possession. A less obscure way to formulate this would be to say that one's cultural heritage can appear, from the standpoint of the individual, as something inorganic in the sense of fixed and finished. This is the way that customary practices tend to strike a novice, as unyielding and immune to future influence. "Inorganic" can here be contrasted with "living" in the sense of malleable, flexible, capable of change. So when Hegel speaks of an "inorganic" nature, he does not mean things that are inanimate, like tables and chairs. Rather, he seems to have in mind aspects of cultural life, products of the activity of past generations, that have ossified, or at least appear to have ossified.

This construal would suggest that *Bildung* can be understood as a process of incorporating this inheritance in such a way that enlivens it and restores its malleability. Interestingly enough, what Hegel stresses is that this process of enlivening cannot be reduced to the individual point of view, as if it were merely a matter of becoming successfully integrated into a given culture. It is also a process that shapes "spirit as substance," namely, the objective culture into which the individual is being integrated. Relatedly, this process also should not be reduced to that of habituation, as if it were merely a matter of making this objective culture into a second nature. Although customary practices are only fully one's own when they have become habitual, Hegel's idea seems to be that heeding them habitually cannot prevent them from becoming "inorganic" in a further sense, namely, empty rituals to which we are no longer actively committed and which have therefore grown dead to us, even though they have not literally perished.

A relevantly pedagogical example might be the custom of reciting the pledge of allegiance at the start of the school day. This custom can appear inorganic to an immigrant child because it involves a fixed code of conduct to which she better adjust her posture and movements. But this custom can also appear inorganic to those who are practiced in its performance, if they are merely going through the motions in principle no differently from the way they brush their teeth. If we take "inorganic" in this double sense, then we can see two ways in which *Bildung* is supposed to turn the inorganic into something organic. It does it by successfully acculturating an individual into a set of given customs. But it also does it by preventing those customs from becoming rituals that we indifferently repeat. Although Hegel's definition does not yet specify how exactly this is supposed to happen, it characterizes this process of "taking possession" as a "reflection into itself," suggesting that it introduces a reflective relation to that of which we take possession – namely, our cultural inheritance.

What this means becomes clearer in the chapter that is specifically titled "Bildung." The configuration of spirit analyzed in this chapter follows on Hegel's discussion of Greek character and the Roman person. Because of its position between the ancient world and the French Revolution, the account of *Bildung* that this chapter provides contains numerous features that seem to be peculiar to the epoch he is describing. That epoch begins with medieval Christianity and evolves through various stages, such as the knightly ethic of honor, the aristocratic manners of the seventeenth century, and the emergence of absolute monarchy. Moreover it tracks the development of a bourgeois class that became increasingly rebellious and hostile toward the *Ancien Regime*. These peculiarities, in addition to this configuration's deficiency, are going to present a challenge for gleaning a more general account of culture.

In its opening pages, however, Hegel stresses that culture emerges at a particular juncture that makes it relevant for our purposes. It introduces a different relation to custom, a relation that differs from that characteristic of Greek ethical life. In this previous configuration, "Essence has the simple determinateness of *being* for consciousness, which is directed *immediately* upon it and whose custom it is" (PG ¶484). Although the project of culture will consist of an effort to redeem customary practices, it will establish a less immediate relation to custom. This relation will be less immediate because it will make explicit the productive activity in which subjects themselves engage, an activity that shapes customs into what they are. The contrast between Greek ethical life and the world of culture is thus very telling:

We see that these essences correspond to the community and the family of the ethical world, but without possessing the local spirit [*heimischen Geist*], which these have; in contrast, while destiny is foreign to this spirit, here self-consciousness is and knows itself as the actual power of these essences. (PG ¶492)

When Hegel speaks of "essences" in this context, he has in mind the institutions that give individuals objective orientation by prescribing the duties to which they are subject. This is what the state and the family provided in Greek ethical life and it is what made them "substantial" and "essential" in this configuration.[23] As Hegel tells us, cultured subjects retain such a social context,

---

[23] I postpone a more thorough analysis of Greek ethical life for the next chapter.

but they regard it as their own achievement. Culture provides them with a standpoint from which to see these essences as not determined by destiny, but by a human power to form.

So this chapter speaks to this key relation between customs and those who participate in them in a way that transcends the particular historical moment under scrutiny. Later I will examine how Hegel characterizes this time of *Bildung* and why he thinks it involves alienation (*Entfremdung*) and externalization (*Entäusserung*). My aim is to show that modern culture serves as Hegel's model for *Bildung* in general because it highlights crucial features present in all cultural life, for – unlike its predecessors – modern *Bildung* rests on the discovery that every culture is culture through and through.[24]

2.2 Self-Cultivation

Hegel describes the world at the outset of *Bildung* as one that has become "external" and "alien," "the negative of self-consciousness," and so introduces an unprecedented experience of alienation.

> [The] world has here the determination of being something external, the negative of self-consciousness. But this world is a spiritual being, it is in itself the permeation of being and individuality; this its existence is the *work* of self-consciousness; but likewise an immediately present and alien reality, which has its peculiar being and in which it does not recognize itself. (PG ¶484)

Self-consciousness is alienated because it regards the world as something "alien" and "external," a perspective that prevents it from recognizing itself in the world it inhabits. But self-consciousness is mistaken, for the world is in fact a "spiritual being" [*geistiges Wesen*] because "its existence is the *work* of self-consciousness, but at the same time also an immediately present and alien reality, which has its peculiar being and in which it does not recognize itself." *Bildung* can provisionally be characterized as the project of overcoming alienation by recognizing that what looks to be an immediately present and alien reality is in fact its own work. Of course, this is not merely a shift in

---

[24] Hegel's strategy for exploring the relevant features of modern *Bildung* depends on his contrast between the moderns and the ancients. This may raise certain doubts about Hegel's account, considering that his characterization of the Greeks is at best highly schematic, and often clearly inaccurate. It is, however, important to remember that Hegel does not purport to be doing empirical history and is in a certain sense indifferent to whether his description of the Greeks really fits what we otherwise know about them. I will address some of these worries when I deal with Greek ethical life more explicitly. What matters at this point is that Hegel perhaps exaggerates its simplicity, uniformity, and immediacy in order to emphasize certain important elements of modern ethical life, which – even if they were already present in Greek *Sittlichkeit* – acquire an unprecedented status in modernity.

perspective. It is by making it our work that we recognize it to have been our work all along.

In order to understand what kind of alienation Hegel has in mind, we first need to examine its source. Michael Forster interprets the emergence of this alienated world as the aftermath of skepticism, specifically the "skeptical culture" that developed in ancient Greece and Rome.[25] According to Forster's reading, members of Greek ethical life enjoyed a particular form of cognition in which the community was in agreement regarding its fundamental principles and individuals deferred to its authority in their private judgments. In virtue of this pervasive convergence, the Greeks were never conscious of these principles *as* principles. They were not aware of them as products of thinking and thus potentially erroneous, and they were not aware of the fact that there could be competing principles about which disagreement was possible. Skepticism undermined this form of cognition by presenting equally compelling arguments for and against a given principle and thus shattering the immediate and absolute authority it was thought to have. In doing so, it gave rise to a new form of cognition, which saw in the world nothing but the "harshness and objectivity of everyday reality," to use Forster's formulation. According to Forster, individuals came to regard their world as "objective" and "harsh" because it was no longer inhabited by the gods and because they had to acknowledge that their principles might be mere projections that fail to accord with reality.

One way in which they came to cope with this alien world was to construct another world over and above this one, a realm inhabited by an omniscient and omnipotent God. In fact, Hegel defines the world of *Bildung* as one that is fundamentally divided in two: "This spirit thus forms (*bildet*) for itself not just *one* world, but one that is doubled, divided, and opposed" (PG ¶486). Forster argues that this second world is meant to solve the epistemological problems raised by skepticism because we would no longer have to figure out which principles to follow, but need only heed God's commands, since God as the ideal knower possesses the justification of these principles that we are unable to discover. The formation of this other world can be described as a process of self-alienation, for the world of God is alien to our own. We constructed it, and yet we cannot recognize ourselves in it, for the perspective it affords is inaccessible to us. It turns out that this self-alienation is already the work of *Bildung* in its effort to overcome its initial alienation.

Although Forster is able to explain how the construction of a second world responds to the alienating effects of skepticism, he stops short of exploring other aspects of alienation at stake in this chapter. The subject must also find a way of recognizing herself in her own world and so overcoming its objectivity and

---

[25] Forster (1989).

harshness, and this problem is not settled by merely erecting another. In other words, his interpretation can explain the construction of a double world and the rising significance of religious faith, but not the kinds of social structures that were concurrently developed. Hegel casts this failure of self-recognition in two different but related ways. First, he suggests that the problem has its roots in the abstract formalism of Roman law, in which each is treated as a person, a mere bearer of rights devoid of any particularity and indistinguishable from any other. The alienation from "substance," so from the ethical world with its laws and institutions that bestow an individual with a differentiated position, is already experienced within the framework of legal personality. In Hegel's formulation, "he is a person, but a lonely person, who stands over and against *everyone*" (PG ¶481). Persons are alienated from the community in virtue of their formal equality, which robs them of socially recognized self-expression. I am unable to make myself known as the particular individual that I am if my true essence is limited to my equal standing before the law, and I have this standing irrespective of anything I have done. According to Hegel, "Legal personality thus experiences [*erfährt*] ... its substancelessness" (PR ¶482). Hegel casts this as a problem of particularity and universality: I need to win a version of universality that does not come at the expense of particularity. I need to become something real, which means someone in particular, but also someone who is publicly known and acknowledged.[26]

From this point of view, overcoming alienation is a matter of acquiring a particular status or position in the eyes of others. This position is differentiated and so sets me apart from some other members of society, while nevertheless giving my individuality a social expression. Since it is through *Bildung* that I hope to achieve this goal, *Bildung* here becomes synonymous with self-cultivation. Interestingly enough, Hegel describes this process as one of self-alienation, suggesting that I overcome alienation by alienating myself:

Self-conscious is only *something*, it only has *reality* [*Realität*] to the extent to which it alienates itself; thereby it posits itself as universal, and this its universality is its validity and actuality [*Wirklichkeit*]. This *equality* with everyone is not thus not that equality of legal right, nor that immediate recognition and validity of self-consciousness only because it *is*; instead that it counts is through the alienating mediation of having made itself suitable to the universal. (PG ¶488)

Unlike Greek character, I am not immediately recognized, nor is my recognition mediated by my formal standing. Rather, the cultured person becomes recognized in virtue of a process of self-cultivation to which she has subjected

---

[26] A similar problem can be found in Rousseau's *Second Discourse*, according to which socialized individuals develop a passion for recognition which cannot be fully satiated by formal equality, since individuals seek ways to distinguish themselves. See Neuhouser (2014).

herself. Self-cultivation allows me to see my position as my own work, as something that I have achieved. But what I achieve is situated within a social frame – I am simply trying to make myself suitable to the universal. In other words, I am trying to live up to standards that are given to me by the world I inhabit. I assume these standards and measure the success of my self-cultivation by their lights.

Hegel stresses the role of evaluative judgments because social differentiation is so central to this project. What matters is that my position is not occupied by just anyone, and this is in part why those who are cultured pass judgment on those in other social positions. But even among those who occupy the same position – for example, among the "nobles" – there is competition for the attainment of honor, at first through victory in war, and later through battles of wit. What he wants to emphasize is that, in order to attain a socially recognized position, I must become a "type," and this requires subduing what is idiosyncratic about myself. For example, in order to become a courtier, I need to be able to discipline my speech and manners in such a way that they meet the expectations to which a courtier is held, so that the monarch – as well as the servants, serfs, and other courtiers – can recognize me as a courtier. I want to be a "good" courtier, "good of my kind" [*in seiner Art gut sein*] (PG ¶489). Although the standards associated with these types are prescribed to me by the social world I inhabit, turning myself into a type is my own doing and so counts as an achievement worthy of praise.[27]

Hegel describes this process of cultivation as one of self-alienation, for – as was already quoted – "we may say that self-consciousness is only *something*, it has *reality* only to the extent to which it alienates itself" (PG ¶488). One way to understand this is to say that, in order to become cultured, I must relate to myself as an object to be formed or reformed, even if I only ever explicitly attend to some specific aspect of myself. I must also be able to regard myself from an external standpoint and assess my own worth from the perspective of others. Recognition is of course already an important element in upbringing, which presupposes that the child comes to desire the parents' approval. But here I know exactly whose approval I desire – namely, that of a small set of people. Cultivation involves considering one's own behavior and actions from an increasingly anonymous point of view, even if this point of view is relative to class. We no longer want to do merely what a particular individual asks of us, but we want to perform actions that any cultivated person will recognize and esteem. Hegel calls *Bildung* a process of self-alienation because it requires

---

[27] "This individuality forms itself [*bildet sich*] into that which it is in itself, and only by doing so is it in itself and has an actual existence; the degree to which it has culture is the degree to which it has actuality and power" (PG ¶489).

adopting this alienated perspective on one's own conduct and considering how it would look to an observer, even if only to those who are similarly cultured.

This process of self-cultivation can be described as an exercise that echoes reflection in the *Logic*: in taking myself as my object, I am looking in a mirror, so to speak. In other words, I am stepping apart from myself, distinguishing myself from myself. It is this distance that allows me to evaluate myself, to ask myself whether what I see in the mirror reflects my own aspirations. And in reshaping my own "appearance" or "seeming," I am reconstituting its identity with my "essence," confirming that what is visible to others accords with the way I see myself.

Hegel also suggests a second way of interpreting the failure of self-recognition, which *Bildung* is supposed to mend. He claims that agents do not recognize themselves in the world because they do not see it as a product of their work, even though "this its existence is the *work* of self-consciousness" (PG ¶484). We can understand this as an alienation from the standards by which I am measuring the success of self-cultivation. Even if it is I who make myself into a courtier and become a good version of my (social) kind, the relevant kind does not seem to be up to me. I find this position and its standards of success given and inflexible. "[The becoming of the actual world], even though it has come about through individuality, is for self-consciousness one that is immediately alienated and has for it the form of an unshakable actuality" (PG ¶490). The roles themselves strike me as unshakable. What is up to me is whether I become good at embodying these roles, whether I manage to become cultured or not. The objective culture is there already, setting the measure.

But this contrast between personal self-cultivation and the process of cultural formation rests on a misunderstanding of their connection. When Hegel claims that the actual world has come about through individuality, he is pointing out that there would be no world of culture if there were no cultured people in it. Culture itself becomes realized through the self-cultivation of its participants. In other words, it is only because we subscribe to its standards and struggle to meet them that those standards are something real, something that has an actual impact on the structure of social life. Conversely, if we refused to participate in the process of self-cultivation, those roles and their corresponding standards would vanish as well. For Hegel, the very same process of self-cultivation can be also seen as the process of cultural formation, when regarded from the standpoint of substance. These are two sides of the same coin: "What in relation to a single *individual* appears as his cultivation, is the essential moment of *substance* itself, namely, the immediate transition of its universality in thought into actuality. ... His cultivation and his own actuality is therefore the actualization of substance itself" (PG ¶490). This interdependence of self-cultivation and cultural formation has another dimension: the culture I inhabit is revealed to be as malleable as I prove to be in virtue of my capacity for self-cultivation.

This insight into the nature of all culture – its irreducible malleability – is one that modern *Bildung* affords for the first time. This is its significance. Although what it reveals is true of all cultural life, modern *Bildung* is the first culture to foreground it.[28] The discovery made is a genuine one, though it invites a particularly destabilizing form of skepticism with pernicious implications.[29] Thus modern *Bildung* lapses from self-cultivation into an indulgence in artifice. The cultured individual grows so preoccupied with perfecting her own qualities that she honors no limit to the project of forming herself.[30] Hegel argues that the process of cultivation, which started out as a desire to become someone in the eyes of others and so gain an objective existence in the world, evolves into the fantasy that the individual is thoroughly self-made and that there are no constraints on this process, whether imposed by nature or culture. Thus the cultivated individual becomes the enlightened self, "which grasps nothing but the self and everything as the self, i.e. it comprehends everything, it cancels all objectivity (*Gegenständlichkeit*) and transforms all in-itself into a for-itself" (PG ¶486). This highly *self*-reflective form of *Bildung* ends up undermining the very reflection it was meant to afford. *Bildung* had the aim of enabling the individual to find herself in the world, not by "canceling all objectivity," but by expressing herself in objective form.

Although *Bildung* in this chapter of the *Phenomenology* ends up betraying its own nature, it is possible to glean some elements of *Bildung* in general that seem to hold true even for cultures far less self-reflective than early modern Europe. While the Greeks did engage in reflective practices of various sorts,[31] they did not regard their culture as a whole as culture, namely, something of human making. As we will see in greater detail in the next chapter, in the *Phenomenology*, Hegel characterizes Greek culture as divided into two sets of norms, the human law and the divine law, and while the human law – which Hegel identifies with "custom" – could perhaps be reevaluated, the divine law was certainly immutable and inscrutable because it was authored by the gods.

---

[28] As György Markus (1986) puts it, "the view which regards modernity as the *world of Bildung*, contains the correct insight that only modern society knows itself *as* culture, recognizes its institutional world as one which came about in, and is sustained by, human activities. ... But this view at the same time misses the fact that *all* historical worlds are worlds of culture, even if they do not know it" (119).

[29] Here it is worth recalling Forster's term "skeptical culture."

[30] Robert Pippin (2008) points out that in the world of *Bildung*, "possible ethical worlds are understood as if all were mere theatrical masks, as if freedom were not, could not be, a matter of any deep, non-alienated identification with who one is, but a complete and permanent state of alienation, of not being anybody and so potentially being anybody" (146).

[31] They produced works of art, most notably tragedies, that reflected their culture.

Modern culture is marked by the gradual discovery that all laws (of ethical life) are human laws, and so in principle revisable. This does not mean that they *should* be disregarded or even abolished, only that they can be, should grounds for revision emerge.[32]

Thus the initial attitude toward cultural norms as stable reference points by which to assess the success of my self-cultivation gradually crumbles. This increasing realization that culture is no more fixed than I am is a realization that has significant political consequences, since Hegel is tracking the emergence of a revolutionary ideal that adopted an exclusively negative attitude toward cultural inheritance. This realization that culture is sustained by nothing over and above our own participation in it clears the ground for a radical restructuring of social life. Nevertheless, the truth of *Bildung* is that it takes work – work that has simultaneously a subjective and an objective dimension. As Hegel writes in the *Lectures on the Philosophy of World History*, "The individual finds the work as a completed world before him, which he has to incorporate for himself" (VPG, 45). And the individual already does this, not only when she undertakes a revolutionary project, but simply by engaging in self-cultivation. In fact, the revolutionary project of building culture from scratch fails to do justice to the truth of *Bildung* because it rests on a failure to see that the culture we inherit is already a work, a spiritual achievement of prior generations.

2.3 Work

Given our previous description of self-cultivation, it might seem far-fetched to characterize it as a form of cultural contribution. Of course working to become cultured does mean that one is implicitly honoring and perpetuating certain social practices, but this does not seem enough for actively shaping a culture in a way that reveals its essential malleability. Moreover, Hegel described self-cultivation as highly self-absorbed. If what I work on is myself and not something other than me, it does not look like this process of self-cultivation gives rise to anything like an objective culture over and above the community of cultured people. Although the cultured people Hegel describes in this chapter

---

[32] Recognizing that the world is a work has two important implications that escaped less self-reflective cultures. First, it entails that no part of culture can exempt itself from reevaluation and should not be perpetuated simply because it is in place, or because it is commanded by some external authority like the gods. Second, it entails that no practice is in principle unrevisable. But this does not mean that we can simply create or eliminate any and every practice or even construct an entirely new culture from scratch. Moreover, Hegel is worried that our reevaluations can become a source of confusion, for they can mislead us in various ways, giving rise to shallow criticism and blinding us to the true value of a given practice. I will return to this issue of revisability in the next chapter.

are not exactly productive members of social life and seem concerned primarily with their own appearance and status, the artistic interests of the later nobility do point in another direction. One could even say that wielding witty phrases is already a kind of production, though speech as such is relatively ephemeral. But Hegel also mentions the nobility's active support of the arts. Though the artists themselves were usually members of the bourgeoisie, which was thought to lack culture, the nobles nevertheless displayed their degree of cultivation by appreciating the artistic creations of others.

Since Hegel is describing an age for which "culture" became an explicit ideal, it should not be surprising that *Bildung* is here taken as synonymous with what we would call "high culture." This kind of discrimination is already contained in the phrase "being cultured" (*gebildet*), which does not apply to all "acculturated" members of a society. In the context of Hegel's chapter, the arts would rank higher than other artifacts because the standard at stake for the early moderns is closely tied to social class. The kind of society Hegel is here describing is one that is divided into the nobility, which has the leisure to pursue less material ends, and the emerging bourgeoisie, which is occupied solely with the acquisition of wealth. Thus the arts became a mark of culture precisely because they were elevated above the "base" economic activity of the bourgeoisie. But this class antagonism and its accompanying evaluative judgments prove increasingly untenable – again, foreshadowing the collapse of entrenched social distinctions in the wake of the French Revolution. So the kind of formative work that contributes both to self-cultivation and to cultural life is not confined to members of a leisure class that can afford to work only on themselves.

In fact it is the production of objects other than oneself that better illuminates this dual benefit of work, its capacity to culture me and shape culture at one and the same time. In order to investigate this formative function of work, I want to turn to Hegel's chapter on "Lordship and Bondage." Although it occupies a very different stage in the *Phenomenology*, this chapter already introduces the topic of *Bildung* and its relationship to productive activity. The framework in question is rather impoverished by comparison, confined to three elements: the lord, the bondsman, and the thing. First we need to review the background briefly. In the framework of desire – the first form of self-consciousness – I wanted to prove my independence from the thing by consuming it and so negating its status as something self-standing. Because this kind of consumption had the contrary effect of revealing me to be the dependent party, I sought something that could mediate this relationship to the object of desire and so ensure my own status as a self-standing being.[33] The only thing that could

---

[33] At this stage I am looking for something that can guarantee that I remain *independent* from the material world, while at the same time satisfying my material needs. Whatever this turns out to be would thus be "mediating" my relation to the object of desire.

88   Culture

perform this mediating task turns out to be another self-consciousness. After a "life-and-death struggle," one self-consciousness enslaves the other and positions the latter between itself and the object of desire. Now it is the bondsman who has direct dealings with the material world, whereas the lord merely enjoys the product of the bondsman's labor. Most importantly, the lord enjoys continual recognition as an independent being, which the thing on its own could not provide.

But in Hegel's famous diagnosis, it is precisely the bondsman's engagement with the thing that makes him freer – or in a better position to realize his freedom – than the lord. Whereas the lord shrivels into a parasite completely dependent on the bondsman, the bondsman's work in fact transforms him into a (relatively) self-standing being.[34] Hegel emphasizes that it is *work* that has this formative effect. He writes:

> Work ... is restrained desire, arrested disappearing, or its forms [*bildet*]. The negative relationship to the object becomes its form and something permanent, precisely because for the one working the object is self-standing. This *negative* middle or the formative [*formierende*] activity is at the same time the singularity or the pure for-itself of consciousness, which now through work steps outside itself into the element of permanence; so the working consciousness arrives in this way at a perception [*Anschauung*] of its own independence in the independent being [of the object]. (PG ¶195)

Hegel is here contrasting unrestrained desire, which was the downfall of the prior configuration, with the restraining effect of work. Because the bondsman has first to reshape the purely natural object in order to make it fit for enjoyment (despite the fact he himself will never get to enjoy it), he inevitably learns to inhibit his desires and so gains control over them. In this respect, work has a formative effect on the bondsman himself.[35]

But what Hegel wants to stress in saying that work forms (*bildet*) is that it gives rise to products and turns parts of nature into human artifacts. This is what he means when he claims that through labor, self-consciousness is able to "step outside itself into the element of permanence." By making something that continues to exist once I am done making it, I am externalizing some aspect of myself in the form of an object distinct from me. This in turn makes possible objective confirmation of my own self-conception. In the object I worked on, I see a reflection of who I take myself to be. In the case of the bondsman's thing, this reflection is very dim, considering that his productive activity is directed by the will of another. The lord's will is not only someone else's will, but it is

---

[34] Of course this is by no means Hegel's last word on freedom. In fact, the *Phenomenology* as a whole suggests that the kind of freedom whose potential is embodied in the slave is still very primitive and ultimately inadequate.

[35] For an especially lucid presentation of this chapter, see Neuhouser (2009).

directly opposed to the will of the bondsman. Pursuing the lord's ends comes at the bondsman's expense. Moreover, the lord's will is that of a single (and relatively asocial) individual, and so determined by his particularities, peculiarities, and idiosyncrasies, which are arbitrary and contingent. Nevertheless, Hegel stresses that the bondsman does behold himself in the object, because the object is something he made through his own effort, even if he made it to satisfy the lord's demands. It is this capacity to form that is manifest in the formed object, made visible in it.

Labor for Hegel has to be understood in relation to death, or fear of it, which is the reason the bondsman entered into bondage in the first place. According to Hegel, it is labor as formative activity that dispels this initial fear because it allows the bondsman to leave an enduring imprint on the world and in this way to transcend his own mortality. But this fear of death also enabled an important insight into the essence of self-consciousness. As Hegel puts it, through this fear the servile self-consciousness "*experienced* its own essence. For this consciousness has been afraid, not concerning this or that or just at this or that moment, but for its whole being; for it has felt the fear of death, the absolute lord. Through this it has become internally dissolved, has trembled in every fiber of its being, and everything fixed has been shaken." He adds, "this is moreover not a universal dissolution in general, but in service [the servile consciousness] actually brings it about" (PG ¶194). It is through labor that the bondsman actualizes this insight – the realization that he cannot be definitively fixed – by reshaping objects in a way that mirror this aspect of himself back to himself. By shaping objects, he demonstrates that the objective world is similar to him in this important respect: both he and it are capable of transformation.

Let us now gather the central lessons of this chapter: First, the bondsman himself becomes formed (or educated) into a free being by forming an object. It is his labor that teaches him to be self-disciplined and self-sufficient, a lesson of which the lord remains deprived. Second, the bondsman's labor results in the creation of an object distinct from himself. The thing is initially already there, found in nature, and the bondsman merely works on it. But through his labor he gives the thing a new form. The bondsman is thus "externalizing" himself by forming something external to him. Laboring activity establishes a certain distance between the bondsman and the "thing" he has produced, a distance that makes visible a crucial kinship between them.

Third, this distance becomes integral to *Bildung* because it introduces a reflective relationship. Hegel describes this relationship as one of "becoming conscious" [*kommt zum Bewußtsein*] and "finding again" [*Wiederfinden*]. So even though Hegel does not use the term "reflection" in this context, what he describes is once again structurally akin to reflection in the *Logic*. His term for it is *Anschauung*: the object serves as mirror image in which the bondsman is able to "behold" himself. This object is distinct from me, but at the same time the product of my own laboring activity and so evidence of the kind of formative activity of which I am capable. As Hegel puts it, "the form, by becoming externalized [*hinausgesetzt*], does not become something other [*ein Anderes*] than he; for in fact it is *his* pure for-itself, which thus becomes truth for him" (PG ¶196). Although this is clearly a reflective relation, it does not necessarily coincide with what we usually mean by reflection. It does not seem to involve evaluation, let alone criticism, except perhaps by the standards internal to the craft involved. In calling it an "Anschauung" or beholding, Hegel emphasizes that this version of reflection appears in a comparatively unreflective guise. The bondsman beholds himself in the product of his work because this product reflects him, even if he continues to be fully absorbed by his productive activity.

This seems to be another version of Hegel's central thesis that a degree of distance is necessary for the possibility of genuine identification. As we have seen in the context of habit, it is only once I have risen above my determinations and made them *mine*, and no longer simply *me*, that I can regard them as my own properties. Here Hegel is making a similar move, although one with bolder implications. He is arguing that the bondsman can become free and know himself as free only because he has externalized herself in the form of an object. Only when he is confronted with something other than he that is at the same time of his own making can he attain self-knowledge and find confirmation of his own self-conception. Even though this thing is not an object of contemplation, his relation to it is nevertheless a reflective one. And it remains reflective in a way in which habit on its own does not, because the distance it introduces endures as long as the object sticks around.

Although Hegel alludes to work in the *Bildung* chapter, in that context he says surprisingly little about the structure of work and its contribution to *Bildung*. But I think that the picture of labor that emerges in the context of bondage can supplement Hegel's remarks about the centrality of work in the later chapter. There he proposes that the alienation (*Entfremdung*) from which modern individuals suffer can be cured only through externalization (*Entäußerung*). I initially confront a world in which I cannot recognize myself because I cannot see it as my own work, and I can only overcome this alienation by appropriating this world through work. In order to make the world hospitable to my own capacity for self-cultivation, I need to externalize myself in the world and so give this capacity an objective expression – namely, by actively giving objects a new shape. We have seen in the case of the bondsman's labor that this process has two dimensions. On the one hand, work contributes to my own *Bildung*, for it makes me self-disciplined, capable of self-cultivation, through my transformative engagement with objects. On the other hand, work contributes to objective *Bildung* because it produces artifacts and so gives a new shape to what was initially found as already there, whether in nature or in culture.

This second dimension is relevant to understanding what it means to say that the world is a work, a work that is already an accomplishment, and yet one on which we continue to work. Because work turns things into a lasting expression of their producer's own self-conception, Hegel characterizes it as the formation of a shared culture. In order to make sense of this claim, it is important to note that the relevant self-conception that is being expressed is significantly shaped by the social dimensions of labor and ceases to be merely that of an individual. This is to some extent true of the bondsman's labor as well, since the bondsman is expressing an essential feature of self-consciousness and not laboring to satisfy his idiosyncrasies. But what makes culture shared is not only the fact that the self-conception at stake is a social one. It is also important that this culture is a material one, a culture made up of artifacts, although Hegel does not mean this in a narrow sense. As Hegel writes in his Introduction to the *Lectures on the Philosophy of World History*,

Spirit is essentially active, it makes itself into that, which it in itself is, into its deed, into its work; in this way it becomes an object to itself, has itself as an existence before itself. Thus it is with the spirit of a nation [*Geist eines Volkes*]: it is a determinate spirit, which builds itself into a present world that now stands and persists, in its religion, in its cults, in its customs [*Gebräuchen*], its constitution und its political laws, in the whole complex of its institutions, in its events and deeds. That is its work – that *is* what a nation is. (VPG, 99)

So Hegel provides an extensive list of the different modes of cultural self-expression and he argues that a culture is nothing over and above its own objective manifestations, which include the religion, law, language, custom, art, etc. that it has produced. This means that cultural objects are constitutive of a culture because they embody a cultural self-conception, making this self-conception something real. But because these products are expressive of a culture, they also serve a reflective function – they provide its participants with reflections of themselves. We have encountered this reflective aspect of work on the individual level in the bondsman's labor. But in this context Hegel is making a stronger claim. He argues that cultural objects both make up a culture and mirror it. There is in a sense no culture prior to and independent of its works, but these works at the same time reflect the culture in which they were produced. To put this in terms of the "*Bildung*" chapter of the *Phenomenology*, "substance" becomes "cultured" through work that on one hand constitutes a culture and on the other hand reflects it. This is what I take Hegel to mean when he defines the *Bildung* of substance as the "acquisition of its self-consciousness" and the "bringing-about of its own becoming and reflection into itself." According to Hegel, participation in a culture always involves a reflective relation to it, for the objects we form provide us with a speculum of our cultural context.

Earlier, I emphasized that *Bildung* has two central aspects, that it forms both subjects and objects. This double aspect of *Bildung* should remind us of the definition that Hegel gives of it in the "Preface" to the *Phenomenology*, where he defines *Bildung* from two complementary standpoints. We can either view it as the formative education of the individual, or we can consider this very same process in relation to social substance, and in this relation *Bildung* turns out to be the formation of a (cultural) world. Hegel insists that becoming cultured and forming a culture are merely two ways of characterizing one and the same process. This double aspect reappears in the *"Bildung"* chapter, for the individual's *"Bildung* and his own actuality is for this reason the actualization of the substance itself" (PG ¶490). They are both achievements that take work, work that transforms them both in turn.

We should also call to mind that this process had the aim of devouring something that had turned "inorganic," of taking possession of it. One central insight won through modern culture's heightened self-awareness is that culture can avoid ossification only through ongoing participation. One way to understand this requirement would be to say that inheriting a culture is a matter of reaffirming it, or recommitting oneself to it in order to prevent it from becoming an empty ritual. But what the process of *Bildung* reveals is that this affirmation is first made possible through production, for productive activity introduces a sufficiently reflective relation to one's own cultural context that puts participants in a position to reaffirm it or recommit to it. Being a participant in a living culture requires that one is also actively contributing to it. This contribution can range from the mundane to the elevated, and so can be satisfied by cooking a meal, performing a play, or instituting a policy. And these forms of contribution open up the space for reaffirmation of and recommitment to inherited customs precisely by transforming them in (usually subtle) ways. In short, traditions change – and have to change – as long as they have people actively participating in them, rather than merely going through the motions.

This structure of cultural participation already indicates the degree of its continuity with and divergence from habitual modes of engagement. Clearly cooking, performing, or instituting have a habitual component. These activities are also a part of our second nature. For example, cooking is in many respects paradigmatic of habit, for it is ideally something that comes "naturally" to me, and yet something that requires simultaneous attention and inattention in the ways we have seen. At the same time, these habitual forms of cultural participation are not as unreflective as they appear, for they establish a reflective relation to custom that surpasses mere immersion. These are relatively inconspicuous forms of reflection. We catch a glimpse of our culture in the periphery, so to speak, even when fully absorbed by habitual activities. But it is these forms of reflection, as inconspicuous as they may be, that are meant to sustain our commitment in the face of growing indifference.

Before I turn to the role of *Bildung* in the *Philosophy of Right*, I want to raise and address how narrowly we are to understand work, whether it needs to take place within the public sphere and whether it needs to issue in the production of objects. To be more specific, does Hegel's account exclude the cultural contribution made by those who tend to domestic chores and childrearing?[36] As Simone De Beauvoir disparagingly put it, "Few tasks are more similar to the torment of Sisyphus than those of the housewife; day after day, one must wash dishes, dust furniture, mend clothes that will be dirty, dusty, and torn again. The housewife wears herself out running on the spot; she does nothing; she only perpetuates the present."[37] De Beauvoir is thereby denying that housework counts as a contribution of lasting significance. For her, it as well as childrearing are too closely tied to the repetitive cycle of life. But I do not think that this has to be Hegel's view. As we are about to see, *Bildung* in the context of ethical life admittedly does take place in the institution of civil society, from which women are officially excluded. At the same time, the account of cultural activity we have seen so far is general enough that it can include all sorts of work, even that which is unpaid and undervalued. In the case of both housework and childrearing, it is obviously a mistake to think of them as merely repetitive activities that do not demand creativity and that do not produce anything of lasting value. So I see no reason to saddle Hegel with a narrow view of work, despite the fact that his interest is primarily in the kind of work that takes place in the economic sphere.

2.4 Civil Society

The next task is to investigate the place of culture in ethical life, so in a sufficiently rational social order. This will involve searching out *Bildung* in the *Philosophy of Right* and determining its resemblance to *Bildung* in the *Phenomenology*. In this context, I will also return to a question that I flagged but have not yet explicitly addressed: is ethical life hospitable to cultural *pluralism*, so to differences in customary ways of life? Can it accommodate these differences, or does it do away with cultural bases of identification?

To the extent to which the "Bildung" chapter of the *Phenomenology* corresponds to an identifiable historical epoch, it appears to be a time of transition, a world between the *Ancien Regime* and the French Revolution. So *Bildung* is not only taking place among the nobles who abhor economic activity. Its world is also marked by the emergence of a new institution, namely civil society.

---

[36] I am grateful to Estelle Ferrarese for raising this important question to me.
[37] De Beauvoir (2010), 474. Thanks to Georgia Warnke for bringing this passage to my attention and for discussing it with me.

Hegel characterizes this world as divided into two social spheres, the nobility that seeks honor, power, and recognition, and the bourgeoisie that is in pursuit of wealth. Members of the opposing groups judge each other's aims to be "bad," but it turns out that they are not as different as they wanted to believe themselves to be. Moreover, we discover that the whole social order, including the high-minded nobility, depends on the self-seeking activity of the bourgeoisie. Echoing Adam Smith's "invisible hand," Hegel argues that self-interested motives produce wealth that ends up benefiting everyone, even if the individuals who are producing this wealth are completely indifferent to the public good. So this entire society, including its higher "cultural" aspirations, is ultimately indebted to this "base" economic activity.

Its relation to the bourgeois market serves to confirm that Hegel does ultimately consider *Bildung* proper a uniquely modern phenomenon, even if it exposes a pervasive dimension of all cultural life. According to Hegel, it is civil society that distinguishes modern ethical life from its predecessors and that prevents it from suffering their fate. Although Hegel reserves his more developed account of civil society for the *Philosophy of Right*, his earlier characterization of the emerging bourgeois class in the *"Bildung"* chapter incorporates strikingly similar elements.[38] But in the *Phenomenology*, civil society is still cast as a necessary evil because it remains uncultured, even if it makes culture possible. In the *Philosophy of Right*, Hegel describes civil society as itself the site of *Bildung*, and not merely an unfortunate yet necessary condition for its flourishing. The *Philosophy of Right* identifies civil society as the sphere in which *Bildung* (rather than mere *Erziehung*) takes place.

Hegel positions civil society as a point of transition between the family and the state, even though its basic principle looks to be radically opposed to those of either sphere. Kin take the good of the family to be their personal aim, and citizens orient their activities toward the good of the social order, while "the concrete person, who as a *particular* is his own end ... is the one principle of civil society" (PR §182). Civil society provides an outlet for the particular and arbitrary wills of individuals, allowing them to make the satisfaction of their subjective needs and desires their primary concern. But it turns out that I cannot attain private satisfaction without entering into relations with others, whose needs and desires place constraints on my will. In Hegel's words, "in civil society is each his own end, everything else is nothing to him. But without

---

[38] This resemblance has already been noted by Rózsa (2001), who argues that the concept of *Bildung* provides an important point of continuity between the two works. She writes, "die Bildung steht in enger Verbindung mit dem wirtschaftlichen Status der Selbstbestimmung und Selbstidentifikation des modernen Individuums überhaupt" (205). ["*Bildung* stands in close connection with the economic status of the self-determination and self-identification of the modern individual in general."]

relation to others he cannot attain the scope of his ends; these others are thus means for the end of particularity" (PR §182A). Although the principle of universality remains operative in civil society, it is treated as a mere means for the satisfaction of particularity. If this were indeed all there is to economic activity, it would imply that "the ethical is here lost in its extremes" (PR §184A).

Here, too, Hegel echoes Adam Smith when he characterizes such "self-seeking" (*selbstsüchtig*) activity as inadvertently benefiting everyone else. He claims that "by earning, producing, and enjoying for himself, each precisely thereby produces and earns for the enjoyment of the rest" (PR §199). But this argument can at best prove that civil society is rational at the institutional level. There still seems to be a disconnect between the two perspectives, that of the institution as a whole and that of its individual participants. Even if they do as a matter of fact contribute to the public good, they need not care about this good, need not be motivated to pursue it. In fact, it might be better if they are not, since self-seeking activity tends to be more effective in materially contributing to it. Like animals, their behavior conforms to the laws of the market without their knowing or willing it. So Hegel goes beyond the tradition of political economy when he insists that participation in civil society must also be shown to be subjectively free, if the institution itself is to count as fully rational. He writes, "the interest of the idea [of freedom], which does not lie in the consciousness of the members of civil society as such, is the *process* of raising their singularity and naturalness ... to formal freedom and formal universality of knowing and willing, of forming (*bilden*) subjectivity in their particularity" (PR §187). He calls this process *Bildung*.

Although Hegel considers *Bildung*, unlike *Erziehung*, a form of self-education, this can sound misleading. For example, Hegel is not talking about what we think of as being self-taught rather than taught in educational institutions. Moreover, he is not even talking about an education we decide to undertake. Neuhouser correctly points out that "it is intrinsic to the nature of *Bildung* that it takes place unconsciously and involuntarily, behind the backs, so to speak, of the very subjects who undergo the process of formation."[39] *Bildung* must take this unconscious and involuntary form not only because unformed individuals at first lack the desire to be formed, but also because they lack the capacities necessary for making a conscious and voluntary decision. According to Neuhouser, civil society is especially suited to this educative task precisely because individuals *must* enter it in order to satisfy their basic needs and so have no choice but to undergo this process.

But there is an important sense in which *Bildung* can be described as *self-directed*. For Hegel this has to do with the close connection between *Bildung*

[39] Neuhouser (2000), 149.

and work, a connection he repeatedly reiterates. He even defines *Bildung* as a subject's own liberation through "hard work against the sheer subjectivity of behavior, against the immediacy of desire as well as against the subjective arrogance of feeling and the arbitrary will (*Willkur*) of pleasure" (PR §187). Hegel identifies several aspects of work that are central to its formative power. The first has to do with its submission of desire. As we have seen in the bondsman's laboring activity, work has the effect of postponing the fulfillment of desires because the desired object must first be produced before it can be enjoyed. The better we become at ignoring our desires, the more control we gain over our own will. But work also generates new and higher desires, such as the desire for luxuries beyond the satisfaction of natural needs. Moreover, Hegel claims that work generates a significantly different kind of desire, namely, the desire to be busy. Thus Hegel remarks that "the barbarian is lazy and is distinguished from the cultured person (*Gebildeten*) by his brooding stupor, because practical education (*praktische Bildung*) consists precisely in the habit and in the need for activity" (PR §197A).

Finally, work trains specific skills and so gives individuals a sense of personal self-worth and pride in what they do. This acquisition of specialized skills seems to be an artifact of the division of labor, specifically the growing social interdependence, which Hegel associates with "abstraction." He calls this process "abstraction," even though it is not undertaken by anyone's conscious and deliberate efforts, because it involves abstracting *away from* more and more of an object. In the process of abstraction, needs and desires becomes increasingly particularized and directed not only at specific objects, but even at specific features of objects. I no longer want simply a shirt, but a shirt made out of silk or linen. This is accompanied by a growing demand that labor be "socially productive," to borrow Neuhouser's phrase. This means that my labor must be responsive to these highly specialized demands and that the goods I produce must satisfy the desires of others, if my own desires are to be met. It also implies that my own work stands in relation to the work of others. While labor remains an engagement with the world of objects, consumption becomes a social matter, in which the human being relates first and foremost to what has been produced by other human beings.

Although becoming industrious and self-disciplined are important aspects of this education, it is really the social context of work that is crucial to the *Bildung* individuals undergo. As in the *Phenomenology*, Hegel characterizes *Bildung* primarily as a process in which the individual is educated to the level of the universal. Much like the person of culture in the "*Bildung*" chapter, the member of civil society can only distinguish herself as a particular individual by entering into a certain profession and so committing herself to a specific social position. Hegel even emphasizes that it is only in virtue of this position that she counts as *someone*. But unlike the person of culture, the member of civil society cannot merely keep to her professional sphere and measure herself solely by its standards. Because of the growing economic interdependence among all parts of civil society – which Hegel calls the "system of needs" – each member is brought into relation with every other member and so must learn to adjust her behavior according to a wider set of norms than the self-cultivated individual was willing to acknowledge.

Hegel characterizes this transformation in several different ways. For example, he argues that *Bildung* consists of learning how to take the perspective of others into consideration and he contrasts this with the manner of the uncultured person, who tends to offend people easily. Although it is not her intention to cause offense, she has "no reflection for the feelings of others" (PR §187A). This is of course reminiscent of the cultivation Hegel described in the *Phenomenology*, since being cultivated also involved considering one's own behavior from an impersonal standpoint. But as I already mentioned, there are more of these others that a member of civil society must take into consideration, because her economic activity puts her in direct or indirect contact with everyone else. Hegel also describes this as a process of adopting an increasingly universal point of view toward the situation at hand. What this means is that the cultured person is able to take more aspects of a particular situation into account. He echoes this claim in the *Lectures on the Philosophy of World History*:

The cultured person [*Gebildeter*] approaches objects and considers the different sides; they are present to him. Cultured reflection [*gebildete Reflexion*] has given them the form of universality. ... Thus the cultured person can in his behavior grant the individual circumstances their right, while the uncultured person – though with good intentions – clings to one side, but in doing so offends many other sides. (VPG, 43)

One way to paraphrase this would be to say that the cultured person becomes more attentive to the multiple facets of the specific circumstances she confronts, because she is able and willing to consider how that situation looks to those who occupy perspectives different from her own. This "cultured reflection" can itself become habitual, so it does not mean that I have to stand back from the situation in which I find myself in order to gain a distanced view of it. So what Hegel is here saying is not in tension with the role of attention to the universal that is a part of ethical habits. Hegel is just pointing out that this attention can be more or less cultured. The cultured person does not usually have to run through the multiple standpoints in her mind before she proceeds to respond. If I am cultured, I know how to avoid offending people without having to exercise great reflective effort.

Interestingly enough, this process of cultured reflection is one that unfolds gradually, as I come into contact with new perspectives and incorporate them into my own, thus making mine less and less provincial. *Bildung* does not involve a leap from my particular standpoint to a universal one. Rather, I am reshaping my take on situations through increased exposure to the ways in which others see similar situations. For example, I become sensitive to the racist or sexist dimensions of a text, even if these would at an earlier time not have stood out to me. And I internalize these new sensitivities into my second nature, so that I do not have to keep reminding myself to look out for racist or sexist implications or undertones. So this process is a gradual one, and it involves incorporating perspectives as I come into contact with them, rather than attempting to purge my own of all particularity through reflective abstraction. And participation in civil society puts me into such contact. Within the growing interdependence of economic activities, the circle of those, to whose perspectives I am exposed, widens. This is a central formative dimension of civil society, its contribution to individual *Bildung* (beyond the familiar benefits of work as such).[40]

But *Bildung* issues not only in a perspectival shift; it also transforms our customs. According to Hegel, participating in this vast system of needs requires that one adopt the manners, customs, and even opinions of others:

Everything particular becomes to that extent something social; in the manner of clothing, in the time of eating, there lies a certain convenience which one must adopt, because with respect to such things it is not worth the trouble to want to show one's own opinion, rather it is wisest to proceed in them like others. (PR §192A)

My self-interest compels me to conform to certain informal practices and codes of conduct, which has the effect of standardizing and disseminating them throughout the whole of civil society. This conformity to shared customs even affects what objects we come to need or desire. In other words, the general effect of *Bildung* is the emergence of shared standards on the level of individual development as well as on the social level. This suggests that participation in civil society is not merely a matter of an individual's self-cultivation, but does have directly cultural effects. Not only are we producing goods that others can enjoy, we are also transforming our very customs in this process.

It is sometimes assumed that Hegel believes that the members of ethical life must already share a set of richly cultural practices and his comments about the centrality of custom at the beginning of his chapter on *Sittlichkeit* can confirm that impression. But Hegel considers the modern state capable of incorporating various levels of divergence and diversity. In fact, Hegel distinguishes

---

[40] Similarly, Hans-Georg Gadamer (1989) emphasizes that *Bildung* is "keeping oneself open to what is other – to other, more universal points of view" (50), and that "to distance oneself from oneself and from one's private purposes means to look at these in the way that others see them ... The universal viewpoints to which the cultivated man (*gebildet*) keeps himself open are not a fixed applicable yardstick, but are present to him only as the viewpoints of possible others" (17).

between a state and a nation precisely on the basis of what its members must have in common. According to Hegel, a state is founded on merely "juridical relations" whereas a nation is a community that shares "speech, mores and customs (*Sitten und Gewohnheiten*) and culture (*Bildung*)."[41] Mark Tunick has made much of this distinction and argues that, for Hegel, modern social ties cannot rest on a common cultural heritage, which includes history, tradition, language, taste, and even to a certain extent values.[42] Although he is right in stressing that, for Hegel, the modern state must be able to incorporate a diversity of cultural backgrounds, he overlooks the fact that part of the function of civil society is precisely to homogenize customs and so give rise to a shared culture, even where there may have been none before.

Hegel claims that this convergence of individual conformity with cultural homogeneity brings about a "formal universality" of willing. In calling this universality formal, Hegel wants to emphasize that the public features of civil society set the formal constraints on my economic activity, which I continue to pursue with the aim of satisfying my particular needs and desires. Shared customs limit my pursuit of individual wealth, because I cannot achieve my private ends unless I conform to them. But it might seem as if I continue to view them as mere means that I cannot circumvent, but that I do not consider valuable in their own right. As Hegel put it, "with respect to such things it is not worth the trouble to want to show one's own opinion, rather it is wisest to proceed in them like others."

Although this perhaps captures our initial attitude toward the universal, Hegel suggests that submitting my conduct to shared practices brings about a transformation in my attitude toward others. In a striking passage he writes: "It belongs to *Bildung*, thinking as an individual's consciousness in the form of the universal, that I am grasped as a *universal person*, in which *everyone* is identical. The *human being counts, because he is a human being*, not because he is Jewish, Catholic, Protestant, German, Italian, etc." (PR §209). This seems to be the most explicitly ethical effect of *Bildung*, for it goes beyond merely taking the perspective of others into consideration. According to Hegel, participation in the market compels us to disregard those features that distinguish people from one another, particularly their nationality, ethnicity, and religion. In other words, *Bildung* allows us to regard every human being as first and foremost a human being, and only secondarily as the member of some narrower community.

---

[41] See Tunick (2001). This distinction is also important to the interpretation offered by Moland (2011).
[42] Tunick (2001).

Because this attitude is clearly cosmopolitan in spirit, Hegel is careful to disavow this association between his view and cosmopolitanism in the political sense. There is a sense in which the cultured individual becomes a citizen of the world insofar as she does not restrict her dealings to those who inhabit the same community as she does. At the same time, Hegel does not take this to be an argument in favor of a world-state, which is what he believes political cosmopolitanism would require. Moreover, he thinks that worldliness is not at odds with membership in smaller communities defined by richer customs than those that bind the members of a nation-state or even partners in international economic interactions. As Hegel puts it, "The consciousness, for which the *thought* counts, is of infinite importance – and is only then deficient, when it becomes something like cosmopolitanism and fixes itself in opposition to the concrete life of the state" (PR §209). The issue of cosmopolitanism is especially pressing in this context because civil society does not seem to respect the political borders of a nation-state. Through trade, it aims to establish a marketplace of global scope, and so the kind of relationships it fosters could be regarded as threatening to patriotism and to other local bonds. But Hegel is so eager to distinguish cosmopolitanism from *Bildung* precisely because the two have crucial features in common. In learning to adapt to the ways of life of others and to take their perspective into consideration, the cultured individual also gives up particularities that would make her stand out. Thus Hegel invokes this dual sense of universality in civil society through a memorable metaphor comparing *Bildung* and money: "Cultured people [*gebildete Menschen*] look alike, like coins which have been in circulation for a long time" (VRP, 310). While giving up certain particularities, namely individual idiosyncrasies, is a necessary and positive effect of *Bildung*, Hegel is worried about the dissolution of all concrete ways of life. According to Hegel, becoming "cultured" cannot require becoming detached from any culture in particular.

We can discover the significant role of particular attachments even within the economic activities of a single state. Although, for Hegel, civil society remains a sphere in which each individual is free to indulge her particularity, he emphasizes that this institution must exhibit a differentiated internal structure. As we have seen, this is a feature that Charles Taylor is eager to emphasize, that Hegel thinks individuals participate in civil society as members of what he calls "estates" (*Stände*). Estates are in some respects akin to social classes because they are determined by the kind of professions its members pursue. Thus Hegel divides civil society into three estates, the agricultural or "substantial" estate, the business estate, and the "universal" estate of civil servants. Members of the first estate share a commitment to religion and to the earth, and Hegel even ascribes to them a specific attitude of gratitude and trust in God for the fruits of their labor. The second estate is differentiated into further professional domains – craft, manufacture, and trade – though its members all share a sense that what they possess is something they themselves have earned. Since the third estate (not to be confused with *the* third estate)[43] does not engage in economic life directly but is employed by the state, it can focus its attention on universal interests.[44]

Because each estate involves different professional spheres, they value different things and subscribe to different codes of conduct, all of which can coexist within civil society. In fact, it looks like, at least in the *Philosophy of Right*, cultural pluralism in modern ethical life enters more at the level of estates than at that of ethnicity or nationality. Hegel argues that such estates are more compatible with the freedom at issue in civil society because membership in an estate is at least in part up to an individual. Conversely he criticizes the caste system in India for condemning people to a certain social class without leaving any room for their own preferences in the matter.[45] Of course what estate one ultimately joins will also depend on talent and upbringing, and so is not reducible to individual preference. But, for Hegel, it is important that an individual can view her membership in an estate as at least in part a personal achievement. Recall the praiseworthy success of self-cultivation in the world of early modern *Bildung*.

This suggests that estates cannot be simply equated with cultural communities in the traditional sense, as Taylor seems to do. While members of an estate do in a sense share "culture, values, and modes of life," these are not something an individual merely inherits. Moreover, they are a product of the professional ties that bind the members of an estate. We have seen that in his account of civil society, Hegel emphasizes the transformative effect of participating in the market. According to Hegel, the customs shared by participants in a society's practices are to a large extent shaped by their economic activity and interaction. At the same time, estates for Hegel do serve a role similar to the one that Taylor envisions. According to Taylor, Hegel thinks that differentiation provides a basis for identification and that we cannot simply conceive of ourselves as citizens of a state, but must also identify with our own partial communities and their local customs.

---

[43] As in Abbé Sieyes's pamphlet, "What Is the Third Estate?"

[44] There is a passage in the *Philosophy of Right* that could look like a direct challenge to the interpretation I put forward in the previous chapter: "The people, insofar as one means by this term a particular part of the members of the state, refers to that part *which does not know what it wills*. To know what one wills, and furthermore what the will that has being in and for itself wills, i.e., reason, is the fruit of a deep understanding and insight [*Erkenntnis und Einsicht*], which is the very thing the 'people' lack" (PR §301R). But here Hegel is simply making an elitist point about the difference between the estates, that one has to be trained in the right way in order to be suitable for political leadership.

[45] See PR §206.

Hegel certainly gives us reasons to think that this is his view. Estates are so central to Hegel's account of civil society not only because they enable something like communal life within a sphere of rampant individualism, but also because they demand a commitment to a particular way of life rather than another. "In saying that the human being must be *something*, we mean that he belongs to a determinate estate" (PR §207). This is reminiscent of Hegel's claim in the *Phenomenology* that one can only become "someone" by adopting a specific social position and conforming one's behavior to its standards. In other words, commitments to a particular profession or professional community provide us with a more determinate self-conception. If we regard estates as cultural communities, this would mean that cultural membership is indeed integral to an agent's identity. But, for Hegel, our allegiance to our estate cannot exclude other bases of identification. Since such local communities form part of a larger social network that generates shared customs, our identities are never exhausted by our membership in them.

Thus Hegel's views about the formative effects of participation in civil society have interesting implications for cultural pluralism. As we have seen, Hegel's account of ethical life, especially his account of civil society, shows that a certain degree of pluralism is not only permitted, but even required. Becoming a member of civil society involves entering an estate that differs from other estates in cultural respects because it represents a distinct outlook, privileging certain concerns over others, and embodies a concrete way of life. For example, the agricultural estate expresses an attitude of trust, faith, and gratitude, privileges family and tradition, and partakes in certain religious practices that the other estates do not. According to Hegel, becoming a member of an estate is important precisely because its outlook differs from those of other estates. Without such differentiation, our participation in civil society would fail to provide us with a sufficiently determinate self-conception. So becoming formed or *gebildet* does involve becoming a member of a "local" community in this sense.

That said, we have seen that Hegel frequently identifies *Bildung* with the attainment of a universal point of view. In other words, our commitment to our local communities cannot come at the cost of participation in broader social practices that are required by ethical life. This could mean that we must be willing to adjust some of our practices to those of others in order to cooperate in the wider system of needs of which we are a part. It could also mean that we must be willing to consider how our customs look to someone who does not share them. So *Bildung*, for Hegel, consists not only in the acquisition of a determinate and differentiated identity, but also in the ability to regard oneself from the outside, so to speak. This is in part why *Bildung* shares so much with cosmopolitanism and why Hegel wants nevertheless to distinguish the two. According to Hegel, this "universal" perspective must be compatible with particular commitments and cannot result in an indifference toward one's local forms of membership. To achieve *Bildung* is precisely to attain and sustain this balance between worldliness and concreteness.

2.5 Cultural Identity

I want to conclude by returning to a question I raised at the very outset of this chapter about the tension inherent in the very idea of a cultural identity – a tension noted by Anthony Appiah and Samuel Scheffler. They claimed that full-fledged cultural members do not relate to their own practices as cultural and in that sense do not explicitly identify with the culture they inhabit. One could say that to assert one's cultural identity is to take an external perspective on that culture because it involves adopting a reflective attitude toward it. In my reading of the *"Bildung"* chapter, I emphasized one sense in which reflection could be regarded as a part of all cultural participation. There I argued that, for Hegel, participating in a culture involves producing objects, broadly construed, that "mirror" the culture in which they are produced. I also suggested that Hegel privileges modern culture because it has achieved an unprecedented self-awareness. While all cultural participants practice mundane forms of reflection about aspects of their culture, whenever they engage productively with it, it is the participants in the world of *Bildung* who become aware of the fact that their culture as a whole is a culture. In other words, they discover something that was in a sense true even of their predecessors, namely, that all of their customs depend on human activity for their origin and endurance.

But being aware that your culture is a culture is not quite the same as being aware of your cultural identity. Claims to cultural identity seem to involve an emphasis on the particularity of one's culture and on its being one's own. Although Hegel does not explicitly consider the nature and status of this kind of cultural self-consciousness, I do think his view has challenging implications for such claims. Here I want to return to Michael Hardimon, whose discussion of the difference between Hegelian and communitarian conceptions of identity is especially illuminating. According to Hardimon, it looks as if the communitarian view accords with Hegel's depiction of the Greeks, for Hegel claims that the Greeks were unable to abstract from and reflect on their social roles and communal membership. But these similarities can be misleading. As Hardimon points out, communitarians tend to argue that (some) people believe that they are unable to abstract from and reflect on their roles and membership, and this is quite different from saying that they are in fact unable to do so. It is very well possible that they are mistaken in their belief. Although Hardimon does not draw this conclusion, one could say that the communitarian conception is even verging on incoherent, for forming an explicit belief about your identity is already to have abstracted from that identity – it is to have adopted a reflective relation to it. So it looks as if you are performatively contradicting yourself when you assert that you believe yourself to be incapable of disassociating from your own culture.

Since modern *Bildung* evolves into the Enlightenment, Hegel thinks that it has far-reaching effects that make this kind of immediate relation to culture untenable. In a very evocative passage Hegel compares the Enlightenment "to a silent expansion or *diffusion*, like of a perfume in the unresisting atmosphere. It is a penetrating infection which does not make itself noticeable beforehand as something opposed to the indifferent element into which it insinuates itself, and therefore cannot be warded off" (PG §545). In this context, he is talking about the impact of the Enlightenment attitude on religious faith, but it seems to me that this metaphor can be expanded beyond that specific context. What Hegel is here saying, in other words, is that reflection is a bit like an infectious disease. Once it appears on the scene, one cannot protect oneself against it, cannot retain the immediate relation to culture one may have previously enjoyed. But, as Hardimon rightly emphasizes, communitarians at the same time exaggerate the extent to which we are self-conscious of our own identities. It is Hegel's view that to have an identity, for example a professional role, is to have incorporated this identity to such an extent that you no longer need to think about it, even though your work reflects it. We can miss the extent to which we do identify with our various forms of membership precisely because we are not calling them perpetually to mind. Let us not forget the significance and dominance of second nature in Hegel's account of ethical life. If we have successfully incorporated our various roles, even when these roles are richly cultural, we are not usually thinking about their corresponding principles as principles, let alone the roles themselves as roles.

Moreover, Hegel suggests that our explicit self-conceptions can be at odds with and so misrepresent our own true identities. This is another version of his worry that we tend to misunderstand our own true commitments, commitments that are better visible in how we behave than in what we avow. Although Hegel would clearly say that those who believe that they are unable to abstract from their cultural identities are mistaken, they are not merely ignorant of their own capacity for abstraction. The identity they ascribe to themselves is itself a mark of confusion. Throughout the *Phenomenology*, Hegel explores various dissonances between how we conceive of ourselves and who we turn out to be and in this way emphasizes the fantasies we are prone to indulge. For example, we have seen in the "Lordship and Bondage" chapter that the lord becomes a victim of such ignorance, for the independent status he ascribes to himself is falsified by the dependence his actions (or inactions) exhibit. Coming to have a clear view of oneself is clearly a difficult task, one that is often thwarted by the disorientation that reflection itself introduces. To recall Hegel's point from the *Logic*, stepping apart from one's own mirror image can generate the illusion that one is not as one seems, that there is a fundamental gulf between appearance and essence. So the practice of beholding or examining oneself is not necessarily to be trusted.

In conclusion, I want to propose one way in which these sorts of illusions can bear on the idea of cultural identity. Although it is certainly possible that someone could be correct in ascribing a particular cultural membership to herself, Hegel gives us reasons to distrust such self-ascriptions. Identifications with a culture tend to be framed in exclusive terms. This is especially vivid in the context of immigrant communities, which sometimes seek to isolate themselves from the dominant culture in which they are housed. We have seen that Hegel emphasizes the transformative effects of *Bildung* not only on individuals, but also on the culture itself. As he points out, economic life gives rise to shared customs that push beyond cultural divides, ethnic as well as professional. So when we conceive of ourselves as members of one particular culture and no other, our self-conception fails to reflect the transcultural practices in which we are already engaged. As he stresses in the *Bildung* chapter, culture is a work, a work that requires continued work. And as he stresses in the chapter on civil society, it is a work that requires cooperation beyond parochial divides. All of this strongly suggests that, even though Hegel leaves room for cultural participation in his account of ethical life, he is asking that we reconceive of culture in a deep way and recognize that culture is better understood as *Bildung* – an open-ended process that shapes the world of human making as well as those who make it.

3 Critique

Even though we have seen some of the ways in which reflection can be, or even must be, integrated into ethical life, one might nevertheless feel dissatisfied, as if we have been dodging the most crucial issue. One could respond that it is not reflection in general that has been our concern – reflection in the sense of deliberation about how to apply given norms, or reflection in the sense of an implicit affirmation of them in the way of cultural participation. What Hegel's critics suspect is that his account of ethical life fails to incorporate reflection of the *critical* sort. Does Hegel allow for the possibility of criticizing our social world, for positively objecting to it? More specifically, does Hegel allow for the possibility of criticizing not just some practice or another, but the norms that lie at their basis? In short, how deep can criticism run and what course is available to it?

In this chapter, I propose a response to this set of concerns that is Hegelian in spirit, even if it requires going beyond the letter of Hegel's text. I should note at the outset that there is a hermeneutic difficulty here. Although Hegel focuses in much of his work precisely on the possibility of assessing, contesting, and changing a given normative framework, he never offers an explicit account of what such a critical stance would look like and what role it could play in the context of a distinctly modern form of ethical life. This could invite the impression that Hegel deems it superfluous in an already rational society, where it was not so for our predecessors. I do not think that our social order, as Hegel sees it, has by any means obviated the need for critical reflection once and for all, as no order ultimately can. Nevertheless, this means that developing a suitable conception of critical reflection will require leaving behind the central work in question – the *Philosophy of Right* – and drawing on other resources Hegel has left at our disposal, especially those in his earlier *Phenomenology of Spirit*.

I admit that it may not seem obvious that Hegel needs an account of social criticism in modern ethical life, that this is an omission on his part. Even those who hold that critical reflection must remain possible often argue that such reflection is already accommodated by what Hegel calls "true conscience."[1]

---

[1] Moyar (2011) has offered an excellent defense of this line of thought. According to Moyar, conscience is an exercise in "immanent negativity" because it has the capacity to destabilize

Hegel undeniably disparages appeals to conscience in his treatment of the moral point of view.[2] But he takes issue only with "formal conscience" – namely, with a form of conscience that claims to be able to determine the good through exclusively subjective resources, thus asserting that its duty is nothing over and above whatever it thinks its duty to be. True conscience, in contrast, does not make claims to such peerless authority, but it does impose a subjective requirement on what can count as the objective good. As we have seen in the first chapter, this version of conscience takes the form of a right – the "right of the subjective will" – according to which I must be in a position to grasp the goodness of whatever I am to recognize as good.[3] So this right seems to grant a space to critical reflection, to a questioning of social norms, in which case there would be nothing lacking in Hegel's official account.[4]

But true conscience and its corresponding right of subjectivity strike me as inadequate concessions to critique. Hegel does identify conscience with a critical attitude when he describes it as an activity of "evaporation." And its preservation in ethical life has implications for the role of critical reflection, for it does indicate that we must be in principle permitted to ask ourselves whether a given norm is valid, whether it is indeed a good one to continue following. Hegel is quite clear on this point by designating it as a "right." However, this is all its preservation can tell us. It does not yet tell us how we can ever settle the question, namely, how we can figure out whether a given norm is indeed valid. The perspective of conscience is not a full-fledged perspective at all, not a point of view that grants us substantive insight into how to proceed, should our norms come into question.[5] This is what Hegel implies when he describes

---

existing social norms. "Conscience cannot be an original source of norms, but it can be a source for transforming, through processes of negation, the existing norms. It is an *activity of liberation* rather than the basis for a construction from the ground up of a society's ethical norms" (30).

[2] In addition to Hegel's specific objection to conscience in the chapter on "Morality," conscience also seems to be one of his central targets in the *Philosophy of Right* as a whole. His preface is largely a polemic against the *Überzeugungsethik*, or ethic of conviction, dominant in his day. So its status in ethical life is obviously a significant question that the work itself raises.

[3] This is not a "right" in the political sense, for it is not one that the state must overtly sanction. Rather, it is a requirement for the full realization of the kind of freedom that "morality" promises.

[4] There are numerous variations of this reading, but the baldest is perhaps Allen Wood's. Although phrased rather cryptically, this is at least how I understand the following claim: "At least in its mature form, the conception of ethical life is intended to include rather than exclude individual moral reflection. Sittlichkeit, as Hegel means it, is a special kind of critical reflection on social life, not a prohibition against reflection" (Wood 1990, 196).

[5] Hegel does mention conditions under which "what counts as the right and the good in actuality and custom cannot satisfy the better will" (PR §138), and these do seem to him to justify retreating into oneself in search of the right and the good. But this does not mean that he thinks such a search can ever succeed. He seems to imply that "in times when actuality is a hollow, spiritless, and unsettled existence" (PR §138A), we lose any means for distinguishing the moral genius from the sheer fanatic.

this right as merely "subjective" and so as lacking an objective criterion for distinguishing truth from opinion and error.

Moreover, it does not yet tell us whether occasions for raising this question could ever even arise. In other words, it could very well turn out that we never encounter grounds for doubting the validity of our norms. This means that we have not hereby demonstrated the genuine possibility of criticisms. This right can (and usually is) satisfied through the ethical disposition, or at least through cultural participation that involves reflective affirmation. At most I need to be able to pause for a moment in my habitual adherence and abstract away from a given norm in order to inquire into its validity. But this does not yet indicate that I could ever discover this norm to be invalid. So making room for criticism requires more. It requires showing something about the social world we inhabit, and not only about our available attitudes toward it – namely, that even modern ethical life could prove objectionable, and so in need of criticism.

My reasons for wanting to develop a Hegelian conception of critical reflection are not exclusively hermeneutic, so as to supplement his official theory or mend a textual gap. I think such a reconstruction and reconsideration is worth undertaking because it can offer a conception of critical reflection that takes full account of its virtues and drawbacks. As I read him, Hegel stands in the tradition of thinkers who are wary of an unlimited exercise of critical reflection and who contest its unconditional value. I suggest calling them "critics of critical criticism."[6] Although his wariness may not be as deep-seated as that of some, he is not convinced that it is always a good idea to scrutinize our social world with a critical eye, namely, with a view to *revising* its norms. He suggests in various ways that such reflection has destructive repercussions because it incites us to doubt what we may have no reason to doubt, and because it tends to spread from doubt about the validity of one contested norm to doubt about the social order as a whole. So a valuable form of critical reflection would need to be constricted in the face of its tendency to dissipate far and wide.

The conception I propose can meet the challenge posed by Hegel's fellow critics in offering a form of critical reflection that keeps to its proper bounds and questions only what has proven questionable. In short, the thesis I am here advancing is that critical reflection, for Hegel, does occupy a valued place in ethical life, but that its value is not unconditional, for it is not a good thing to exercise under any and all circumstances. Rather, Hegel thinks that critical reflection must be motivated not by the mere possibility that there could be

---

[6] I am taking this phrase from the subtitle of Marx' work *The Holy Family* (1844). Although Marx's target differs from Hegel's, and he even has a certain strand of Hegelianism in mind, I think that Hegel is perhaps more of an ally than is generally acknowledged, for both are concerned with excessive abstraction, as well as with the practical limitations of philosophical reflection.

something wrong with our norms, but by a confrontation with objective problems.[7] It is such problems that call for and in turn justify the activity of reflecting critically. And this may seem a thoroughly reasonable view to hold, one that few would be inclined to challenge. It would, after all, be highly impractical, to say the least, to engage in perpetual social criticism. Such a critic would be like the skeptic who does not know how to close the door to her study and reenter social life. Who would object to caution against unhindered reflection? And if no one would, why should a Hegelian response be of special interest to us?

Here I want to point to two conceivably controversial dimensions of the view I am ascribing to Hegel. The first concerns the conception of ethical knowledge that lies at its basis. If we really have no grounds for reflecting on our social norms until they produce problems that prove them worthy of reflective assessment, then we are *right* to adhere to them even before we ask ourselves whether the ways in which we ordinarily justify them are adequate – even if we in fact never ask ourselves whether they are. This confirms that there can be ethical knowledge at the unreflective level, knowledge that is not first earned through the exercise of reflection. It is easy to see that this would not be an uncontroversial claim, for it runs counter to a dominant intuition that we can only claim to know what we can fully justify. Of course this is not to say that Hegel thinks we can claim to know what we can in no way justify. All he holds is that we need not interrogate our ordinary modes of justification themselves before we are entitled to employ them.[8]

The second concerns the picture of critique that emerges from his account. Even if we accept that this is indeed how we as a matter of fact reflect and revise, one might still question whether such ordinary forms of critique are self-sufficient, or whether they need to be supplemented by a critical *theory* that lends them the perspective necessary for diagnosing and proceeding in the right way. Although I will insist that critique should not be modeled on a philosophical account of social life, at least not on the kind that Hegel himself advances, it leaves open the further question of whether critique can accomplish all it seeks through its own resources, from its correspondingly embedded perspective. For example, the proponents of a critical theory tend to argue that

---

[7] This is one important sense in which Hegel can be said to accord with later pragmatist thinkers. For example, Peirce argued that we need to have positive reasons for doubt, beyond the mere (Cartesian) maxim that all is in principle dubitable until proven certain. In Peirce's famous words: "Let us not pretend to doubt in philosophy what we do not doubt in our hearts" (Peirce, "Some Consequences of Four Incapacities," *Journal of Speculative Philosophy* [1868] 3, 140).

[8] This may seem inconsistent with Hegel's notoriously demanding epistemic standards, his thesis that we only truly know that which we can situate within his highly complex and complete "system" of mutually justifying elements. Anything short of it does not yet count as knowledge, because somewhere down the line we always end up depending on a presupposition that we cannot at all justify. I will take this issue up in the following chapter.

there is something inadequate about partial and piecemeal forms of criticism, because they lack a grasp into the deeper structure that is responsible for the practical problems such criticisms target. By taking up this line of argumentation, I hope to highlight Hegel's reasons for resisting it.

What I propose is that we think about ordinary forms of criticism along the lines of "immanent critique" in Hegel's *Phenomenology of Spirit*. Immanent critique can be provisionally defined as a process of evaluating a practice in light of its normative commitment, or conversely, evaluating a norm in light of its practical application. In the *Phenomenology*, this process takes on a consistently critical form, for the whole work explores those practices and norms that cannot do each other justice and in this way reveals their respective inadequacies. What makes such criticism "immanent" is that it needs nothing outside of the framework in question in order to expose these inadequacies. The framework is itself responsible for generating the kinds of conflicts between norm and practice that provoke its adherents to rethink both. The framework, moreover, provides its adherents with the critical standards for rethinking them, or at least for recognizing that they need to be rethought.

My aim in this chapter is as follows. I will begin by returning to my suggestion that Hegel should be read as a "critic of critical criticism," clarifying what I mean by "critical criticism" and positioning my reading within the spectrum of scholarship. I will then outline a conception found in the *Phenomenology of Spirit* that I think can satisfy a "critic of critical criticism" of Hegel's frame of mind, namely, immanent critique. Next I will illustrate immanent critique at work in the context of the Greek polis before assessing its relevance to the modern context. This last move is also the most contentious, for it is precisely the continued need for immanent critique that is in question. I will motivate it by returning to the institution of civil society and exploring the kinds of contradictions it generates, specifically poverty. Finally, I will take up the question about the relationship between critique and theory. In this context, I will assess whether ethical life could be permeated by ideologies that make ordinary forms of critique inadequate and in need of theoretical supplementation.

3.1 Critical Criticism

In his *Ethics and the Limits of Philosophy*, Bernard Williams raises doubts about the value of critical reflection, which he broadly defines as a skeptical interrogation of our ordinary ways of justifying what we do, or into our justificatory reasons. Critical reflection does not necessarily lead to criticism in the narrower sense, for it could very well turn out that, once we have interrogated our reasons, we find them justified. All it does is open up the possibility of reaching the opposite conclusion.

But this on its own is not what renders critical reflection suspect in Williams's eyes. Rather, it is its revisionary aspiration. Williams thinks this aspiration is a drive toward developing a moral theory, namely, toward arriving at a single normative standard by which to assess all actions. He also describes this as a drive toward "systematicity," and he claims that, unless it is somehow curbed, this drive directs all critical reflection. This means that, even when it does not debunk a given justificatory reason, critical reflection proceeds by replacing a rich reservoir of evaluative concepts with a narrower and thinner set. For example, rather than characterize someone's behavior as "rude" or "warm," we are asked to justify judging it favorably or unfavorably in terms like "right" and "wrong." Williams's point is that we have ways of justifying our judgments by means of traditional concepts. The problem arises as soon as we begin to look upon these concepts themselves as in need of a further justification. And narrowing our normative resources just is a basic feature of critical reflection, regardless of whether its conclusion is ultimately affirmative or not. For Williams, this is a destructive process.[9]

Is Hegel a "critic of critical criticism" in Williams's sense? Is he doubtful of the value of critical reflection, and if so, does he doubt its value on the same grounds? There is no consensus among his readership on this point. While most would likely deny that he could be rightly classified as such a critic, others have suspected him of being of the most conservative variety. And it is indeed difficult to overlook that Hegel often speaks against the exercise of critical reflection. His primary target tends to be criticism in the domain of philosophical thought, and he notoriously distinguishes philosophy's proper task of comprehending the social world from that of issuing corrections for it.[10] In this vein, he describes his own project as follows: "As a philosophical text, it must be farthest away from attempting the construct a *state, as it ought to be*; the instruction, which it can contain, cannot consist in teaching the state, how it ought to be, but instead how it, as the ethical world, should be understood" (PR, 26). It is not difficult to see that he has the "critical critic" of the state in

---

[9] Williams (1985): "I come back now to reflection itself and its relation to ethical knowledge. Earlier I said that reflection might destroy knowledge, because thick ethical concepts that were used in a less reflective state might be driven from use by reflection, while the more abstract and general ethical thoughts that would probably take their place would not satisfy the conditions of propositional knowledge. ... Knowledge is destroyed because a potentiality for a certain kind of knowledge has been destroyed" (167).

[10] This is somewhat misleading, because Hegel does condone and even advocate a form of philosophical critique, but one that is directed at the abstractions generated by reflection, rather than directly at the social world. As he puts it in his introduction to the "Critical Journal," the task of critique is to extract the idea of philosophy from its various deficient manifestations in contemporary thought. I will return to this critical task of philosophical reflection in the next chapter.

mind, namely, a philosopher who purports to know its current faults and to be able to construct a better version, at least in thought.

But warnings against such hubris extend beyond his programmatic remarks regarding the proper aims of philosophy, and Hegel often criticizes critical reflection in broader strokes, describing it as essentially restless and ultimately empty. For example: "[it] is only too easy to indulge in criticism, and it helps to confirm men's estimates of their own superior knowledge and good intention" (VPG, 66). Here it sounds as if he is not merely discouraging philosophy from becoming a critical enterprise, but considers it shortsighted and misguided in other contexts as well. Though this is not yet to call it destructive, the kind of condescension Hegel associates with the critical attitude points in that direction. Moreover, in the background is his worry that reflection tends to generate abstractions that have damaging repercussions because they lead to forms of confusion he diagnoses as "one-sidedness." As soon as we begin to reflect, we inevitably narrow the range of standards we think we can rightfully employ, preferably until we arrive at a single measure. This, for Hegel, has to do with the close proximity between the activity of reflection and that of abstraction, which is an essential moment of all reflecting.[11] In this respect, he seems to anticipate Williams, who sees reflection as equally directed by what he calls a "systematic" drive toward a first principle that can serve as a criterion for every evaluative judgment.[12]

Another reason to call Hegel a "critic of critical criticism" has to do with his positive appraisal of unreflective attitudes associated with habitual conduct. As we have extensively seen, he states in a key passage that

[in] the simple identification of individuals with actuality (*Wirklichkeit*), the ethical (*das Sittliche*) appears as their general manner of conduct (*allgemeine Handlungsweise*), as custom (*Sitte*) – the habit (*Gewohnheit*) of the ethical appears as a second nature, which is put in place of the first purely natural will and which is the soul, meaning, and actuality permeating its existence. (PR §151)

Here it sounds like he is privileging a rather extreme form of unreflectiveness, for if overt criticism lies on one end of the spectrum, habit is surely found on the other. Although I take myself to have already shown that an emphasis on habit is not incompatible with reflection, including critical reflection, I admit

---

[11] Recall characterization of the free will in PR §5, where he associates "abstraction" and "reflection-into-oneself."

[12] This conception of reflection is one Hegel frequently associates with *Reflexionsphilosophie*, and he also calls it "abstract" precisely in order to distinguish it from forms of reflection that he does not consider equally problematic, and in order to suggest that such reflection generates "abstractions" that lead us astray. I should also add that Hegel's own conception of a system does not fall prey to Williams's worry because it is not meant to be founded on a first principle, again a subject to which I will return in the next chapter.

that it is not exactly conducive to it either. Even if being habitually immersed and adopting a critical distance can in principle coexist in ethical life, fixed habits may make the latter more difficult. So it is not unreasonable to suspect that the more immersed in our habitual ways we become, the more resistant we grow to ever questioning, let alone altering, those ways. And even if we could move from habit to reflection with some ease, it would still not be possible for us to do both at once, to be both immersed and critical at the same time. So his preference for habit does seem to come at an indirect cost to critical reflection.

It is passages like these that have inspired two types of charges against Hegel's account of modern ethical life. On one hand, it has looked to some as if Hegel were denying the very possibility of critical reflection, suggesting that those who inhabit modern ethical life are so immersed in its practices that they are simply unable to distance themselves sufficiently from them. On the other hand, one might raise the slightly milder worry that Hegel, while not denying that it is in principle possible for social agents to engage in critical reflection, nevertheless discourages them from doing so. Both versions are contained in Ernst Tugendhat's famous accusation that

> Hegel does not allow for the possibility of a self-responsible, critical relationship to the community, to the state. Instead, we are told that the existing laws have an absolute authority, that a community determines what each individual must do, that each individual's own conscience must cease to exist, and that trust must replace reflection.[13]

Although worries about the possibility of critique and about its value may look distinct, I take them to be importantly linked. For what someone like Tugendhat demands is not merely an explanation of how we, as participants in ethical life so understood, can come to engage in critical reflection at all, but of how we can come to do so rightfully. So I take it that the question about the available sources of critique is at bottom also a question about its positive import.

But there is a further, third question here. In asking about the possibility of critical reflection, we are not only questioning its value, but also its standpoint. In other words, what we want to know is what resources we have at our disposal for engaging in critique, and how we can criticize society in a rational, rather than in an arbitrary or haphazard fashion. This is a version of the problem of finding and vindicating the appropriate standard or *Maßstab* that so preoccupied Hegel throughout his work. Many of his methodological discussions revolve around the necessity and difficulty of establishing just such a standard. In this context, the question can be put in the following way: to which normative measure can we appeal when critically assessing given social norms? Moreover, we ask this question as participants in the world Hegel is

[13] Tugendhat (1986), 315.

114   Critique

here describing, for what we want to know is what place for critical reflection remains *within* his account of ethical life. Thus our concern is really with a critical reflection that is suited to and appropriate for social participants who are practically entangled in the very practices they seek to assess and who remain so entangled even while assessing them.

I think Tugendhat's accusation exposes a significant gap left open by the *Philosophy of Right* and so raises a genuine challenge, one that is no longer taken sufficiently seriously. What it reveals is that Hegel has told us too little about what critical reflection would entail for us, how it can even emerge within the practices of modern ethical life, and what tools we have for engaging in it. But much of the recent scholarship has vehemently rejected the type of reading Tugendhat represents, arguing that Hegel merely disparages certain forms of critical reflection and that the very project he undertakes in the *Philosophy of Right* illustrates an alternative he favors. What these scholars point out is that Hegel seems to be engaging at least in a highly reflective enterprise, even if not in a narrowly critical one. The standard strategy has been to argue that Hegel is indeed holding the social world he wants to understand to rational standards of assessment, in order to show us that we can rationally endorse our own participation in it. Even though he ultimately concludes that this world is as it ought to be, there was always the possibility that his reflections could have yielded a different result and shown that it in fact fails to measure up. According to such readings, Hegel is undoubtedly reflecting critically, despite the fact that his final verdict is an affirmative one.[14]

Although I grant that such efforts to show that Hegel is no enemy to critical reflection have been important in moving beyond the straw man that Tugendhat attacks, I have reservations about looking to Hegel's own philosophical project as a model for how to think about critical reflection within ethical life. While I have to postpone a more thorough discussion of this project to the following chapter, I want to point to one significant reason for resisting such a strategy in the first place. This has to do with the connection between critical reflection

---

[14] Two examples of this reading: Michael Hardimon (1994) begins by arguing that Hegel's hostility toward critical reflection pertains merely to philosophy and has no implications for other domains of life and inquiry. But even if "[social] criticism might not be a *philosophical* activity in Hegel's view ... his social philosophy provides the tools that enable one to engage in *philosophically informed* criticism of the social world" (p. 29). Fred Neuhouser (2000) suggests an even stronger affinity between philosophical and critical reflection. According to Neuhouser, Hegel's effort to demonstrate that the social world is rational is meant to satisfy the aforementioned "right of subjectivity," which is the right of individuals to follow only those norms they can see as good. Neuhouser's claim is that this right requires a form of reflection that is best exemplified by philosophy as Hegel conducts it. So not only is Hegel engaging in a critical project, he is also promoting the same kind of critical reflection for social participants themselves, even if many of them are as a matter of fact unequipped to attain its highest (philosophical) form.

broadly speaking and criticism in the narrower sense. I do not dispute that these two need to be distinguished, for simply asking whether a social practice is justified does not yet imply that it is not. Hegel looks to be the perfect counterexample, for he is after all both interrogating the adequacy of our social world *and* seeking to redeem it in our eyes.

At the same time, to be worried about the status of critical reflection in ethical life is to want to know, not whether those who partake in it are capable of abstracting from and evaluating the norms they habitually heed, but whether they could plausibly and legitimately *criticize* them. Tugendhat's challenge goes beyond the possibility of mere evaluation, a possibility Hegel seems to be demonstrating. Rather, Tugendhat accuses Hegel of precluding that we ever could legitimately object to aspects of our social world and judge them to be in need of change. I take this to indicate that, even if there is some sense in which Hegel is exercising critical reflection, it cannot be the relevant sense, for the philosophical perspective for him is unable to yield genuine criticism. He expresses this idea in a famous passage: "To say a further word on the subject of *issuing instructions* on how the world ought to be, philosophy anyway always comes too late for it. ... When philosophy paints its grey in grey, a form of life has grown old, and it cannot be rejuvenated [*verjüngern*], but only understood; the owl of Minerva begins her flight only with the onset of dusk" (PR, 27–28). Hegel here wants to emphasize a crucial difference between the philosophical and the ordinary standpoints. While he may be conceding that we are capable of rejuvenating our form of life, he is discouraging us from looking to philosophy for guidance on how to do so.

3.2 Immanent Critique

My suggestion is that we search out a more suitable model for ordinary critical reflection in the *Phenomenology of Spirit*, specifically in its take on "immanent critique" – a term often ascribed to Hegel, though he himself never uses it. Immanent critique is usually identified with the tradition of critical theory tracing itself back to Marx's Hegelian roots, and defined as a method of evaluation that appeals only to norms that are internal to the object of evaluation. This is taken to be preferable to the "naiveté of openly evaluative and prescriptive inquiries."[15]

While part of what makes immanent critique "immanent" is indeed that its criteria of evaluation are internal, I do not think that naiveté is Hegel's primary concern. We get a better understanding of Hegel's reasons for preferring immanent critique if we focus on its indebtedness to *practical contradiction*. Hegel

---

[15] Benhabib (1986), 9.

thinks that any form of critical reflection that seeks to criticize our norms, and not just our practices, must confine itself to practical contradictions, for it is only through them that it learns what is worth criticizing, and so it is only from them that it gains its proper orientation. In other words, we must await the emergence of practical contradictions before we are in a position to criticize our norms. Prior to their emergence, we often do not know which norms are at work in our practices, so to which norms we are "internally" committed. And prior to their emergence, we rarely know which among our norms are objectionable. We need to appeal to experience, specifically experience of contradiction, in order to attain the requisite critical standpoint on our normative framework. So an account that links immanent critique to practical contradiction is in a much better position to explain its advantages from Hegel's point of view.

One might think that, when I speak of immanent critique, I have in mind what is commonly referred to as "internal criticism." Following the work of Rahel Jaeggi, I want to insist that the two are significantly different.[16] Internal criticism, or the "criticism of practices by appeal to understandings, norms, and values that are, at some level of generality, widely shared,"[17] does at this very general level resemble the kind of process of reflection at issue here. It is, moreover, a form of criticism that we frequently exercise whenever we fault an institution, say, the academy, for failing to live up to its own ideals and falling prey to economic interests at the expense of education and scholarship. But this is nevertheless not to be confused with immanent critique. Though internal criticism objects to practices for violating the standards they espouse, this type of objection differs from those voiced by an immanent critic in at least two relevant respects.

First, it is effective only when we presuppose that there is a merely contingent connection between a practice and its standard and that a failure of application has no implications for the validity of the standard itself. An example might be calls for campaign finance reform, which do not challenge our political ideals themselves, only their implementation. As we will see more closely, immanent critique is interested in those failures that indicate that there is something wrong with our very standards, and that these – and not merely their implementation – are in need of revision. Of course not all failures will be of this kind, and when there is only an issue of application, internal criticism is

---

[16] Jaeggi (2014), 261–301. Jaeggi stresses that "immanent" critique is anchored in "contradictions" and "crises" that are of an objective nature. My interpretation of Hegel's conception of immanent critique and social criticism is greatly indebted to her work.

[17] Here I am adopting the definition from Joshua Cohen (1997), 108, even though he himself dismisses this notion as too underdetermined to be of use.

usually sufficient. But such criticism falls short of touching the norms that are being inadequately applied.[18]

Second, internal criticism seems to presuppose that we are self-conscious of the "understandings, norms, and values" we share and that we are already ready to avow our commitment to them. Immanent critique, by contrast, often invokes norms that, albeit in a sense widely shared, are not always overtly acknowledged. So engaging in immanent critique can require that we first be made aware of commitments to norms we may not have even known we had. Although these norms must be operative in our practices for them to become critical resources for us, this does not mean that we must be self-conscious that they are operative, or that our practices commit us to them. Immanent critique can thus be understand as a method that has in part the task of highlighting these commitments, though it is practical contradictions that first bring these commitments to light.[19]

But if immanent critique is not confined to "shared understandings, norms, and values" in this self-conscious sense, from what is it being distinguished? Does it have an outer limit? And what would even count as an "external" form of criticism? There are different ways of characterizing an external standpoint, and the most vivid might be that of the literal outsider, such as a tourist who judges foreign ways by comparing them to those of her compatriots. In this case, one is still employing local standards of assessment, only not local to the society being assessed. Although this is perhaps the most extreme example, it does echo Hegel's own reminders to the "critical critic," namely that she is being too hasty in her condemnation and should refrain from dispensing verdicts until she has at least made a sincere effort to understand the modes of justification already at work in the practices before her.

One could also describe the standpoint distinctive of morality as external in a more sophisticated sense, for moral norms are thought to transcend any specific set of social practices one happens to inhabit. As his infamous "emptiness charge" against Kant's moral law[20] already suggests, Hegel is a rather harsh

---

[18] There are also different ways of classifying the relevant forms of criticism that can be mapped roughly onto this distinction between immanent and internal. For example, Luc Boltanski and Eve Chiapello (2007, 32–33) speak about criticism in terms of "corrective" and "radical" – where the former intend to make our "tests" (rules for competing within a social order that include justificatory constraints) stricter, and the latter to replace the given test with another. My sense is that this taxonomy is meant to capture the same distinction.

[19] As we will see, Antigone is an example of this. She believes that she is committed only to the divine law, but her crime reveals that she was implicitly committed to the human law as well, even though she failed to acknowledge it. This means that "to be committed to" is not always the same as "to identify with." We could be committed to many more principles than we are prepared to affirm simply because we participate in practices in which they are operative.

[20] Hegel famously accuses the moral law of being too indeterminate to be able adequately to single out good from evil principles. For further discussion, see, for example, Ameriks (2000) or Wood (1989).

critic of moral criticism. But his main complaint is that moral criticism cannot amount to *social* criticism. In fact, in the chapter of the *Phenomenology* called "Reason as Law-Tester," Hegel attempts to employ the categorical imperative (which he interprets as the purely formal "principle of non-contradiction") in evaluating institutions. He concludes that the categorical imperative can at best expose a contradiction between a social practice on one hand, and a personal maxim on the other. For example, it can show that theft is wrong only against the background assumption of private property. But it cannot tell us whether private property is worth upholding. So Hegel takes the further step of trying to employ the categorical imperative to determine whether the institution of private property, or rather that of non-property, can be shown to be contradictory. It turns out that both institutions can be made to pass and both can be made to fail, and that with equal success.[21]

At the same time, it seems possible to construe Kant's reflective procedure itself in immanent terms as a way of exposing commitments I already have in virtue of being an agent, even if I fail to acknowledge them when I act. This is nothing other than the transcendental move from what I happen to value to the very conditions that enable me to value it.[22] It is in a sense immanent, for it exposes implicit commitments. Nonetheless, this transcendental procedure differs from immanent critique, for it departs rather quickly from my concrete commitments. In other words, for it to work, it does not really matter what I happen to value – my particular point of departure – as long as I value anything at all. To be more precise, the determinate standard, to which it appeals, does not depend on the content of my given commitments, only on the fact that I have some commitment or another. Immanent critique, in contrast, is not indifferent to our starting points, nor does it automatically privilege the abstract over the concrete, the formal over the substantial.

Nonetheless, its kinship with this transcendental move should lead us to question whether the distinction between "internal" and "external" norms is all that helpful for understanding immanent critique. What sets it apart is perhaps less the norms to which it appeals, and more the way in which it appeals to

---

[21] I should note that Hegel is departing from Kant's own understanding of the categorical imperative, for Kant never meant to apply it to institutions, but to maxims of action. Hegel's point is, however, that the categorical imperative can reveal contradictions in our maxims only if we take certain background institutions for granted, institutions that the categorical imperative cannot effectively evaluate.

[22] Here I have specifically Christine Korsgaard's adaptation of Kant in mind. In *Sources of Normativity*, she begins with what she calls our "practical identities," namely the particular ways in which we conceive of ourselves and that provide us with ends and obligations. She then goes on to argue that these practical identities are not themselves the source of the authority they have for us, but that their authority derives from our identity as human beings. It is meant to show that, if we value anything at all, we are thereby committed to valuing our own humanity.

them, namely, by drawing the kinds of connections that show them to be part of our evaluative scheme, despite varying depths and distances from what we explicitly accept. Thus the critical resources available to an immanent critic remain immanent to the society under scrutiny, even if the divide between what lies inside and what lies outside is neither sharp nor fixed. This indicates that immanent critique is perhaps better understood as a method, one that might not always find a criterion ready to hand, but one that nevertheless searches out its measure in the object of criticism itself.

In the *Phenomenology of Spirit*, Hegel explicitly advances such a mode of measuring as his preferred methodology. As I mentioned in the Introduction (and as I will explore in greater detail in the next chapter), this text officially investigates "actual knowledge of what truly is" (PG ¶73). Initially, this task is interpreted in exclusively theoretical terms as the knowledge of some independent object that stands over and against me. But it comes gradually to incorporate practical knowledge, knowledge of genuinely binding social norms. Throughout, Hegel focuses on what he calls "appearances" of knowing, which is meant to carry two connotations. On one hand, he has in mind claims to knowledge that have actually been made and to their corresponding standards that have underwritten these claims. On the other hand, he also has in mind *false* claims to knowledge. In other words, appearances of knowing prove *mere* appearances.[23]

Key here is going to be Hegel's plan for proving that these claims are indeed false, that the standards to which they appeal are invalid, and so that the knowledge they purport to offer is not "real."[24] He does this by showing them to be self-undermining. In other words, he recommends that we follow him in adopting the standard that is already on the table and asking whether this standard can be met, whether it can be successfully applied, so whether it can attain the knowledge it seeks. In Hegel's words, "Consciousness provides its own criterion [*Maßstab*] from itself, and the investigation thereby becomes a comparison of [consciousness] with itself" (PG ¶84). In this way, we can challenge a given standard simply by exposing its inability to meet its own measure. One advantage of Hegel's method is that it can dodge the charge of arbitrariness that other forms of evaluation inevitably invite, namely, that they are merely assuming some criterion or set of criteria by which they are evaluating another. His

---

[23] "But science, in entering the stage, is itself an appearance; its entrance onto the stage is not yet [science] in its developed and unfolded truth.... It is for this reason that a presentation of how knowledge makes its appearance will here be carried out" (PG ¶76).

[24] Hegel describes the *Phenomenology of Spirit* as "an investigation and examination into the reality of knowing," adding that "it would seem that [such an investigation and examination] cannot take place without some presupposition, which can serve as its underlying criterion" (PG ¶81).

method also has the further advantage of persuasiveness, because it can convince someone committed to the standard under investigation that this standard is invalid, even by her own lights. "Hereby we are not required to import criteria and to apply *our* ideas and thoughts during the investigation; it is by leaving these aside that we succeed in considering the matter at hand as it is *in and for itself*" (PG ¶84).

But the main advantage of this method is its orientation toward practical contradictions, which provide it with both: an appropriate object of criticism and a suitable criterion by which to do it. So given their centrality in Hegel's method, it is worth trying to give some account of what would count as a practical contradiction for him – despite the fact that this (like "immanent critique") is not exactly his term.[25] A practical contradiction is something more specific than a failure to apply a given standard. It involves, first, an actual *inversion* of the expected result, not just a falling short of expectations. In other words, I am contradicting myself practically when what I do turns out to be the opposite of what I set out to do, and not just not quite what I set out to do. Second, I am contradicting myself practically when I betray the standard *in* enacting it. It is important that I am actually trying to live in accordance with it, and so that betrayal of it is not merely accidental. Third, I am contradicting myself practically when there was no way to avoid the failure, when it is not as if I should have, or could have, tried harder to remain faithful to the standard. The inversion must be a necessary one, one that any effort to enact the standard would have suffered.

A preliminary and familiar example of a practical contradiction is Hegel's dialectic between the lord and bondsman. The lord has a certain conception of what it means to be free. He imagines that to be free is to be free from direct engagement with the material world. But enacting this vision involves putting the bondsman to work for him, and so inadvertently makes him dependent on the bondsman's laboring activity. He also imagines that to be free is to be recognized by someone to whom you don't have to accord recognition in turn. But even enacting this vision proves impossible, because you have to value the

---

[25] The term "practical contradiction" is usually associated with Korsgaard's reading of the categorical imperative, specifically its universal law formulation. According to Korsgaard, the categorical imperative test reveals that the maxim would be "ineffectual" if universalized, because you could never achieve your private end. This is supposed to suggest a contradiction that is weaker than a strictly logical one, but that can nevertheless be determined through a formal examination of the maxim in question. Although I grant that my use of this term invites a comparison, I mean it in a very different sense. Most obviously, it is not maxims that are being tested, but norms operative in social life. But equally importantly, practical contradictions as I characterize them cannot be determined by examining the norm alone, because they consist of a discrepancy between norm and practice, and this discrepancy can be identified only once the practice has unfolded.

other's recognition and so implicitly recognize him as worthy of granting it to you. So the lord entangles himself in a practical contradiction because the life he ends up living is the inverse of the one he had hoped to win.

Hegel clarifies the structure of such contradictions in the "Introduction" to his *Phenomenology*, where he places them at the center of his methodology. What we are evaluating in this text turn out not to be just free-floating standards, but "configurations" (at first of consciousness, later of spirit) that are probably best described as normative frameworks of varying complexity, initially founded on one principal norm, which is taken to be a self-sufficient standard of knowledge. Each such configuration consists of two discrete but related poles – a conception of what would count as knowing (which he calls "certainty") and instances of knowing (or "truth") – and "comparing consciousness with itself" involves weighing its two poles against each other. Throughout, we discover systematic inversions between the two poles that make the configuration untenable.

There are two further structural features worth noting: first, Hegel stresses that consciousness is brought to reflect on its own configurations when it runs into contradictions that it cannot endure. In other words, the need for evaluation is not imposed by the readers, or, for that matter, by the writer of the *Phenomenology*, but has already been acknowledged by those who espouse the perspective under investigation.[26] This will turn out to be an important aspect of what it means to call such contradictions *practical*. Second, the criticism leaves neither the practice *nor* the norm unscathed. For Hegel, when we do stumble upon a failure to meet our own measure, this is no coincidence, nor is it a contingent outcome that could be remedied if we simply tried a little harder. To repeat, Hegel is interested in those failures that point to a necessary connection between a criterion and its enactment. When we fail to do justice to certain standards, it reveals not our own imperfection, but the imperfection of those very standards. Thus in this process, "the criterion for testing changes, when that for which it was supposed to be the criterion fails to pass the test; and the test is not only a test of knowing, but also of its criterion" (PG §85).

An especially vivid, though also highly abstract, illustration of this method can be found in the first section of the *Phenomenology*, "Sense-Certainty." Sense-certainty is, for Hegel, the most minimal conception of knowledge, for it claims that knowledge is nothing more than the immediate apprehension of what is, and that what is itself something immediate – i.e., not mediated by relation to anything other than itself, including both the knower and other

---

[26] In his influential commentary on the *Phenomenology*, Terry Pinkard (1996) stresses this point, arguing that Hegel's theory is fulfilling an aim that "must be shown to *emerge* as a requirement itself, as something that those accounts themselves generate out of their own failures to make good on the terms they have set for themselves" (10).

objects. So "immediacy" is its basic criterion, the measure it hopes to meet, its "knowledge-for-itself." In order to assess this criterion, we need to examine its application, what would count as an instance of knowing for it. Its actual instances of knowing are limited to the expressions "This," "Here," and "Now," since any other expression would invoke concepts and so would violate both the immediacy of our apprehension and the immediacy of the object to be apprehended. Note that the one demand that Hegel does impose from outside, so to speak, is that we be able to say what it is that we know, and he takes for granted that we cannot be said to know what we cannot in principle articulate. It is at this point, when sense-certainty tries to put its knowledge into words, that it is compelled to contradict itself.

Without spending too much time on its various efforts, it will suffice to say that the verbal expressions of knowledge available to sense-certainty – namely, "This," "Here," and "Now" – prove highly general, indeterminate, and without content, in the absence of concepts. For example, there is no way for me to pick out a particular object, say, a framed painting, merely by means of the expression "This," since "This" could equally well refer to the whole wall on which it hangs, or to the rural cottage it depicts. And employing more fine-grained ways of pointing, namely, by differentiating the spatial "Here" from the temporal "Now," leaves us no better off. So sense-certainty arrives at the very result it hoped to avoid. It sought a form of knowledge that has sacrificed nothing, has not omitted anything from its object. It wanted to represent the object exactly as it is, in all its particular richness. But "this *certainty* in fact gives itself away as the most abstract and poorest *truth*" (PG ¶91).

What becomes especially clear in sense-certainty, however, is not just the discrepancy between the two poles (when we "compare consciousness with itself," so a criterion with its application), but the inevitability of failure. Its proponents purported to have the richest knowledge, but they were called out as having the poorest, lacking any content whatsoever. The contrast between certainty and truth, or between norm and practice, could not be starker. But they failed through no fault of their own. It is not as if they were hypocritical in their avowals, or sloppy in their application. We now see that this criterion, with its entire corresponding conception of what it means to know, cannot be applied. It will produce the inverse every time.[27]

---

[27] Nonetheless, our failure has taught us something. We learn that, if we want to know particular objects, we have to conceive of them as possessing a more complex structure than sense-certainty attributed to them. At the next stage, this is interpreted to mean that we need to think of an object as that which underlies the sum total of its sensible qualities, qualities it might share with other objects. So in the transition from "sense-certainty" to "perception," we continue to be interested in a world of objects standing over and above us. But we have come to

The doomed efforts of sense-certainty illustrate exceptionally vividly Hegel's methodology in the *Phenomenology*. This method shares a lot in common with immanent critique as I have previously characterized it, but it is crucial that it not be conflated with immanent critique in the sense that will become relevant to the *Philosophy of Right*. In order to get a better sense of the difference, we need to disentangle two processes operative in the *Phenomenology*. For the sake of perspicuity, let us call the one "critical" and the other "reconstructive." The first process is conducted at the level of "consciousness" (or, as we will soon see, at the level of "spirit") itself and involves stumbling into problems that consciousness cannot overcome without abandoning its configuration. Another way to put this, and I will return to this shortly, would be to say that consciousness *experiences* contradictions when it makes the effort of applying its criterion or living out its norm and discovers that this cannot be done.

The second is conducted by Hegel himself and involves rationally reconstructing the critical process that consciousness has already undergone. This reconstructive process facilitates a form of evaluation that may not have been available to consciousness itself. It is often the case that those committed to a given configuration do not manage to see their own failure as a case of contradiction, so as a failure that could not have been avoided. It is also often the case that they do not voice their own criticisms in the form of a contradiction. To be more specific, social practices (including practices like slavery) need not be criticized for being contradictory, even if they are, and even if the fact that they are makes them objects of criticism in the first place. So presenting them in their contradictory form seems to be a contribution that a rational reconstruction might be able to make. In any case, rational reconstruction makes the *necessity* of failure more transparent.

This should not, however, be taken to imply that from the standpoint of consciousness we are in no position to identify the contradiction as a contradiction. Since the relevant contradiction is a practical one, and so consists of an inversion between norm and practice, it is a contradiction we can discover in the activity of trying to enact the norm. It just that we often experience a problem without grasping it as a contradiction. This experience tends to be more of a sense of unease, discontent, and frustration. Here rational reconstruction can expose what was true of a configuration all along, namely, that it contains a contradiction that could not have been overcome without abandoning the configuration in question. But it is also clear that Hegel's method is derivative

recognize that an object cannot be thought of as a bare particular we passively apprehend, that we can know an object as the particular object it is only by relating it to other objects, and so only by employing concepts.

of the hard work of confronting and overcoming failures in practice through the effort of trying to inhabit the configuration in question. Hegel's own evaluation of these configurations is indebted to such prior accomplishments, which produced the contradiction in the first place, and in this way revealed that the configurations were contradictory all along. Without this effort, the contradiction between norm and practice could never have even emerged, and so could never have been reconstructed.

The unique task of rational reconstruction, however, is to retrace the *transition* from one configuration to another and in this way show this process of normative change to be a rational one, one in which the new configuration is an improvement on the last. These transitions can only be seen as rational when viewed retrospectively. But they must have first been undergone by consciousness (or, more precisely, spirit) itself. One clear advantage of the "critical" process is its revisionary upshot, which the "reconstructive" process does not afford. When evaluation is exercised from the standpoint of consciousness, it is never merely negative, a dead end, but produces a new configuration that has taken stock of its previous failures. Once we encounter a problem within our normative framework, no matter how deep-seated it may be, it does not mean that we must now compose a new framework from scratch. Rather, "what emerges from this process is the *determinate* negative which is thereby a positive content" (PG ¶59). Hegel calls this transformative moment "determinate negation."[28] But this description can be true only of the "critical" process, not of Hegel's own philosophical methodology, which can never be prospective, only retrospective. It can never guide normative change, only grasp its progressive direction in hindsight. A rational reconstruction thus depends on the earlier, genuinely revisionary process of stumbling into and emerging out of contradictions.

All of this indicates that there are going to be serious limits to the extent to which Hegel's method can be thought of as a *test* in any strict sense, since it can only evaluate configurations in retrospect, not in advance. Hegel's evaluative procedure cannot be applied in abstraction from what Hegel calls "experience." What makes practical contradictions practical is that they are encountered in experience, an experience that cannot be predicted or anticipated before it has

---

[28] This notion of "determinate negation" is central to Hegel's dialectic, a term I do not foreground in this context, but that is closely connected to the movement I am here describing. According to Hegel, the progression from one configuration of consciousness to another cannot be conceived as a linear improvement, but *must* work through contradictions that emerge within it. At the same time, these contradictions generate a new content and a new configuration that salvages elements from its predecessors. Thus Hegel's answer to the question: "Why bother with the false?" (PG ¶38) is that even a configuration that is on the whole untenable contains some truth worth preserving.

been (for lack of a better word) experienced.[29] Hegel in fact calls the very movement of uncovering and overcoming contradictions a kind of experience, by which he has at least three things in mind.

First, criticizing a norm is going to involve weighing it against its practical enactment. This means an experience of actually enacting it is necessary in order for us to know what it would look like in practice. This need not have been my own experience, but someone at some point would have had to try it out before anyone is in a position to evaluate it. Second, encountering contradictions is not merely something we do when we choose to contemplate our norms, but is rather something we are positively compelled to confront in our attempts to apply them. In other words, it is our experience of living in accordance with inadequate norms that provokes us to adopt a reflective attitude toward them. Third, this experience is importantly a historical one, and the movement of critical revision one we have already exercised in our history. I believe this final sense of experience suggests most clearly that Hegel's talk of a "test" must be misleading, since he does not think we can formulate a set of criteria that can be applied independently of the real transformations we have undergone. This is so because the inadequacies of a given framework are rarely visible at the outset. So any exercise of "comparing consciousness with itself" benefits from the long historical experience at its disposal, without which it would be highly limited, if not useless.

Where, then, does immanent critique occur within the *Phenomenology of Spirit*? What conception of it does this text offer us? According to my reading of the Introduction, the relevant process of critical reflection – the process that has the power to revise a given configuration – is the one that Hegel is trying to reconstruct. In short, immanent critique refers to the activity at the level of consciousness (or spirit), not at the level of philosophical evaluation. Unlike the latter, the former represents the motor of normative change, remaining forward-looking, directed at problems as they arise and invested in their overcoming, even if it has no way of testing proposed solutions in advance. At the same time, there is significant overlap between the two processes, which makes Hegel's method an especially illuminating illustration of the basic structure of immanent critique. His method exposes the contradiction as a contradiction, and in this way explains what actually propels critical reflection, even when this process does not take a fully self-conscious form.

---

[29] For an admirable and illuminating study of experience in Hegel's *Phenomenology*, see Emundts (2012). In this work, Emundts clarifies the sense in which claims to knowledge have to make an appeal to and ring true to experience, so that experience plays an ineliminable role in this investigation.

3.3 Beautiful Ethical Life

Despite the clarity of the early sections of the *Phenomenology*, it is important to take note of the fact that these configurations are what Hegel calls "abstractions" from configurations of "spirit." Even though Hegel characterizes sense-certainty as the standpoint of "natural consciousness," he cannot mean that people ordinarily conceive of knowing in this way, that this is a starting point his readership shares.[30] I think the main reason Hegel begins with this configuration is not because it is most common or pervasive or mundane, nor because it is the earliest in history, but precisely because it is the most minimal, primitive, and crude.[31] So its clarity is also its limitation, and it is not until the chapter on "Spirit" that Hegel turns to worldviews rich enough that they could have been pervasive in actual societies. Thus it is also first in the "Spirit" chapter that we begin to see what it means to call immanent critique an experience in the compulsory and historical sense, rather than an exercise we can choose to undertake.

I announced at the outset that my concern in this chapter is with critical reflection in modern ethical life, and I alluded to some of the peculiar difficulties this context poses for Hegel. In short, modern ethical life is supposed to constitute a fully rational social order, whereas the configurations of "spirit" that comprise the *Phenomenology* do not.[32] But before we can address these dissimilarities, we need to get a better sense of how immanent critique works when it arises in actual societies, even in those that proved less rational than our own. The next step is thus a detour via the Greeks, as Hegel describes and diagnoses them, in order to examine the emergence of critical reflection in their midst. The Greek polis differs significantly from its modern successor, though this does not make it irrelevant for us. In fact, one reason to look to the Greeks is in order to highlight the difference between an inadequately and an

---

[30] Many have argued that this is what Hegel means. See, for example, Bristow (2007). I find this highly implausible, because Hegel thinks that this standpoint is already the product of excessive abstraction, abstraction in which we engage only when we step back from our practical involvement with the objective world.

[31] For an explanation of why Hegel needs to begin in this way, namely, why the initial account of knowledge needs to also be the most minimal, given his epistemological aims, see Rolf-Peter Horstmann (2011). According to Horstmann's reconstruction of the critical procedure, Hegel hopes to demonstrate the "primacy of the maximally complex over the elementary simple" by revealing that a more complex conception of both the subject and the object is already implicit even in the *most* simple. This would make the procedure transcendental in some sense, because it exposes the preconditions of even the simplest conceptions. But it would also make this procedure revisionary, for the simpler conceptions end up giving way to the increasingly complex. Thus Horstmann calls it "transcendentalistic."

[32] To be more precise, these configurations are also rational, but in an incomplete sense. One can find *aspects* of a rational social order even within the *Phenomenology*, for example in the *Morality* chapter that appears later in the section on "Spirit."

adequately rational social order. As we will see, this will amount to the difference between a society that is at bottom inhospitable to critical reflection and ill-equipped to cope with its effects, and a society (such as our own) in which critical reflection can be more easily accommodated.

Thus in the following I will focus on the first configuration of spirit, which Hegel calls "beautiful ethical life." Although I suggested that configurations of spirit do not lend themselves to the same simple analysis, it is possible to extract some general criteria that Hegel takes to be definitive of beautiful ethical life. In a familiar vein, one could say that its participants identify "immediately" with their social order, though "immediacy" is understood somewhat differently here. It is no longer a matter of knowing a world of independent objects, but of knowing an objective social world. But given that I also take part in this social world, my knowledge of it is supposed to yield self-knowledge. In others words, I look to the world in order to find out how to behave, and my duties are prescribed to me by the role I occupy within it. So each individual has no trouble figuring out what to do in any given situation and she inhabits her role so seamlessly that she always performs her duty decisively, without any hesitation. The aim of action is to sustain the internal harmony of this order by fulfilling one's particular role, and action is guided by a knowledge that is immediate because it does not need to be acquired through any kind of reflection, including deliberation.[33]

This criterion for ethical knowledge has to be understood against the background of "social substance"[34] that forms the context of its application. This substance is divided into two distinct spheres that are both equally essential to beautiful ethical life and so need to be able to coexist harmoniously without infringing on each other's terrain, if order is to be maintained. Hegel identifies the two spheres as the family and the state, and he claims that each is governed by a different set of laws, the family by the divine law and the state by the human law. The human law, which Hegel also calls the "prevailing custom," is

---

[33] As we have seen in Chapter 1, not all of these criteria for ethical knowledge are themselves problematic, and Hegel in fact reintroduces many of them in the *Philosophy of Right*, implying that decisiveness and lack of hesitation should be regarded as essential features of modern virtue as well.

[34] I do not have sufficient space to elaborate this notion here, but I do want to point out that the presence of "substance" is a new element that sets configurations of spirit apart from those of mere consciousness. According to Hegel, substance is the social order that individual agents and knowers inhabit. Substance can on one hand be distinguished from its individual members because it both precedes and outlives them, but on the other hand it is a work produced and sustained by their actions. In this context, Hegel defines substance in the following terms: "the universal, self-identical, and abiding essence is the unmoved and solid *ground* and *starting-point* of action of all and their *purpose* and *goal*. ... This substance is in the same way the universal work, which produces itself through the action of all and each as their unity and sameness" (PG ¶439).

publicly known and acknowledged. "Its truth is the validity that is open and in broad daylight" (PG ¶448). What this means is that everyone knows not only the content of the law – which sorts of actions it commands – but also its origin, which is a human one. In short, the human law is one whose source of validation is not obscure because it is posited by human beings. The divine law, on the other hand, is also known immediately, but its origin is unknown, since it is authored by the gods. What this means is that, while its adherents know what it commands of them, they do not know why. This law is, moreover, timeless, unwritten, and infallible, and so remains off limits to human evaluation and revision.

Hegel stresses that neither law has a privileged status because each depends on the other. Moreover, the authority of each is derived from the underlying social substance, which in turn requires the jurisdiction of both for its own survival. But the fact that there are two competing sets of laws is not supposed to compromise the criterion of immediacy, for it cannot generate conflicts of duties within one individual, since no individual is ever subject to both laws. Everyone is assigned exclusively either to the family or to the state. One important aspect of beautiful ethical life is that social roles depend on the natural distinction between men and women. "Nature, not the accident of circumstances or of choice, assigns one sex to one, and the other sex to the other law" (PG ¶465). While women belong to the family and have the task of protecting divine law, men are participants in the state and so comply first and foremost with the dictates of human law. This is why it is never unclear to which social roles one is assigned, since assignment is based exclusively on biological facts about the individual. And since one's sex determines whether one is a member of the state or of the family, no individual can belong to both spheres and so experience a conflict between the duties each prescribes.

Next, I will follow Hegel's own narrative in order to trace the structure of his argument. So let me begin with Hegel's account of the family, to which he devotes considerable attention. Hegel calls the family a "natural community," by which he means more than merely that its members are connected by blood. He claims that the family must possess its own unique ethical function and that this function cannot lie exclusively either in childrearing or in the acquisition of wealth, since both of these activities point beyond the family toward public life. He concludes that what distinguishes the family from the state is its commemoration of the dead. Burial is for Hegel an ethical act because its aim is to preserve the social standing of a deceased family member in spite of his or her natural death. As Hegel puts it, "the blood-relationship thus supplements the abstract natural movement by adding the movement of consciousness, interrupting the work of nature, and rescuing the blood-relation from destruction" (PG ¶452). This gives us another sense in which the family stands in close relation to nature. Although its task is primarily to "interrupt the work of nature," this in turn gives ethical significance to something natural about us – our mortality.

But the state's unique ethical function, which Hegel identifies as war, can also be described as an effort to "interrupt the work of nature." First, war prevents individuals from lapsing into their natural state of self-seeking drives, appetites, and desires by pushing them to orient their activities toward public ends. Second, Hegel argues that there is a particular value in putting one's own life at risk.[35] The individual is forced to assert his own independence from life and so prove that he is not merely a living creature and natural organism. Those who survive the battle are awarded the honor of becoming citizens with a publicly acknowledged standing. Unfortunately, women cannot achieve this recognition in public life, since their "destiny lies in the home." So it must be possible for them to become recognized as participants in ethical life within the constraints of the familial structure.

Although this premise is never explicitly stated, Hegel seems to hold that such recognition is essential to ethical agency, including that available to women within this world, for without it one remains a merely natural creature without any duties at all. In order for women to be able to regard themselves as subject to the divine law, their self-conception must be confirmed through recognition by another. But most familial relations prove inadequate in this regard. That between husband and wife is too wedded to feeling, desire, and procreation, and so to nature. And that between parent and child is a relation among vast unequals. So the only remaining candidate is the relationship between brother and sister, because such a bond, albeit natural, remains free from the intrusion of sexual desire. As Hegel puts it, brother and sister "are the same blood which has, however, in them come to its rest and equilibrium ... they are free individualities toward each other" (PG ¶457). And yet a sister's role is still significantly different from that of her brother. Brothers leave home, go to war, and participate in political life, while sisters become the principal guardians of the divine law.

It is probably clear that Hegel is setting the stage for his reading of Sophocles' *Antigone*, which comprises the kernel of his argument in this chapter, since this tragedy presupposes the significance of this filial relationship. But Hegel also turns to it because it focuses on a conflict between two individuals who embody

---

[35] As Hegel states in the chapter on "Lordship and Bondage," "It is only through staking one's life that freedom is preserved.... The individual who has not risked his life may well be recognized as a *person*; but he has not attained to the truth of this recognition as an independent self-consciousness" (PG ¶187). This moment of risk serves to draw a dividing line between freedom and life and demonstrates that the ends of freedom are my true priority, even if in the end I can be free only so long as I am alive. But Hegel also offers another argument, namely, that it is the confrontation with death that reveals to us our essential indeterminacy and capacity for abstraction. This is what the bondsman learns as he trembles before the "absolute lord."

the two central spheres of beautiful ethical life. Antigone is a woman who disobeys Creon's edict that her brother Polyneices remain unburied because he died in an effort to overthrow the throne. At night she attempts to bury Polyneices, though fully aware that this deed is punishable by death. From the perspective of the state, which Creon as king represents, Polyneices was a rebel who acted out of self-interest and so must be denied this "last honor," which in turn makes Antigone's act likewise one of rebellion. But from the perspective of the family, the state is permitted to punish only the living. The dead properly belong to the family and so must be returned to its fold. In leaving the corpse in broad daylight, Creon has violated the divine law, which commands that the deceased be buried by his relatives.[36]

Prior to this collision between the family and the state – personified in Antigone and Creon – this social order encountered no problems that it could not settle by appeal to justice, a function of the human law intended to restore social equilibrium. This is what makes it a "beautiful" form of ethical life. He writes, "This ethical realm is in this way in its enduring existence a world that is immaculate, not sullied by any antagonism" (PG ¶463). But the conflict we see in *Antigone* cannot be settled in this way because both sides have committed a crime and so neither is in a position to arbitrate justice. Moreover, Hegel thinks that these crimes could not have been avoided and so have little to do with Antigone and Creon as individuals, or with the specific circumstances in which they found themselves. What their actions reveal is that, within this form of ethical life, every ostensibly dutiful action carries the prospect of guilt, for it could very well turn out to be a crime, no matter how dutiful it may have been. As Hegel puts it, "Innocence is therefore only non-action, like the being of a stone, not even that of a child" (PR ¶468).

This is a strong claim, but it is not as implausible as it sounds. Hegel argues that, as long as one refrains from acting, it is possible to feel certain of what duty demands and to remain committed to one law at the exclusion of the other. But as soon as one acts out of this "simple certainty of immediate truth" (PG ¶468), one enters a social space that is far more complex than one's own

---

[36] There is some textual evidence in support of Hegel's reading. For example, Sophocles' version stresses this conflict between two sets of laws and the ensuing disagreement about their rightful jurisdiction. As the chorus leader reassures Creon, "Law and custom, as I see it, are totally at your disposal to apply both to the dead and to us survivors" (250: 1–3). But when Creon asks Antigone why she dared to break this law, she gives a reply that Hegel loves to quote: "Yes, because I did not believe that Zeus was the one who had proclaimed it; neither did Justice, or the gods of the dead whom Justice lives among. The laws they have made for men are well marked out. I didn't suppose your decree had strength enough, or you, who are human, to violate the lawful traditions the gods have not written merely, but made infallible. These laws are not for now or for yesterday, they are alive forever; and no one knows when they were shown to us first" (550: 1–12). Hegel alludes to Antigone's speech in the *Philosophy of Right* when he describes the laws in the objective sphere of ethical life (§144A) as equally eternal.

attitude reflects. Since each agent acknowledges only one law, she is merely lucky if she avoids transgressing the provisions of the other. Antigone reveals that it is only a matter of time before our well-intentioned deeds make us guilty of a crime. So every particular action is at least vulnerable to this threat. What this means is that such a world does not allow for any purely ethical actions, because each action can – from the point of view of the other law – be legitimately interpreted as a violation.

The conflict that emerges between the two sides of beautiful ethical life is irresolvable and so initiates its downfall. We already witness a certain level of destruction within the play itself, since the whole family perishes as a consequence of Creon and Antigone's misdeeds. But Hegel thinks this particular conflict is merely a harbinger foreshadowing the death of the entire Greek configuration because it exposes ineradicable inadequacies within it. At the beginning of this chapter, Hegel announces that beautiful ethical life will come to exhibit two kinds of contradictions, for it is divided not only into two sets of laws, but also into two types of self-consciousness, each one aligned with only one law. "Thus [self-consciousness] experiences [*erfährt*] in its deed both the contradiction of those powers, into which substance divides itself, and their mutual destruction, as well as the contradiction between its knowledge of the ethical nature of its action and that which is ethical in and for itself, and so finds its own downfall" (PG ¶445). Although he calls both "contradictions," only one of them is ultimately responsible for this downfall. The first contradiction that emerges between the two powers or sources of authority does not yet disclose that there is anything inherently wrong with this evaluative framework. The fact that there are two sets of laws, rather than one, is not as such a problem, especially given that each set is tied to a distinct institutional domain.

This suggests that the relevant contradiction is rather the one between a certain conception of ethical knowledge and the only possible actualization of this knowledge, which turns out to be an essentially *criminal* action. Let us take a closer look at Hegel's diagnosis. What, according to Hegel, makes this attitude deficient and incapable of enduring conflicts like that between Antigone and Creon? At the end of the chapter, he writes, "This downfall of ethical substance and its passage into another configuration is thus determined by the fact that the ethical consciousness is oriented toward the law in a way that is essentially *immediate*" (PG ¶476). What Hegel has in mind is that single-mindedness prevents such an agent from performing the act of abstraction, namely, from stepping back from one law and evaluating his or her action from the perspective of the other. Antigone was exclusively a sister and thus unable even to entertain Creon's point of view, and Creon was in turn unequipped to take Antigone's standpoint into consideration. This incapacity accounts for their subsequent failure to see that the other's action accords with norms that are equally essential to the social order they share. While this ability to abstract may not have been sufficient for resolving this particular conflict, Hegel suggests that it is revealed to be a necessary condition for sustaining a common social world in the face of ethical conflicts that will inevitably erupt in a society that exhibits even a minimal degree of pluralism, as beautiful ethical life clearly does.

While it is right to conclude that the exclusivity of commitment is at fault, Hegel thinks there is an even deeper contradiction at the core of this self-understanding that such conflicts bring to the fore. Antigone may think of her identity as exhausted by her familial roles, but Hegel argues that she is in fact committed to the human law as well. Though her action is a violation of the human law, it likewise reveals that she is not only a sister, but also a member of a broader society that includes the human law as a legitimate and essential source of authority. Hegel's point is not simply that the other law is equally legitimate and essential, but that neither law is self-sufficient and that each needs the other for its own authority. The divine law needs the state for its public actualization, just as "the publicly manifest spirit has the root of its power in the underworld" (PG ¶474).[37] Because the two laws are ultimately codependent, Antigone cannot be committed to the one without thereby committing to the other, which in turn compromises the simplicity of her self-conception. In Hegel's words, "In the *deed* [the two powers] are as a self, but a diverse self, which contradicts the unity of the self and constitutes its unrighteousness and necessary downfall" (PG ¶472). So Antigone is in a sense in contradiction with *herself*, even if not with her explicit self-conception, and not just with her action as it is interpreted by the world she inhabits. And since "neither power has any advantage over the other that would make it a more essential moment of the substance" (PG ¶472), the same can be said of Creon as well.

We can learn from Hegel's discussion of *Antigone* what it means for a society to undergo immanent critique. The society in question invokes a standard of "immediacy" in knowledge – namely, an immediate grasp of objectively binding norms – that it has to meet if it is to count as ethical by its own lights. But in its effort to adhere to its standard, it discovers that upholding it produces unethical actions, actions that are inevitable crimes committed against the social order as a whole. Even though such a society requires that the

---

[37] This is an obscure moment in Hegel's argument, but I think we can make some sense of it. It is perhaps easier to see why the gods would require the state in order to actualize their aims, since they do not otherwise have a public presence. Hegel calls them a "bloodless shade." So when Creon violated their law, they needed the assistance of other states surrounding Athens in order to avenge the wrong committed against them. Beckoned by the gods, these other states "rise up in hostility and destroy the community which has dishonored and shattered its own power, the sacred claims of the family" (PG ¶474). This in turn gives us some insight into the dependence of the state on the divine law. Since the divine law is in a sense more universal, a law that holds for other communities as well, any particular state needs to respect it in order to maintain its harmony with the other states surrounding it.

attitude of agents be undivided, its social structure is divided into what look like relatively autonomous spheres, even though they turn out to be significantly interdependent. According to Hegel, problems erupt when agents try to act out their uniform convictions within this complex structure. Although it may initially appear as if it were possible to avoid interfering in each other's domains of governance, Hegel suggests that they will eventually encounter a situation in which both laws have a stake and discover that they lack the resources they need to assess the two competing claims. When such a situation arises, it becomes clear that actions that express an "immediate" attitude are in principle divisive because they oppose the integrity of the whole. Moreover, it becomes clear that this attitude could never have been truly "immediate" in the first place, for it always already incorporates an unacknowledged commitment to the opposing law.

Since modern social participants do not share this insistence on "immediacy," it is not immediately clear how the experience of beautiful ethical life is supposed to bear on its successfully rational successor. Here it is worth recalling that this difference is in part what makes the Greeks so relevant. Earlier, I characterized it as a difference between a society that is inhospitable to critical reflection and one that is capable of accommodating it. We can now see that the fatal flaw of beautiful ethical life was nothing other than its incapacity to integrate critical reflection. It held fast to "immediacy" to such an extent that critical reflection could only appear as an interruption and intrusion, even when it was beckoned by contradictions that were fully its own. Here immanent critique had to adopt a radical form, for it could not resolve the central contradiction without thereby undercutting this society's basic self-conception.

3.4 Modern Contradictions

Though modern social participants might be quite accustomed to reflecting critically, it is not at all clear that the forms of criticism available to them count as instances of immanent critique. Immanent critique is the main mechanism of normative change in the *Phenomenology*, including later configurations of spirit, so even once we move past the simplicity of beautiful ethical life. But it is notably absent from the *Philosophy of Right*. And to many this looks like no omission. Even if they accept that Hegel leaves room for criticizing existing institutions for betraying their ideals, given that modern ethical life is supposed to be rational in its foundations, all that remains to be done is to engage in internal criticism and demand that our practices accord more faithfully with our normative commitments.[38] This does not mean that we cannot also evaluate

---

[38] This seems to be Hardimon's proposal for a "philosophically informed" criticism of the social world (1994, 29).

these norms themselves, as an extracurricular activity of sorts. All we would discover, however, is that they are in order – namely, that we know what freedom requires, even when we do not manage to live free lives. So critical reflection at this deeper level could at most yield approval of modern ethical life, one to which Hegel himself arrives.

Let me first note that it is easy to overstate Hegel's theoretical ambitions. In order to determine what Hegel even means in calling modern ethical life rational, we would first need to examine his methodological aims, which I will do in the next chapter. As we will see, he is in no position, as he himself admits, to dispense any final verdict on modern ethical life in any given form. Hegel has traditionally been read as locating his own standpoint at the "end of history," as if there were no unknown future facing his contemporaries. But this is a misunderstanding of his project. As I intend to show, Hegel's conception of philosophical method gives us a very different picture, one according to which any available justification of ethical life is and necessarily remains provisional. This means that the *Philosophy of Right* cannot in principle rule out the possibility that contradictions may surface at a later stage in our own historical development.

At the same time, this text also offers us a different basis for being confident in the resilience of modern ethical life in the face of future contestation. It hopes to demonstrate that whatever problems have emerged, and continue to emerge, will never necessitate a revolutionary transformation of our basic evaluative framework. In other words, Hegel wants to convince us that modern ethical life is sufficiently flexible to accommodate revisions without issuing in overhauls of the sort we witness in the *Phenomenology of Spirit*. But what makes it so flexible is less the invulnerability of its current norms and more its high estimation of critical reflection itself. If it proved inimical to critical reflection and unequipped to cope with the challenges it presents, that is when it would fail thoroughly by its own lights. One could say that modern ethical life is less fragile than its ancient counterpart, not because its laws are guaranteed to stand the test of time, but because it has dispensed with the standard of immediacy. This means that there is a sense in which a radical form of critique is no longer possible for us, if for no other reason than that it is no longer needed. And it is no longer needed because critique itself has become a core value.

That said, Hegel does not consider modern ethical life immune to problems altogether, problems that may even challenge its justifiability as it stands. On one level, it is true that the chapter on "Ethical Life" in the *Philosophy of Right* is meant to present a vision of a successful social order, but even there it is not seamlessly so. This is clearest in his section on "Civil Society," in which Hegel admits that among a string of more or less worrisome repercussions, the rise of poverty is a direct consequence of the modern market. It is, moreover, not a contingent one either, for it is due to its "inner dialectic." As he puts it, "It comes therein to the forefront that despite the *excess of wealth* civil society is *not rich enough*, i.e. it does not possess enough of its own resources to check the excess of poverty and the creation of a rabble" (PR §245). Although Hegel himself does not go so far as to call this a contradiction, stated in such terms, it sounds like a serious challenge to the justifiability of this institution, even in the provisional sense.

In blaming civil society for poverty, Hegel seems to have two things in mind. His first point is that under modern conditions, poverty assumes a new form, appearing as the "rabble." The rabble for Hegel comprises a constituency of those who, in losing their employment, recede entirely from social participation. Such a constituency is a uniquely modern phenomenon because of the status that civil society assumes. With the introduction of a relatively autonomous market, the economic function of the family (as well as that of the state) diminishes, and so there is no longer a safety net for those who fall on difficult times.[39] But Hegel also wants to say something even stronger, namely, that poverty itself rises as a consequence of the market, and not merely that the market makes poverty more difficult to bear. What he suggests is that civil society tends toward overproduction of goods, which in turn leads to mass unemployment. So it is the very efficiency of the market that is responsible for its rise.[40]

Even if we accept this diagnosis in its stronger form, it is not obvious what conclusion we are to draw from it. Hegel himself remains remarkably reticent. Since he mentions poverty only toward the end of his analysis, he avoids confronting the difficulty it presents and assessing the threat it poses to his previous account. This has led many commentators both to praise him for his bold diagnosis, and to criticize him for his refusal to draw the conclusion it warrants. For example, Schlomo Avineri admires Hegel's premonition into the fate of commercial culture, even if Hegel himself refrains from offering a solution to the problem of poverty.[41] But many remain divided over the status of poverty in Hegel's philosophy, some arguing that the problem of poverty indicates Hegel's half-hearted acknowledgment of a class conflict,[42] others suggesting

---

[39] See, for example, PR §238: "Initially, the family is the substantial whole whose task it is to provide for this particular aspect of the individual, both by giving him the means and skills he requires in order to earn his living from the universal resources, and by supplying his livelihood and maintenance in the event of his incapacity to look after himself. But civil society tears the individual away from family ties, alienates the members of the family from one another, and recognizes them as self-sufficient persons. ... Thus the individual becomes a *son of civil society*, which has as many claims upon him as he has rights in relation to it."

[40] To spell this out more explicitly, the idea seems to be that the increasingly efficient production of goods leads to layoffs, which in turn means that fewer and fewer can afford to purchase the goods being produced. So there is a reciprocal interaction between overproduction and impoverishment.

[41] See Avineri (1972), 150.

[42] See Wartenberg (1982) and Westphal (1992).

that Hegel does provide viable solutions to poverty, and so is able to overcome this problem within the framework of his official account.[43] Despite Hegel's reticence on this point, I think his admission that poverty is a structural feature of civil society indicates a certain foresight on Hegel's part, a foresight that implicitly concedes the continued relevance of immanent critique in modern ethical life.[44] If we accept his diagnosis, we discover reasons for thinking that poverty is more than an unsavory side effect at the periphery of civil society, that it even exposes a contradiction at its center. I will now try to motivate this reading by identifying the contradiction at stake.

In order to charge this institution with being contradictory, we would have to be able to show that participating in it hinges on a commitment that its actual practices systematically violate. So we must first consider the kind of subjective attitude that this institution requires for its successful functioning. It is tempting to think that civil society, which corresponds to the economic market, need not measure up to any ethical criteria in the eyes of its participants. The market is notoriously amoral. Marx captures this in his formal principle of capitalist accumulation (M – C – M'), a principle that looks to be without ethical content. Though Hegel was not working with a concept of capital, he did conceive of economic activity as propelled by individual self-interest, so as having the "infinite" structure of ceaseless desire.[45] Given that such activity is governed by an insatiable drive for more satisfaction, we might conclude that individuals have a self-evident motive to participate in this institution. Simply put, it accords them a sphere in which they can unapologetically prioritize what is already of interest to them.

Hegel, however, gives us reasons to think that such a motive would be insufficient to perpetuate this institution. His view in this respect resembles the one recently advanced by Luc Boltanski and Eve Chiapello, who have argued that capitalism demands a corresponding "spirit" – a spirit that *justifies* capitalist practices to the agents responsible for perpetuating them – in order to sustain a commitment to continued participation. Neither brute self-interest nor inertia could be enough, for capitalism must prove itself "worth the effort of being lived."[46] Boltanski and Chiapello develop this thesis in a slightly different

---

[43] See Anderson (2001).
[44] Marx thinks through the implications of Hegel's account of civil society more generally, but it is striking that he does not explicitly take up Hegel's discussion of the "rabble." For a helpful discussion of the connection between Marx and Hegel on this front, see Melamed (2001), 33–36.
[45] "Particularity in itself is boundless extravagance, and the forms of this extravagance are themselves boundless. Through their representation and reflection, human beings expand their desires, which do not form a closed circle like animal instinct, and extend them to false [*schlechte*] infinity" (§185A).
[46] Boltanski and Chiapello (2007), 11.

direction, for they go on to deny that this spirit could appeal to something as theoretical as the "common good," and to propose that we think of it as serving an ideological function. These are not directions Hegel will himself pursue. Hegel seems to think that theoretical accounts like those proposed by political economists manage to capture the way we ordinarily justify our social participation to ourselves. He also does not discredit these forms of justification as ideological. But he nonetheless shares their basic insight, namely, that those participating in the market, regardless of how much material satisfaction they gain, must be able to find some good in their participation. Otherwise, they would be unable to find what they do to be worth doing, or, to put this in Hegel's own terms, to see their own activity as free.

This requirement seems to follow from Hegel's general thesis that subjective freedom is satisfied only when the right of subjectivity is accommodated, and as we have seen, this right contains the provision that we see the instituted laws or informal rules we are to follow as *good*. He does not defend it specifically in the context of economic practices, but it certainly seems to extend to this context as well. What he suggests is that market activity involves a distinct kind of self-understanding, according to which unhindered individualism is worth indulging because it inadvertently benefits *all*. So long as I am convinced of it, I can continue to regard my own participation in civil society as justifiable. I should qualify that this need not take the form of an explicit belief about the validity of the institution as a whole. Perhaps it is more aptly characterized as a tacit trust[47] that, if *I* work hard, *I* will be rewarded – because everyone who does will. Putting it in these terms can help us see why Hegel is in the end not as puzzled by the ethical dimension of civil society, for he does not think that the principle at the basis of market activity – which he calls the "principle of particularity" – can operate in a self-sufficient manner.

The next step is to clarify the structure of this self-understanding by disentangling the two principles at the basis of market participation. According to Hegel, what sets the market apart from other institutions is its privileging of particularity, its allowance of the pursuit of individual ends, whatever these may be. But it turns out that "particularity in itself [*für sich*] indulging itself in all directions as it satisfies its needs, contingent arbitrariness, and subjective caprice, destroys itself and its substantial concept in the act of enjoyment" (PR §185). So we find that this principle must first become a "right" with its own sanctioned social space, if it is to accrue any authority, and it can accrue such authority only if it is "constricted by the power of universality" (PR §185).

---

[47] Although I have not made this central to my analysis of unreflectiveness in ethical life, Hegel frequently talks about "trust" as a way of characterizing this immediate perspective. See, for example, PR §147 and §268.

It bears noting that Hegel is not simply asserting that self-interested activity requires some kind of justification in the terms of "universality." Rather, he is making a different point, namely, that the principle of particularity would destroy itself – that it could never achieve its particular end in the first place – if it were not so constrained.[48]

The dependence of particularity on universality is revealed in stages, stages in a process of subjective transformation that Hegel considers integral to civil society. This is the very process of *Bildung* that we have previously seen. Initially, universality is merely a means for the satisfaction of particularity, since even the pursuit of my particular ends can succeed only if I take those of others into consideration and coordinate my endeavors around theirs. To be more specific, if I want to secure my own financial success, I must produce only what others want to purchase. In this way, I am made attentive to their needs, though their needs matter to me only instrumentally, because they enable me to satisfy my own. Through this mutual cooperation, I also become embedded in what Hegel calls a "system of needs," a broader network of cooperation that already orients my activity toward the interests of all others, even if at first exclusively out of self-interested considerations.

These considerations, however, gradually change with the growing material interdependence among individuals, their deepening entanglement with one another. As we have seen, Hegel characterizes this as a process through which the participants themselves are made increasingly universally minded. It has an objective and a subjective side. Objectively speaking, economic activity actually produces something of social value on which it in turn depends – namely, what Hegel calls the "universal permanent wealth," "which contains for each the opportunity to take part in it by the exercise of his education and skill in order to be guaranteed his livelihood – while what he thus earns by means of his work maintains and increases the general wealth" (PR §199). As Hegel puts it, "In this dependence and reciprocity of work and the satisfaction of needs, *subjective selfishness* turns into a *contribution towards the satisfaction of the needs of everyone else*" (PR §199). In other words, the self-interested activity of each generates a source of wealth from which all in turn profit, including I. It is from it that I draw my own material satisfaction.

One might wonder whether I have to recognize my own dependence on this universal permanent wealth, whether this needs to be reflected in my attitude, in order for me to contribute to it. But Hegel thinks that this objective process of increasing material interdependence has an essentially subjective side as

---

[48] Thus "in the very act of developing itself in itself [*für sich*] to totality, the principle of particularity passes over into *universality*, and only in the latter does it have its truth and its right to positive actuality" (PR §186).

well, for it alters my conception of others as well as of myself. First, I can no longer view others simply instrumentally, because the system of needs has blurred the line between ends and means, and so the line between them and me. In order for others to provide me with means for the attainment of my ends, I have to provide them with the means for the attainment of theirs.[49] This introduces "the requirement of equality in this respect with others" (PR §193). If I am to enter into economic transactions with others, I have to be willing to grant a formally equal standing, to regard them as beings with needs in this respect no different from me, even if this does not – and should not, according to Hegel – translate into material equality.[50] It is this neediness that we share and that enables us to enter into interactions in which we adopt the abstract roles of "buyers" and "sellers." Hegel's point is that these roles presuppose a formally equal standing and that economic transactions can take place only so long as this formal equality is at least implicitly acknowledged.

Such a shift in attitude toward others affects the way I view myself as well. I now see myself not only as equal to others in my neediness, but, moreover, indebted to them for my sustenance. So the second subjective transformation is a dawning recognition of my dependence on the universal permanent wealth to which I have contributed, and from which I am promised a piece in turn. This universal permanent wealth is that on which I as an individual like any other rest my trust that I will be guaranteed my share. Without this trust, I would cease to see my own activity as worth undertaking, for the universal permanent wealth grounds my conviction that, through my work, my needs will be met. Hegel emphasizes that, in this respect, civil society replaces the function of the family. As he puts it, "the individual becomes a *son of civil society* which has as many claims upon him as he has rights in relation to it" (PR §238).

What precedes is the picture of civil society as a successful social institution, one in which particularity is both constrained and protected by the power of universality. In other words, this is how civil society is, according to its own self-understanding, supposed to operate – a self-understanding articulated in the tradition of political economy and captured most memorably in Adam Smith's metaphor of the "invisible hand." In Hegel's rendition, the story is one in which "each man in earning, producing, and enjoying on his own account is *eo ipso* producing and earning for the enjoyment of everyone else" (PR §199). But heeding the principle of particularity proves to have an unanticipated

---

[49] "The fact that I have to fit in with other people brings the form of universality into play at this point. I acquire my means of satisfaction from others and must accordingly accept their opinions. But at the same time, I am compelled to produce means whereby others can be satisfied. Thus, the one plays into the hands of the other and is connected with it" (PR §192A).

[50] Hegel, in fact, claims that material inequality is an essential and ineradicable feature of civil society. See PR §200R.

consequence. Although doing so may secure the material well-being of *some* individuals, it at the same time relegates many others to utter destitution. So it turns out that civil society is in fact not capable of benefiting *all*, and so cannot avoid violating the principle of universality on which it likewise depends.

There are two senses of universality at issue here that need to be distinguished, but that are ultimately linked. According to the first sense, universality refers to the total sum of individuals, and a commitment to universality involves a commitment to ensuring the livelihood of each and every one. According to the second sense, universality refers to the social order of which individuals, as well as civil society as a distinct institution, form a part. A commitment to universality in this second sense is made to the survival of the broader structure that conditions and sustains civil society as a sphere of particularity. I think, for Hegel, universality in the relevant sense would not have been violated, if it turned out that civil society necessarily produces one poor individual, or at least a very small number of poor individuals. But it has been violated if civil society necessarily produces a number of poor individuals large enough to harm the social order at large. And this is precisely what the emergence of the rabble signals, for the rabble is a class that has become unfit to participate in any other institution, most notably the state,[51] and so has no stake in the survival of this order and may even come to wish for its demise.[52] I say that the two senses of universality are ultimately linked because the rabble consists of individuals who have been cast aside, whose rights against civil society have been denied, even if it is the magnitude of this group of outcasts that makes them a destabilizing element in ethical life.

We are now in a position to determine whether this unanticipated consequence exposes a practical contradiction within this institution. According to the conception we find in the *Phenomenology of Spirit*, a practical contradiction must involve a necessary inversion between practice and norm. In beautiful ethical life, for example, we saw that *every* seemingly lawful action could as well be a crime, or could at least be interpreted as one. Though this may sound surprising, given that not everyone is in fact a member of the rabble, something equally damning can be said of civil society. If civil society cannot guarantee the livelihood of *everyone*, it cannot *guarantee* the livelihood of

---

[51] According to Hegel, "When a large mass falls below the standard of a certain subsistence level ... and when there is thus a loss of a sense of right, of righteousness, and of the honor of maintaining oneself through one's own activity and work, this brings about the creation of a rabble" (PR §244).

[52] This is especially clear in the Addition to §244, in which Hegel defines the rabble in terms of its socially destructive frame of mind: "Poverty in itself does not reduce people to a rabble; a rabble is created only by the disposition associated with poverty, by inward rebellion against the rich, against society, the government, etc."

anyone. So our right against it, which Hegel identifies as central to our sense of trust in it, remains unprotected.

Of course, the right to share in the universal permanent wealth that economic activity generates is contingent on actual participation. You have to contribute to it in order to be owed something in return. At the same time, it could happen to me that I have contributed to it and yet be denied my share. This means that the trust I invest in this institution as its active participant, even while I am faring quite well, proves groundless. Anyone could in principle be demoted to the level of the rabble, despite the fact that this does not as a matter of fact happen – just as in beautiful ethical life, every seemingly lawful action could in principle turn out to be a crime, though most are not. This is the reason it is crucial to show that universal considerations are internal not only to the functioning of civil society as a whole, but also to the satisfaction of individual pursuits. If the principle of universality were entirely extrinsic, it could not be mobilized in any criticism of this institution. Then civil society could not be faulted for failing to meet the requirement this principle imposes, namely, that all benefit from the actions of each.

Much like those we find in the *Phenomenology of Spirit*, this type of contradiction is not a formal one, but takes a distinctly practical form. In the former context, I characterized the relevant contradiction as an ineradicable discrepancy between norm and practice, but here we are dealing with a more complex set of conflicting components. One could say that the contradiction is in a sense between two norms – the principle of particularity and that of universality – rather than simply between one norm and its enactment. What makes such a contradiction nonetheless practical is that we discover (and discover *through experience*) that we are unable to do full justice to both without violating either one or the other, and in this way introducing objective problems for ourselves.

Another way to capture this thought would be to say that the effort of upholding both principles to the fullest extent proves unsustainable. It has become increasingly popular to associate failures in forms of life with the notion of "unsustainability," or the related notion of "uninhabitability." It is, for example, an aspect of social failure that Terry Pinkard has recently emphasized.[53] This way of speaking remains true to Hegel's spirit, for Hegel is explicitly concerned with the livability of particular social arrangements, with their longevity and capacity for survival and regeneration.[54] But there are admittedly dangers in identifying contradictoriness and unsustainability too closely. One reason to question such language is that it sounds too ecological, as if the

---

[53] Pinkard (2012) speaks of alienation in terms of "uninhabitability," which seems to me to be roughly the same idea.
[54] Recall the passage from the "Preface" of the *Philosophy of Right* in which Hegel speaks of shapes of life having "grown old" and immune to (philosophical) "rejuvenation."

issue were primarily an exhaustion of material resources, which is not always the case. Hegel does say that civil society is not "rich enough" to check the excess of poverty, but I take this to be an allusion to the dearth of its normative resources, its inability to overcome this contradiction without sacrificing either the right of particularity or that of universality, so either principle to which it is committed.[55]

Another reason might be the seeming indeterminacy of this concept of unsustainability. The worry is that it lacks a criterion of application and so cannot adequately distinguish between what merely seems unsustainable and what truly is so. For example, some men might not feel at home in feminist familial arrangements, might even claim that they find them uninhabitable, without thereby demonstrating that such arrangements are in fact so. Or conversely, some women may feel perfectly at home in the midst of a patriarchal family structure without this speaking in its favor. But this sort of concern speaks past Hegel. First, Hegel does not hold that we can determine in advance whether something will prove genuinely unsustainable. Our verdict must await the test of time. Second, he certainly would not look to any feelings of discomfort as evidence for uninhabitability. In fact, Hegel's entire project in the *Philosophy of Right* is predicated on the premise that his contemporaries feel ill at ease in their social world and that they consequently need to be shown that their impression is distorted. Third, the notion of practical contradiction is supposed to yield an objective criterion that can be used in social criticism. But its applicability is going to require the presence of objective problems, and not merely on a sense of personal dissatisfaction.

Finally, it may look like contradictory social forms are not indeed unsustainable, since they appear to be, despite all of their contradictoriness, resistant to change. Pinkard notes this when he writes that "however contradictory a form of life may be, and however much of an impact that being true may have on the lives of its participants, people can live with those contradictions and whatever anguish they bring with them for centuries."[56] If we accept this as a fact about social life, it becomes difficult to see what could be meant by calling contradictions unsustainable. I think the best way to think about this is to place emphasis on the *insight* involved. To say that contradictions make a social order uninhabitable is to say that it is impossible to inhabit it without coming to recognize

---

[55] My reading is supported by the context in which this claim appears: Hegel has just enumerated various options for overcoming poverty only to show that each of them would undermine some essential principle of civil society. Charity would rob people of the honor won through work and state-run employment initiatives would only contribute to the source of poverty, namely, overproduction. It is "hereby," i.e., due to the impossibility of solving the problem of poverty in an adequate way, that the civil society proves insufficiently "rich."

[56] Pinkard (2012), 118.

the contradiction, even if only in half-baked way (so not *as* a contradiction). Such recognition may not be sufficient to propel actual change in the institutions themselves, but it does erode our confidence in these institutions, which is integral to their successful functioning. According to Hegel, a form of social life has a chance of survival only so long as it is able to garner the commitment of its participants, a commitment seriously compromised by the emergence of contradictions, even when not recognized as such.

My claim is that contradictions within a social order cannot remain completely unrecognized and that this is what it means to call such an order unsustainable or uninhabitable. The reason that contradictions cannot remain completely unrecognized is that they manifest themselves practically, that they are bound to find a practical expression, thwarting our efforts to sustain or inhabit. So this notion of unsustainability turns out to be fruitful for our purposes, for it sheds significant light on the space left open to critical reflection. It implies, first of all, that it is often not easy to see that two principles are incompatible until we try to live by them. Although we may retrospectively believe that their incompatibility should have been evident from the outset, we now know this only because we tried it out and discovered that it cannot work. To return to our example, it is the phenomenon of poverty that brings to light the irresolvable tension between the principle of particularity and that of universality, at least in their capitalist variation. If we merely contemplate the theoretical foundations of the market economy in abstraction from real economic practices, we may never come to suspect that there is anything wrong with its mode of self-justification and that there is no "invisible hand" ensuring the common good. This goes some way toward explaining why the political economists writing before Hegel's time, and so before the actual emergence of a rabble, lacked his foresight. And it also goes some way toward explaining why it is the further unfolding of capitalism and industrialization that enabled Marx to see Hegel's shortsightedness in turn. The contradictions internal to capitalism were only in the process of surfacing.[57]

A further implication of unsustainability is that we not only discover such contradictions, should we choose to contemplate our norms, but that we cannot avoid discovering them. This implication is crucial, though rarely emphasized. To put this slightly differently, if certain practices of ours are unethical through

---

[57] For example, Marx saw that the problem of poverty lay not primarily in unemployment, but in *employment*. In the *Philosophic and Economic Manuscripts of 1844*, he identifies a number of contradictions that constitute labor under capitalist conditions: "The worker becomes all the poorer the more wealth he produces, the more his production increases in power and range. The worker becomes an ever cheaper commodity the more commodities he creates. With the *increasing value* of the world of things proceeds in direct proportion the *devaluation* of the world of men" (Marx, *The Marx-Engels Reader*, 71).

and through, rather than contingently flawed or defective, this will manifest itself in undeniable ways by generating the kinds of problems that systematically thwart our efforts to inhabit or sustain. We can think of these problems as "crises" of varying depth and scope. And in moments of crisis, it is not reflection that first brings contradictions to light. Rather, it is contradictions that initiate reflection, for it is in the face of them that we find ourselves pressed to reevaluate the conflicting norms. Critical reflection, in short, is a response to the unsustainability of a contradictory way of life, and thus beckoned by our very inability to live it out. This is also clear in the crisis that the emergence of the rabble threatens to provoke, for what emerges is a class of criminals who do not even consent to the very laws according to which they are to be punished. And in the end Hegel nearly admits that they are right to deny their authority.[58]

It might be instructive to consider an example that goes beyond Hegel's own. One that comes most readily to mind is the critique of racial segregation in the early days of the civil rights movement. At that time, segregation was publicly justified in terms of the notorious doctrine of "separate but equal,"[59] which implies, roughly speaking, that having two sets of institutions separated along racial lines does not violate the equal status of each American citizen because both sets can in principle be equally good. While it does not assume that they are as a matter of fact equally good, nor does it offer a positive reason in favor of segregation, this doctrine is meant to vindicate certain social practices by showing them to cohere with our deeper commitment to equality. Interestingly enough, it was after years of actual segregation that this justification came to look *conceptually* incoherent. The Supreme Court ruling in *Brown v. Board of Education* points this out in striking terms, for it states that "in the field of public education, the doctrine of 'separate but equal' has no place. Separate educational facilities are inherently unequal."[60] We can make better sense of this realization, I think, if we look to the role that the experience of segregation came to play. It is precisely this experience of consistently and vastly unequal facilities that demonstrated the incoherence of the doctrine, proving that separate is in fact *inherently* unequal.

The official argument relies explicitly on empirical evidence that shows that racial segregation harms African American children. During the proceedings, research was cited that demonstrated the psychological effects of segregation

---

[58] Hegel's own position is admittedly ambiguous on this point. It is the following comment from his Additions that leads me to ascribe to him the preceding conclusion: "No human being can claim a right against nature, but in the context of society every lack gains immediately the form of a wrong, which is done against this or that class" (PR §244Z).

[59] This phrase was officially established as a justification of segregation in the Supreme Court ruling *Plessy v. Ferguson*.

[60] *Brown v. Board of Education*.

on the self-esteem of students,[61] which presumably has detrimental effects on their academic performance in turn, thus preventing them from achieving results equal to those of their peers, even if both sets of educational institutions were to have comparable material resources (which they as a matter of fact never did). But this evidence was invoked in order to confirm a deeper point about the incompatibility between two norms, that of separation and that of equality – a point not easily defeated by counter-evidence. In other words, the point would still stand, even if it were possible to identify some students who emerged from segregated educational institutions unharmed. What experience reveals is the "inherent" inequality in racial segregation. So it is an experience in Hegel's idiosyncratic sense – an experience of a contradiction between a practice and its supposed justification.

One way to parse this point is to consider the background presupposition against which segregation looks to be worth undertaking. The doctrine of "separate but equal" does not make this presupposition explicit and so does not offer a positive reason in favor of segregation, claiming only that it is permissible because not incompatible with equality. But what experience exposes is the fact that segregation along racial lines is essentially tied to, and thus inseparable from, racist assumptions about the superiority of one race over another. This is what makes segregation incompatible with equality, and so inherently unequal. Empirical studies like the "doll test" foreground this background presupposition by investigating the harmful effects it has on children's self-conception. The explanation for why children in segregated schools come to develop acute forms of self-hatred is that they are being educated in a context in which they are made to feel inferior on the basis of the color of their skin. And it is a presupposition only corroborated by the process of desegregation, during which originally black schools were destroyed and their students required to attend white schools, rather than the reverse. In short, what experience exposes is something that was true of this practice all along – that racial segregation in the context of education could never achieve equality because it presupposes inequality and is only justifiable on a racist basis.

Examples of this kind do more than illustrate the function of experience in revealing contradictions internal to the justifications underpinning

---

[61] The court ruling was influenced by a study called the "doll test" that Mamie Clark conducted as part of her master's thesis. She presented African American children from both segregated and integrated schools with two dolls, one with yellow hair and white skin, the other with black hair and brown skin. They were asked which doll they would rather play with, which one was nicer, which one looked bad, etc. The experiment demonstrated a clear preference for the white doll among all of the children, but exposed an especially acute form of self-hatred among children in segregated schools.

objectionable practices. They also serve to underscore Hegel's inability to safeguard modern ethical life from practical contradictions altogether, and so to obviate the need for immanent critique once and for all. Even if civil society were capable of eradicating poverty without overcoming its own distinction from the state, this does not mean that every practice within this institution has thereby proven beyond question. Contradictions may yet be in store, and that in large part because they stem from practices that are still in the process of taking shape.

That said, there seems to be something different about immanent critique in modern ethical life, which could help explain why this configuration of spirit is not just another chapter in the *Phenomenology*. In the *Phenomenology*, the emergence of contradiction was devastating to the configuration in question, signaling its end. But this need not be so in modern ethical life. For this reason, it is perhaps helpful to think of modern forms of social criticism along the lines of Neurath's ship. In McDowell's appropriation, "the key point is that for such reflective criticism, the appropriate image is Neurath's, in which a sailor overhauls his ship while it is afloat."[62] Neurath had employed this image to point out that our epistemic condition is like that of sailors who rebuild their ship while at sea, rather than from the ground up. The ship, in his context, refers to our body of knowledge. But McDowell extends this image to the nature of criticism as such, especially criticism of our ethical standards. What this image suggests is that we criticize and subsequently revise our standards in an immanent manner, from a standpoint on the very ship we are in the process of altering. But it also suggests that reflective criticism is essentially a piecemeal endeavor – plank by plank, so to speak.

It is worth noting that Hegel would not accept this second suggestion. For him, immanent critique does not necessarily issue in gradual change, but is capable of bringing about a wholesale overhaul of a given "scheme of values." In fact, we witness one such overhaul after another in the *Phenomenology*. This seems consistent with his characterization from the "Preface," where he memorably announces that "the life of spirit is not the life that shrinks from death and keeps itself untouched by devastation, but rather the life that endures it and maintains itself in it. It wins its truth only when, in absolute dismemberment, it finds itself" (PG ¶32). If spirit is not to shrink from death, it must be prepared to risk the demise of its ship. What we can learn from beautiful ethical life, for example, is that there are certain contexts in which ethical failures run too deep to make piecemeal revision fruitful. In such contexts, social criticism must be of a *radical* sort, even when it voices its grievances from an embedded perspective.

---

[62] McDowell (1996), 81.

At the same time, I think this image of Neurath's does aptly characterize modern ethical life. One could say that modern social participants have something in common with his sailors because they can criticize specific principles without thereby destabilizing the integrity of their social world. In other words, normative change for them can indeed take place one plank at a time, or one constellation of norms at a time. Their activity of reflective criticism would still count as an exercise of immanent critique so long as it remains oriented toward practical contradictions. But it would not take a radical form, because it could not throw into question the order as a whole. Modern ethical life might become significantly reconfigured. Its institutional structure, let alone its concrete social relations, may change. But, according to Hegel, modern ethical life itself would not thereby perish. Before we dismiss this as another example of Hegel's alleged conservatism, it is important to keep in mind his reasons for holding this position. It is not that the problems of modern ethical life are never going to be so severe as to require significant change. It is rather that modern ethical life has a peculiar structure that makes it less brittle than those of its predecessors. Unlike the Greek valuation of immediacy, modern ethical life is no longer reliant on a single foundational norm, but incorporates and negotiates a variety of conceptions of freedom whose compatibility with each other remains an open question.

3.5 Theory and Criticism

With this picture of immanent critique in place, I would like to conclude by considering one of its implications – its self-sufficiency. In short, if immanent critique is indeed anchored in practical contradictions, from which it gleans both its object and its standard of criticism, then it appears to be thoroughly self-sufficient. Not only does it not need to appeal to norms external to the social world as such, it does not even need to go beyond the specific constellation of norms that has proven contradictory. In the case of poverty, I can constrict my reevaluation to the two principles at work in civil society – the principle of particularity and that of universality – without needing to have access to any more abstract perspective on my social world. This makes the exercise of critique look like a practice similar to many others, namely, a way of coping with problems if and when they disrupt our habitual modes of engagement. But am I right to characterize immanent critique, even according to Hegel's own conception, as self-sufficient in this way? The tradition of critical theory has argued in one form or another that social criticism, in spite of its immanence,[63] needs to be supplemented by a *theory*. And Hegel has on

---

[63] Not all of the representatives of critical theory subscribe to the idea that criticism needs to be immanent in this sense. Habermas could be described as an exception, since his approach is "transcendentalist" in contrast to "contextualist" (Geuss 1981, 64–65).

occasion been cited as an inspiration for such a project.⁶⁴ The idea seems to be that a theory is necessary in order to identify contradictions, but even more importantly, in order to offer a proper diagnosis of what has gone wrong and so to lend the process of social change a productive direction.⁶⁵

My aim in what follows is to present a consistently Hegelian stance on this issue, even though the terms of critical theory admittedly exceed his own vocabulary – especially the notion of *ideology*, which turns out to be pivotal in motivating a project of this kind. What I hope to show is that Hegel should not be read as a proponent of a critical theory in this sense, for he does not hold that our ordinary critical activities require theoretical supplementation. And even though I also do not think that the theory he puts forward, to the extent that it can be called a "theory," is meant to serve a critical function (at least not as this function has been understood by this tradition), here I will lay out only what I take to be some of his reasons for thinking that a critical theory is not needed from an ordinary point of view.

This commitment at the core of critical theory has surfaced in the debate between Michael Walzer and Axel Honneth about the relationship between theory and social criticism, specifically about the value of the former for the latter. The debate was spurred by Walzer's provocative thesis in his paper "Mut, Mitleid, und ein Gutes Auge" that these are the sole essential ingredients of good social criticism. More precisely, he argues that criticism hinges exclusively on the personal virtues of the critic, virtues that allow her to "say the right thing at the right time." His argument proceeds by showing that a good theory is neither necessary nor sufficient for good criticism, given that plenty of reputable social theories have failed to inspire correspondingly convincing criticisms, and that numerous effective critics had no recourse to any theory, or at least not to a theory as good as their criticisms. Walzer argues that social criticism depends rather on traits of character, specifically on "courage,"

---

⁶⁴ See Honneth (2009), 23. Although he is not tracing precisely this idea back to Hegel, Honneth is suggesting that Hegel saw a deficiency in rationality as a social pathology that his *Philosophy of Right* is meant to overcome. I will return to this proposal.

⁶⁵ These might look to be two distinct points. One could accept that immanent critique as a practice suffices for exposing what needs to be revised, while still doubting whether it likewise suffices for guiding subsequent revisions and ensuring that they are conducted in a rational rather than an arbitrary and haphazard manner. It is worth noting that such a distinction is not really one that a Hegelian approach permits, for it threatens to draw too sharp a wedge between the diagnostic and the revisionary aspects of critique. For Hegel, encountering problems is never a discovery only of what *not* to do, of how *not* to live. The very notion of "determinate negation," which designates the transformative moment in the critical process, refers also to the positive content criticism itself introduces. In other words, our failures already point beyond themselves and indicate how to revise our principles in a way that incorporates these lessons. Even though such revisions may be beset by problems of their own, Hegel is nevertheless committed to regarding them as improvements, and to regarding the very movement of immanent critique as an "educative" path.

"compassion," and a "good eye." It is the last that seems to be most ambiguous, but also the most promising.

Although Honneth objects to Walzer's entire approach, claiming that it fails to set the social critic apart from the "normalized intellectual," he singles out the virtue of a "good eye" as an especially problematic trait from the standpoint of criticism. As Honneth reads him, Walzer means by a good eye a sense of realism about what is politically achievable. This quality, Honneth contends, is not fruitful for social criticism, which requires "the hypertrophic, the idiosyncratic view of those who see in the beloved everyday of the institutional order the abyss of failed sociality."[66] As Honneth understands it, a good eye has the effect of restricting us to the possibilities within a given social context, thus preventing us from asking whether these restrictions are good ones to uphold. Having a good eye thus hinders a so-called critic from challenging the political conditions that make certain moves permissible and thus realizable, and others impermissible and thus unrealizable.

Although Walzer is indeed unclear about what a good eye is, he strongly suggests that it refers to a significantly different sense of realism from the one Honneth attributes to him. It is not prudence about what is politically achievable, but rather "an openness to the real world," to use Walzer's own formulation. This quality involves a realistic attitude with respect to what is as a matter of fact the case, to what the social world is like, which allows the critic to say the "right thing" in the first place. In others words, that about which we need to be realistic is not the potential effectiveness of our criticism, whether or not it will fall on deaf ears, but the very object we undertake to criticize. This suggests that it is its cognitive merits that make this quality vital to critique, for those who possess it are better at seeing the social world as it is, because they are better at resisting distortions – especially distortions produced by theoretical commitments. For Walzer, its value lies less in its ability to inhibit extravagant aspirations, and more in its ability to correct misconceptions by allowing new evidence to falsify a theoretically motivated hypothesis. In short, a good eye directs our view to those features of our social world that genuinely call for criticism.

Although I believe Hegel's view to be sympathetic to some aspects of Walzer's proposal, specifically to his thesis that a critical theory is neither necessary nor sufficient for social criticism, it is difficult to imagine that Hegel would ever have drawn Walzer's conclusion that it is certain *personal* qualities that are needed in its place. Having a good eye might be, from Hegel's point of view, enough for discerning what deserves to be criticized, but this is so only because the relevant problems are in plain sight. In other words, practical

---

[66] Honneth (2009), 188.

contradictions do not need to be first unearthed by any critic, whether one equipped with a good theory or with virtuous traits of character. It follows from the Hegelian account that having a good eye cannot be a remarkable quality that only exceptional individuals possess, but at most a matter of turning one's attention to those norms whose failures have found practical expression, something that any social participant is in principle in a position to do. Many may lack the willingness to confront contradictions, but the same critical insight remains available to each. In order to see why Hegel would nonetheless share Walzer's assessment of the value of theory, we need to take a closer look at the motivations for a critical theory and the considerations in its favor.

Here it is instructive to examine two programmatic texts in the tradition, Max Horkheimer's "Traditional and Critical Theory" and Raymond Geuss's *The Idea of a Critical Theory*, both of which outline the program of a critical theory and make a case for its indispensability.[67] Horkheimer's text is programmatic in a more straightforward sense. Written in 1937, it advocates a "critical" theory by showing its merits over a theory in the "traditional" sense. According to Horkheimer, a traditional theory has exclusively explanatory aims. It tries to account for social facts by generating empirically verifiable hypotheses about why our practices are the way they are. A critical theory, in contrast, has emancipatory aims. Horkheimer seems to understand this as a twofold effort: to make recommendations for social change and to incite the very changes it recommends. So it is both normative and practical in a way in which a traditional theory is not.

One point of similarity between the two is that a critical theory cannot be completely independent of the facts, since it can also only be empirically confirmed or disconfirmed. In other words, its recommendations must prove themselves an improvement on the practices to which it objects. But a critical theory cannot be confined to the facts either, since the evidence relevant to its assessment is not already available. This evidence presupposes a restructuring of society. As Horkheimer puts it, "[In] regard to the essential change at which the critical theory aims, there can be no corresponding concrete perception of it until it actually comes about. If the proof of the pudding is in the eating, the eating here is still in the future."[68] What this suggests is that a critical theory cannot remain purely critical, but must incorporate a utopian element. It is always committed to some vision of a better society.

But even if its normative, practical, and utopian dimensions make a critical theory particularly well suited to emancipation, why would one think that it

---

[67] Geuss perhaps less enthusiastically, though he does conclude that "the construction of an empirically informed critical theory of society might be a legitimate and rational human aspiration" (Geuss 1981, 95).

[68] Horkheimer (1975), 220–221.

is indispensable to it? Although Horkheimer does not make this question his focus, he does hint at an answer. As he points out, the critical theorist's assessment can fail to align with that of the very people he is hoping to emancipate, noting that "[if] such a conflict were not possible, there would be no need of a theory; those who need it would come upon it without help."[69] Without saying it explicitly, Horkheimer seems to be alluding to the familiar Marxist problem that those who are most in need of liberation do not know it, because the world they inhabit has been mystified by ideology. This suggests that it is the presence and persistence of ideology that makes our ordinary critical practices inadequate. In the absence of ideology, a critical theory might still be helpful, but it would not be vital.

Let us consider the simple (and influential) idea of ideology as "false consciousness," the thought that when we are in the grip of an ideology, we cannot help but misunderstand our social reality. Here one is immediately brought to ask what is meant by "false" and by "consciousness." An obvious candidate for consciousness would be a set of beliefs, perhaps beliefs about society. These beliefs would then be false in the same way any belief is, namely, by failing to correspond to the facts. But this not a very plausible conception of ideology, because many beliefs we would be inclined to call "ideological" are not strictly speaking incorrect. For example, the statement "I am proud to be an American" does not involve a factual error, for presumably the person asserting it is both an American and proud of it. Moreover, ideologies do not seem to be limited to descriptions of a world, which they can capture either correctly or incorrectly. Ideologies can also produce the very reality to which they purport to correspond, for they can function as self-fulfilling prophesies. Here I have in mind Mary Wollstonecraft's admission that her female contemporaries are indeed feeble-minded, as men believe them to be, but that because they have been made so by the ideologically informed education they have received.[70]

There is, however, another way to think of ideology as false consciousness. Consciousness can also be conceived along the lines of a "configuration" in Hegel's sense, which we know to refer to a framework that encompasses our norms, principles, and standards, so our evaluative structure within which we form those beliefs in the first place, but also within which we form the social reality to which those beliefs either do or do not correspond. Since a configuration is a view of the world, it must still be possible for it to be truthful or distorting. But given that it consists of an evaluative structure, and one that shapes

---

[69] Horkheimer 1975, 221.

[70] It may sound as if Wollstonecraft is condescending to women when she writes: "My own sex, I hope, will excuse me, if I treat them like rational creatures, instead of flattering their *fascinating* graces, and viewing them as if they were in a state of perpetual childhood, unable to stand alone" (1996, 8).

both belief and reality, it is more challenging to spell out what would make it false. Perhaps the best way to think about the falseness of ideological forms of consciousness would be in terms of the justification and legitimization they lend to aspects of our social world that are actually unjustified and illegitimate. What ideology misrepresents are not primarily the facts of social life, but the validity of a given social reality. It lends the appearance of goodness to that which actually is not good. So what makes the assertion "I am proud to be an American" ideological is its function of vindicating, say, xenophobia at home or militarism abroad. And what makes the assertion "women are silly" ideological is its vindication (among other things) of a limiting program of female education.

One specific conception of "ideology" stresses this functional feature, at times even denying that ideologies involve either falsehood or consciousness at all.[71] According to this conception, ideologies are not defined in terms of a distorting view of the world, but in terms of the very real function they serve in keeping a certain set of social relations intact. What is essential about ideologies is, then, their capacity to stabilize or fortify a given social order, in particular given relations of production. Terry Eagleton, for example, illustrates this point with respect to racial segregation when he concedes that "the ideology, so to speak, is in the bench, not in my head."[72] In other words, segregation is an ideology that is manifest in certain objects like water fountains, schools, and benches, and not first and foremost in the minds of the segregationists.

These two conceptions of ideology – ideology as false consciousness and ideology as materially effective – are usually distinguished from each other and sometimes even cast as mutually exclusive alternatives. But the foregoing characterization indicates that they might be codependent, two sides of the same coin. False consciousness can never be reduced to getting something wrong, even if it is the legitimacy of a given social relations. What make such distortions objectionable are their social consequences, their function of keeping certain practices in place. So a false consciousness would not yet be a case of ideology independently of its material effectiveness. At the same time, it looks like ideologies can be materially effective only because they are also forms of false consciousness. At least a significant part of what it takes to keep unjustifiable practices intact is to make them look good in the eyes of those responsible for perpetuating them. If they did not have the appearance of legitimacy, they would not be able to endure. So ideology's very real function of

---

[71] For a discussion of the disassociation between ideology and false consciousness, see Eagleton (1991), 10–11.

[72] "It is no good my reminding myself that I am opposed to racism as I sit down on a park bench marked 'Whites Only'; by the acting of sitting on it, I have supported and perpetuated racism" (Eagleton 1991, 40).

stabilizing social relations is achievable only through distortion, misrepresentation, falsehood.

In his aforementioned admission, Horkheimer is giving voice to an enduring strand in this tradition, namely, to the conviction that a critical theory ought to be conducted as *Ideologiekritik*. But it is Raymond Geuss's text that explores this connection between theory and ideology in far greater detail. His is not strictly speaking a programmatic text, for it is not meant to promote a critical theory. But it is nonetheless relevant for our purposes, for it reconstructs this program in a novel and perspicuous way. Geuss argues that critical theory can claim to have emancipatory effects not because it moves people to enact its recommendations for social change, but because it initiates a process of reflection that loosens the clutches of ideological illusion. Geuss characterizes its reflective task in genealogical terms. A critical theory is a critique of ideology when it traces our view of the world to the social conditions under which it was formed, showing that *this* view is essentially tied to *these* conditions. Not only does such a process reveal that ideology serves to legitimate, and in this way fortify, the conditions it questions, "Ideologiekritik [also] shows the agents that this world-picture is *false* consciousness by showing them that they could have acquired it *only* under conditions of coercion."[73] In other words, what we discover is that we would not have the worldview we have if we did not inhabit objectionable institutions, the very same institutions our worldview serves to sustain. In this way, a critique of ideology contributes to a critique of the social reality that ideology simultaneously conceals and protects.

In fact, Honneth takes up a similar line of thought in his response to Walzer. He points out that the resistance to theory that has become popular in recent years – and here he seems to have Walzer's own resistance in mind – is "deeply shaken, however, as soon as a causal connection is produced between the existence of social injustice and the absence of any public reaction."[74] Establishing this causal connection seems to bear some resemblance to the genealogical reflection of tracing our legitimizing attitudes back to their basis in exploitative material conditions. But Honneth prefers to speak in terms, not of ideology, but of pathologies of reason, suggesting that the absence of public reaction to "those states of affairs that would otherwise provide particularly urgent grounds for public criticism"[75] partly constitutes the *pathological* character of a social order. To put this slightly differently, it is this widespread acceptance of what should be an object of criticism that makes a given social order especially objectionable, and that gives us ground for calling it pathological.

---

[73] Geuss (1981), 62.
[74] Honneth (2009), 29.
[75] Ibid., 30.

The fact of acceptance also shows that we cannot simply rely on our ordinary modes of social criticism, but need a theory that first exposes the causal connection between injustice and complacency.

One familiar question such an approach to critical theory raises concerns the standpoint of theory. A critical theory seems to be committed to practicing immanent critique, and so to acknowledging its entanglement with its object of criticism. But how can it then claim to be free from the ideology that it attributes to its object? This is one of the so-called paradoxes of *Ideologiekritik*. Once you open the door to ideology, it immediately makes every critical standard look suspect, any to which we might otherwise have unsuspectingly appealed. It is precisely in virtue of their comprehensive character that ideologies are so successful in both distorting and stabilizing. This is a realization aptly captured by the main male character of Wim Wender's film *Alice in the Cities*: "What's so inhuman about television is not that it chops everything up and interrupts it with ads, although that is already bad enough. Far worse is that everything on the air becomes an ad itself, an ad for the existing conditions." If there is no perspective outside of ideology – because everything serves as an ad for existing conditions – then how is a critical theory even possible?[76]

Another question, which is more relevant for our purposes, is how this picture of ideology bears on our ordinary critical practices, practices rarely informed by a theoretical understanding of the genesis of our worldview. Presumably the standards we invoke when we practice immanent critique within a given social order are themselves implicated in the worldview that, from the perspective of critical theory, looks suspect. This gives us one definite reason to think that partial forms of criticisms are bound to be misguided. These forms do not exercise a sufficiently vigilant "hermeneutics of suspicion" so long as they confine themselves to practical contradictions if and when they arise.

One can certainly argue that there are similarities between Hegel's immanent critique and *Ideologiekritik*, even that the latter is indebted to the former.[77] But I think that there is one major point of divergence between the two: Hegel does not have a conception of ideology, nor does he have room for one. There

---

[76] One might think that this problem rests on a false dichotomy between the internal and the external point of view, a dichotomy that the Hegelian notion of immanent critique helps to expose as false. Adorno expresses this clearly when he says that "the alternatives – either calling culture as a whole into question from outside under the general notion of ideology, or confronting it with the norms which it itself has crystallized – cannot be accepted by critical theory. To insist on the choice between immanence and transcendence is to revert to the traditional logic criticized in Hegel's polemic against Kant" (Adorno 2003). Thanks to Karen Ng for drawing my attention to this passage.

[77] See Jaeggi (2009), where she argues that *Ideologiekritik* ought to be modeled on immanent critique because it likewise exposes contradictions between a given ideal and its practical enactment. As she puts it, "the critique of ideology, strictly speaking, does not directly criticize an ideology, but rather a practice that is maintained via this ideology or constituted by it" (69).

are no "socially necessary illusions" in his picture – at least none that has a chance of enduring success. This statement calls for some explanation, since it certainly looks as if Hegel believes us to suffer from various forms of illusion. First of all, he is interested in contradictory configurations of consciousness, those that include inverted relations between self-conception and reality. And relations of inversion seem to be constitutive of ideology, which Marx compared to a "camera obscura" for precisely this reason.[78] But, for Hegel, there is no special difficulty in discovering inversions, or in discovering that they are inversions. In other words, it is not as if the worldview in question holds us captive and prevents us from seeing the way our norms are practically betrayed. A configuration for Hegel, even when it lapses into its opposite, does not share the obstructive side of ideologies. Thus the contradictions that interest Hegel are not to be confused with ideological illusions, even if they involve, at least initially, a misunderstanding.[79]

Second, and more relevant, in the *Philosophy of Right*, Hegel characterizes his contemporaries as subject to a confusion, and he claims that it is his task to overcome it. Honneth cites this aspect of Hegel's project as a forerunner to the notion of social pathology. In Hegel's work, so Honneth argues, the relevant pathology stems from a "loss of meaning" we experience when we do not manage subjectively to appropriate objective institutions, so when we fail to grasp them as rational. This does indeed seem to be Hegel's concern. And the

---

Because of this comparative task of measuring an ideology against the practice to which it gives rise, Jaeggi goes on to agree with Walzer's critics that "to undertake such a critique, one must have not only 'courage, compassion, and a good eye' ... but a good theory as well" (69). I should add that I do not find such a defense of theory persuasive. If our objects of criticism are genuine *contradictions*, all we need to know in order to identify them as such is the relevant ideal and its practical enactment, two pieces of knowledge that any social participant should be in a position to glean. The problem with ideologies seems to be that they are not simply in a contradictory relation with the world, but that they produce a world in their own image, so that comparing them with the world would not suffice to undermine them. Jaeggi's account, in contrast, seems to suggest that ideologies are themselves self-undermining because they generate unsustainable contradictions, in which case we would not need a theoretically informed *Ideologiekritik* in order to bring them down.

[78] "If in all ideology men and their circumstances appear upside-down as in a *camera obscura*, this phenomenon arises just as much from their historical life-process as the inversion of objects on the retina does from their physical life-process" (Marx, *The Marx-Engels Reader*, 154).

[79] There is one passage in which Hegel appears to be thinking about a configuration of consciousness, namely Stoicism, as a worldview that could have emerged only under oppressive social conditions. He writes, "as a universal form of world-spirit, [Stoicism] could only appear in a time of universal fear and bondage, but also a time of universal culture [*Bildung*] which had elevated itself to thinking" (PG, ¶199). Hegel is hereby granting that it might be possible to reflect genealogically about this configuration in the way Geuss outlines, by demonstrating that it is essentially tied to conditions of "universal fear and bondage." But this not yet sufficient for calling Stoicism an ideology, because Hegel gives no indication that it serves to sustain or fortify those conditions in a way that obstructs social change. I am grateful to Daniel James for pointing me in the direction of this passage.

explanation he offers for this loss of meaning is that we have been misled by abstract conceptions of freedom that look to be in tension with our practical lives. These conceptions could be characterized as forms of false consciousness to the extent that they distort the social reality we are in the process of living. But I think it would be incorrect to call them ideologies, as Honneth does,[80] for they lack the functional dimension of false consciousness. These are not *socially necessary* illusions. Ideologies, in contrast, are marked by the service they lend to keeping unjustifiable institutions intact, primarily by making them look legitimate. But the distortions due to excessive abstraction that Hegel hopes to dispel play no such role. In fact, their effect seems to be the inverse: to make good institutions look illegitimate by creating the appearance that they are failing to measure up. Despite all the damage these distortions may wreak on our capacity to find meaning in our lives, they do not serve so sinister an end as masking the unjust. Thus it is not difficult to see that Hegel's approach to social criticism is going to differ significantly from that of his successors, precisely because he lacks the resources for thinking ideology in a way that would be needed in order to motivate such a program.

In his discussion of public opinion in the *Philosophy of Right*, Hegel even explicitly denies the possibility of ideology:

A leading spirit has raised the question for public debate, *whether it is permissible to deceive a people*. One has to answer that it is impossible that a people could be deceived about its substantial basis, about the *essence* and determinate character of its spirit, but that the people can deceive *itself* about the way it knows them [*die Weise, wie es diesen weiss*] and about the way it judges its actions and events. (PR §317R)

In entertaining the question whether it is permissible to deceive a people, Hegel considers whether it is even possible. And although he suggests that various forms of confusion are certainly possible (and that a people can become the source of its own confusion), he denies that "a people could be deceived about its substantial basis, about the essence and determinate character of its spirit." This seems to be a clear statement against the possibility of ideology as a form of false consciousness, at least one that can successfully obscure the essential nature of social life from those who are participating in it, where essence would include both its inner rationality as well as its inner contradictions.

This may look like a limitation of Hegel's account and a reason to prefer the Marxist alternative, but it is not obviously a shortcoming on Hegel's part. In order to evaluate the virtues of his conception of immanent critique against those of his successors, we have to take stock of Hegel's distinct brand of

---

[80] "Hegel saw the outbreak of dominant systems of thought and ideologies in his own society that, by preventing subjects from perceiving an ethical life that was already established, gave rise to widespread symptoms of the loss of meaning" (Honneth 2009, 23).

optimism, his conviction that we will never inhabit an unethical social order without knowing it. It rests on the following line of thought: if our practices are ethically objectionable, they will become practically contradictory, which will in turn make them unsustainable. So ethical failure is identified with contradictoriness, which in turn implies unsustainability. And as we know, unsustainability leads to the recognition that there is something wrong here. Although this might not immediately propel actual social change, it certainly makes the continued perpetuation of those practices increasingly difficult. Note that the way I am characterizing Hegel's optimism does not commit him to a robust conception of ethical progress. It is limited to the unavoidable discovery of ethical failure only, without implying that this discovery is all that it takes to abandon the unethical practice in question, or that the practice that takes its place is necessarily an improvement on the last.

This optimism, even in its limited form, is admittedly not easy to defend, and yet it is integral to the defensibility of his account of immanent critique. Consider, for example, its role in justifying the restriction on critical reflection that I have taken to be central to the immanence of critique. I have insisted throughout that, for Hegel, we need not actively hunt for objects of criticism, that we should in fact refrain from doing so, because these objects will be in plain sight, calling on us to adopt a critical attitude in the first place. Now, it seems like we can accept this restriction only if we also accept Hegel's optimistic conviction that whatever is objectionable on ethical grounds will create problems for its continuation, and so show up as objectionable. In other words, if there is something wrong, this cannot go undetected. What makes this conviction so difficult to defend, however, is that it is based on experience and so inevitably suffers from the problem of induction. As Hume pointed out, the fact that the sun has always risen until now does not guarantee that it will rise tomorrow as well. Similarly, the fact that we have managed to detect our past ethical failures does not mean that we will continue to do so in the future. I think this tentativeness of Hegel's optimistic conclusion cannot be eliminated.

This means that Hegel cannot simply dismiss scenarios like the following: In his novel *Elizabeth Costello*, J. M. Coetzee describes an old woman and renowned writer who is haunted by our treatment of animals and believes herself to be utterly alone in her qualms. When invited to give a lecture at the university where her son happens to teach, she decides to speak on this topic. Given how divisive the issue of animals tends to be, this makes for a very trying visit, full of confrontations with the university faculty as well as with her daughter-in-law – a currently unemployed philosopher of mind – who has little patience for vegetarians. On the way back to the airport, her son finally asks her why she has "become so intense about the animal business." To this question, she gives the following reply:

> It's that I no longer know where I am. I seem to move around perfectly easily among people, to have perfectly normal relations with them. Is it possible, I ask myself, that all of them are participants in a crime of stupefying proportions? Am I fantasizing it all? I must be mad! Yet every day I see the evidence. The very people I suspect produce the evidence, exhibit it, offer it to me. Corpses. Fragments of corpses that they have bought for money.
>
> It is as if I were to visit friends, and to make some polite remark about the lamp in their living room, and they were to say, "Yes, it's nice, isn't it? Polish-Jewish skin it's made of, we find that's best, the skins of young Polish-Jewish virgins." And then I go to the bathroom and the soap wrapper says, "Treblinka – 100% human stearate." Am I dreaming, I say to myself? What kind of house is this?
>
> Yet I'm not dreaming. I look into your eyes, into Norma's, into the children's, and I see only kindness, human kindness. Calm down, I tell myself, you are making a mountain out of a molehill. This is life. Everyone else comes to terms with it, why can't you? *Why can't you?*[81]

Note that Coetzee is not treating Elizabeth's Costello's outlook as authoritative and she is certainly not let off the hook for drawing her comparison. But my interest in this passage has less to do with her specific evaluation of eating meat and its ethical repercussions. Rather, I would like to consider it as a kind of thought experiment that explores the plausibility of such a scenario, one in which we could be partaking in a "crime of stupefying proportions" without any inkling of doing so. Elizabeth Costello believes herself to be watching people perpetuate an atrocity while never detecting a hint of reservation in their demeanor. All she sees in their faces is human kindness. And the practice in question seems to operate smoothly without generating difficulties for us and in this way inviting reservations in the first place. In short, there seem to be no problems, let alone crises, in sight that could compromise its sustainability and throw it into a critical light. Regardless of whether we ultimately regard Elizabeth Costello as some kind moral genius or (as she herself suspects) a bit mad, her description of her own sense of alienation raises the broader question of whether this kind of situation is genuinely conceivable.

The Hegelian answer to such a question would be: yes and no. For Hegel, the objective criterion of ethical failure is practical contradiction in the long run. If a practice is unethical, it will turn out to be contradictory. In this respect, he follows the Kantian proposal expressed in the categorical imperative, that immoral principles contradict themselves. The difference from Kant involves our position with respect to these principles, our capacity to know them to be immoral. Because Hegel is interested in practical contradictions in his idiosyncratic sense, he thinks their emergence awaits the unfolding of experience. This means that we might not be able to figure out that we are committing atrocities

---

[81] Coetzee (2003), 114–115.

until contradictions have indeed emerged, contradictions that make the practice in question unsustainable and in this way draw our attention to the fact that there is something worth criticizing here.[82]

So the situation in which Elizabeth Costello believes herself to be is indeed conceivable. It is possible that in the moment in which she finds herself, experience has not yet shown the practice of eating meat to be objectionable, because the contradiction within it has not yet emerged. It is also possible that her feeling of unease indicates that she is the first to have gleaned an inkling of the contradiction, even if not yet in contradictory form. But it seems to me that she is a bit mad, and that not because of her qualms about eating meat, but because she believes herself to be alone in them. Although she claims that she detects no signs of unease among her family members, it would be difficult to argue that eating meat is a practice that runs as seamlessly as she fears. The meat industry is not exactly the paragon of a sustainable institution. In fact, there is growing evidence that its sustainability is being increasingly compromised and that those who are responsible for perpetuating it are well aware of this.

Consider the measures that factory farms have taken in order to conceal what is taking place inside them. These measures are clearly responses to the damaging effects that exposure has had on the operations of factory farming. In his study of the practice of *Eating Animals*, for example, Jonathan Safran Foer describes his experience of accompanying an activist to a factory farm at night to save a handful of injured animals. Although there is no one anywhere in sight, they find the doors to the factory locked. Foer writes, "In the three years I will spend immersed in animal agriculture, nothing will unsettle me more than the locked doors. Nothing will better capture the whole sad business of factory farming. And nothing will more strongly convince me to write this book."[83] But locked doors are no longer proving sufficient to keep the interiors of these farms hidden. For example, Iowa recently passed "Ag Gag Laws" that make it a crime for investigative journalists to take entry-level jobs in factory farms, in this way attempting more severe precautions against exposure.

The appeal of Hegel's picture derives not only from an optimism corroborated by historical experience. It also derives from its ability to capture most convincingly how we do engage in social criticism. It is important to keep in mind that Hegel is seeking to do justice to the nature of normative change. His

---

[82] To reiterate, this does not mean that one has to recognize that a practice contradicts itself in order to object to it, or that one can only object to it for contradicting itself. But it does mean that social criticism is legitimate only when it is oriented toward practical contradictions, even when the critics themselves do not recognize them as contradictions. The recognition of a practical contradiction as a practical contradiction might sometimes be available to us only in hindsight.

[83] Foer (2009), 87.

philosophical account of it aspires to lay bare how it is actually done, rather than prescribe how it ought to be done. Thus its aspirations are fundamentally different from those of a critical theory whose aim is to become a player in the process of transformation it is simultaneously investigating. For Hegel, these two perspectives, the critical and the philosophical, should never become conflated. This means that the very question with which we began – when social criticism is warranted – is not exactly Hegel's own. His interest in practical contradictions is not meant to be instructive to social agents, outlining the circumstances under which they are permitted to practice critical reflection. It is rather meant to capture how criticism occurs when it does, what occasions criticism, and what form criticism takes when it challenges the fundamental norms of a society, and not merely its success in practicing what it preaches.

4 Science

Hegel opens his *Philosophy of Right* with a highly polemical dismissal of standard approaches to the question of right, approaches he classifies under "theories" of right. He claims that these are far too "instructive," and thus unphilosophical in spirit. Its proponents behave as if the ethical world is eagerly awaiting their "new and unheard-of truths," and in doing so, they make two mistakes: 1. they lack a method, specifically, the method of a "science" (what Hegel calls *Wissenschaft*)[1]; and 2. they fail to see that everyone already knows the truth about right. Hegel's preferred alternative, illustrated in the *Philosophy of Right*, is supposed to overcome these shortcomings: it is supposed to employ a scientific method *and* at the same time stay true to what is already widely known and publicly acknowledged. In fact, Hegel suggests that these two tasks belong together, that only science can adequately capture the familiar truth about right. As he rhetorically asks, "How in this crowding of truths is that which is neither old nor new, but rather that which is enduring, supposed to rise above these formless considerations that keep going back and forth – how is it supposed to distinguish and preserve itself except through science?" (PR, 13).

It is not, however, clear why we would need to employ any kind of method at all, if the truth about right is already widely known and publicly acknowledged. This is a question that Hegel's project raises, given his insistence that his method is not meant to contribute new content, to inform us of how we should be conducting ourselves, at least not in an instructive, prescriptive, or corrective way. First, the picture of ethical life that emerges shows it to be thoroughly self-sufficient and in no need of philosophical guidance. According to Hegel, we are perfectly capable of determining what to do in specific situations, as well as which basic principles to continue upholding, all without his

---

[1] Although I intend to follow the standard translation of *Wissenschaft* as "science," I want to caution against assuming that this term is synonymous to the one in English. *Wissenschaft* in German is a much broader concept that encompasses all forms of theoretical knowledge, including the human and social "sciences." And in Hegel's vocabulary in particular, *Wissenschaft* has a distinctive meaning that is idiosyncratic to his project. Much of this chapter will be devoted to explaining what exactly Hegel means by "science."

help. When in doubt, we can do this by reflecting in the very ways we ordinarily do. Second, Hegel is particularly worried that theoretically informed and oriented reflection leads astray. This should already be a familiar thought. As we are about to see in even greater detail, he thinks that such reflection tends to generate abstractions that distort our evaluative resources as participants in ethical life.

Third, he claims that he is not engaging in this kind of abstract reflection, because his philosophical aim is limited to making the implicit explicit. Hegel's conception of philosophy can be characterized as a form of quietism because it seeks to leave the world as it is, so to speak. As we have seen, this conception of philosophy cannot be incompatible with engaging in critical reflection, though Hegel is clear that he does not think the two should be conflated. There is room in the world – left as it is by philosophy – to reflect critically. Philosophy simply has a very different task. In a different context (in the additions to his *Encyclopedia Logic*), he claims, "The business of philosophy consists only in bringing explicitly to consciousness that which people held to be valid about thought from time immemorial. Philosophy thereby establishes nothing new; what we have here brought forth through our reflection is already the immediate presupposition [*Vorurteil*] of each and every one" (Enz. I §22A).

So why would such a project – the project of making the implicit explicit – be worth undertaking? What contribution is it meant to make to ethical life?[2] These questions will be my focus and I will address them by examining Hegel's scientific method more broadly, as well as in its application to the context of right. As Hegel frequently stresses, science has a formal task, namely, that of exposing systematic relations within its object of investigation. Science and systematization go hand in hand. But a science can only justifiably introduce a form if this form is suitable to its object – if its object implicitly possesses this form. In Hegel's words, "That with which

---

[2] Fulda (2004) has raised a version of this question: "For what are the rights and obligations of philosophy, as a social and political 'institution,' with respect to making its presence felt within the realm of actuality?" (21) Fulda notes that this question has rarely been raised because it is assumed that philosophy has exclusively theoretical ends and so need not have practical value. He disputes this by pointing out that the rights and obligations that distinguish philosophical reflection must be conceived in *ethical* terms. But even though Fulda concedes that this cannot amount to asking how philosophy can serve the ends of the state (since both philosophy and ethical life must possess autonomous ends that are pursued for their own sake), he ultimately ties this ethical task of philosophical reflection too closely to ethical upbringing, making it an integral part of an individual's *Bildungsprozess*. This strikes me as implausible, because it grants philosophy a task that is *too* integral from the practical point of view. Moreover, Fulda ultimately ties philosophy too closely to social criticism, claiming that it cultivates a will that is oriented toward *reforming* the actual world. Although more needs to be said about the proper relation between philosophy and social criticism, we have already seen that it cannot be so straightforward – that philosophers themselves make the best social critics.

this treatise is concerned is *science*, and in science the content is essentially inseparable from the *form*" (PR, 13). To put this a bit differently, Hegel is saying that it would not make sense to give a systematic account of something unless it constitutes a system independently of this account. The relevant object has to already be systematic in order to lend itself to scientific investigation. Hegel applies this program to the specific object of ethical life. As he puts it, ethical life is rational in its content – what it still needs is a rational form, one that fits this content:

> The truth about right, ethical life, and the state is anyway as old as it is exhibited and known in public laws and in public morality and religion. What more does this truth require, to the extent that thinking spirit is not content to possess it in this proximate manner, but to be grasped as well, so that the content which is already rational in itself may also gain a rational form and thereby appear justified to free thinking? (PR, 13–14)

And Hegel is clear that it is science that is to offer this form. So what is this form, how is it introduced, and why does ethical life need it?

Hegel's conception of a science is a familiar topic in the secondary literature. In the context of the *Philosophy of Right*, his scientific aims tend to be brought into connection with his *Encyclopedia of the Philosophical Sciences* and his *Science of Logic*, both of which are mentioned in its Preface.[3] As Hegel explicitly states, his *Philosophy of Right* forms a part of a larger whole that is articulated in his *Encyclopedia*. It is primarily an elaboration of a chapter within the latter work under the title of "Objective Spirit." Hegel moreover indicates that his scientific method, so pivotal to the *Philosophy of Right*, is the same one he explained and defended in his *Science of Logic*. These remarks suggest that Hegel's *Philosophy of Right* cannot be adequately treated as a self-standing work. It is helping itself to numerous concepts, both methodological and substantive, that are vindicated in other parts of his larger system. In particular, this is taken to mean that Hegel's metaphysics is a presupposition of his practical philosophy and so cannot be legitimately set aside.[4]

I will address some of these concerns by considering the extent to which Hegel can be said to be offering a self-standing science of right. Given the way in which I have interpreted the roles of habit, culture, and critique, it

---

[3] Some examples are Thompson (2001) and Lumsden (2001).
[4] This is at issue in the debate between Neuhouser, Dudley, and Kolb in *Owl of Minerva* Fall/Winter 2004 concerning Neuhouser's book *Hegel's Social Philosophy*. I will return to this debate in Section 4.3 of this chapter. Note that there are also more recent studies of Hegel's practical philosophy that treat it as a relatively autonomous work. Moyar (2011): "There would indeed be a severe problem if one could only access Hegel's ethical theory once one had mastered all of his *Science of Logic*. But there worries about the *Logic* are overblown" (7). Moyar's point is admittedly more subtle, namely, that we don't need to understand the *Science of Logic* in all its details in order to grasp Hegel's practical philosophy, but that parts of it are not as foreign to his practical philosophy as they may seem.

should not be surprising that I think Hegel's method in the *Philosophy of Right* is similarly in need of textual supplementation. This means that I will not argue in favor of the self-standingess of Hegel's practical philosophy. At the same time, I think that Hegel's polemic in his Preface to the *Philosophy of Right* is highly relevant to understanding the philosophical aim of this particular work. His diagnosis of his contemporaries, paradigmatically of the representatives of theories of right, shows a different way of motivating his project and procedure. This motivation might also lie at the heart of Hegel's system as a whole,[5] but I will only undertake to show its relevance to understanding his aims in the *Philosophy of Right*.

It is perhaps natural to assume that, when Hegel is speaking about an already rational content, he is referring to the *objective* institutions – institutions we find alienating, confining, unfavorable to freedom. According to this interpretation, Hegel's task is to show us that we are wrong to think that these institutions prevent us from living freely within their confines. Such an interpretation is supported by one of Hegel's concluding remarks in the Preface that he is aiming at *reconciliation* with "actuality" and that this reconciliation is meant to come through rational insight, which philosophy provides. In short, it may look as if Hegel thinks we need to be reconciled with something that is external to us and in which we do not see our aspirations reflected. Michael Hardimon expresses this idea succinctly when he states that "the central aim of Hegel's social philosophy was to reconcile his contemporaries to the modern social world."[6]

In this chapter, I will suggest that there is another way of understanding Hegel's aim, and one that is in a better position to explain his subsequent procedure. According to my interpretation, Hegel does not think we need to be reconciled to a world of objective institutions that are external to us, but that are nonetheless rational. He thinks we are reconciled to this world already. I find my evidence in the following passage:

Now it does indeed happen that those, who live within this actuality of the state and who find their willing and knowing satisfied within it – and among those are many, many more than believe or know it, for in *fact* it is *everyone* – that at least those, who have a *conscious* satisfaction within the state, laugh at such attempts and assurances and take them to be an empty game, now more amusing, now more serious, now pleasing, now dangerous. (PR, 16)

---

[5] In his *Differenzschrift*, Hegel writes, "When the power of unification disappears from the life of people and the contrasts have lost their living relation and interaction and achieve their independence, then the need for philosophy arises" (DS, 22). What Hegel is referring to are processes of abstraction that have severed principles from one another and in this way lent them the appearance of being independent of one another. The term he uses for it in this context is *Reflexion*.

[6] Hardimon (1994), 1.

In this passage, Hegel targets those who are persuaded by theories of right and claims that their demands will seem ridiculous to those who find their willing and knowing satisfied within the social world. But his aside reveals that he believes this to be (more or less) *everyone*. In other words, Hegel thinks that all social participants find satisfaction in actuality, even those who are oblivious of this fact. Hegel's efforts are directed specifically at this latter group of disbelievers, for it is they who are most receptive to theories of right.

This passage has implications for how to understand this already rational content, to which Hegel wants to give a rational form. Hegel cannot be referring to something external to us, namely, the objective institutions of the actual state – at least not *exclusively*. Instead, he must also be referring to something that is internalized. If Hegel thinks that everyone as a matter of fact finds their willing and knowing satisfied in actuality, then there is a level at which we are reconciled to the social world we inhabit, though it is a level that may not be transparent to us. Although this might sound like a far-fetched hypothesis on Hegel's part, it is supported by the relationship between habit and insight. Recall that, for Hegel, our convictions are best demonstrated in our habitual comportment. And as long as we unwaveringly participate in the institutions of ethical life, we demonstrate that we are convinced of their goodness. But the insight revealed in our participation might not be readily available to us. According to Hegel, many of us are divided against ourselves, for there is a gap between the content of actuality, which we have indeed successfully internalized, and our reflective attitude toward actuality. When he claims that he seeks reconciliation, he means that he wants to reconcile these two sides of *ourselves*: our reflective and our unreflective sides.

For this reason, I will argue that Hegel's project is better understood as one of recollection directed at reminding us that we know the truth about right.[7] The concept of recollection appears at various junctures of Hegel's work, but perhaps most explicitly in his *Phenomenology of Spirit*, where he identifies it as the aim of philosophical reflection. As Hegel there argues, what we have been doing throughout the *Phenomenology* is recollecting a process we have undergone. This process is not reducible to a historical one, though it is historical as well. Although recollection so conceived is not an obvious candidate for making sense of a science of right, I want to show that there are more structural similarities than meet the eye.[8] There are also reasons to think that Hegel

---

[7] This has some resemblance to Wittgenstein's meta-philosophical views: "The work of the philosopher is a collection of reminders for a particular purpose" ["Die Arbeit des Philosophen ist ein Zusammentragen von Erinnerungen zu einem bestimmten Zweck"] (*Philosophical Investigations* §127).

[8] Sedgwick (2012) presents the method of the *Philosophy of Right* along the lines of a *Bildungsprozess*, a process of the will *becoming* ethical. Although Hegel is going to be interested in the development of the concept of a free will, I would dispute that this should be

connects philosophy and recollection even in his *Encyclopedia*, though he does not use the same term for it. In one of his Prefaces to this work as a whole, Hegel writes, "For the fact [that philosophy must account for] is knowledge that has already taken shape [*die schon zubereitete Erkenntnis*], and comprehension would be a reflection [*Nachdenken*] in the sense of a retracing in thought [*nachfolgendes Denkens*]" (Enz. I, 17).

There is one final question that no account of Hegel's method can circumvent: does it have normative implications? His contrast between comprehending ethical life and issuing precepts for its improvement leaves ambiguous whether comprehension is meant to include evaluation, even if it excludes prescription. This question is especially pressing in light of Hegel's notorious *Doppelsatz* ("what is rational is actual, and what is actual is rational") from the Preface to the *Philosophy of Right*, which articulates a central tenet of his philosophical program. Most readings of this dictum have focused on the term "actuality," debating what the proper object of Hegel's evaluation is supposed to be. One reading has instead challenged the assumption shared by both sides of this debate, namely, that "rationality" is a normative concept for Hegel.[9] In other words, this reading disputes that Hegel is involved in any kind of evaluation at all, independently of the question of what his object is. I will follow this latter approach by offering a methodological reading of the *Doppelsatz*, while maintaining that Hegel does mean "rationality" in a normative sense. This means that, if Hegel succeeds in his mission, he will have demonstrated that the ethical world is on the whole worth upholding – that it is *good*. This is compatible with the project of recollection, because Hegel thinks that we are already convinced in the goodness of the ethical world, and he is simply showing us that we are *and* that we are right to be. So he is not merely making explicit the fact that we are convinced, but wants to redeem those convictions and show them to be justified.

This chapter will tackle these tasks in the following order: I will begin by examining Hegel's criticisms of what he dismissively calls "theories" of right. He launches these criticisms not only in the Preface to his *Philosophy of Right*, but also in his earlier essay "The Scientific Ways of Treating Natural Law, Its Place in Moral Philosophy, and Its Relation to the Positive Sciences of Law" (also known as the "Natural Law" essay). Although this earlier essay does not include a fully developed positive view in the way the *Philosophy of Right* does, it presents an extensive critical engagement with the two paradigmatic theories of right: formalism and empiricism. Next I will consider what object

---

understood as the ethical education of the will. My emphasis on recollection thus represents an alternative reading.

[9] Stern (2006).

Hegel wants to investigate and whether his investigation is meant to be evaluative. This will involve offering a reading of the *Doppelsatz*, committing to a gloss on the twin terms "actuality" and "rationality," and showing how it fits with the methodological place that Hegel assigns this dictum. I will then turn to Hegel's conception of the "rational form" he is hoping to impose on this rational content, specifically to his conception of a systematic science. In this context, I will address the questions of whether Hegel can isolate his science of ethical life from his broader system and of the extent to which his science of ethical life helps itself to concepts that are elsewhere defended. As I will stress, Hegel's science of ethical life clearly belongs to his *Encyclopedia*, for crucial concepts like freedom, the will, and even actuality presuppose familiarity with it. This means that the *Philosophy of Right* cannot constitute a science in the strict sense, because it itself is not presupposition-less. At the same time, I will emphasize the extent to which Hegel's scientific account of right is nevertheless motivated by a diagnosis of the contemporary frame of mind, one he takes to be corrupted by abstraction. I will defend my core claim at the end, namely, that Hegel's own way of imposing a rational form on a rational content is best understood as an activity of recollection aimed at overcoming the forgetfulness brought about through abstraction.

4.1 Theories of Right

I mentioned in the previous chapter that Hegel can be said to share Bernard Williams's discomfort with reflection of a certain sort. Williams's target is a reflection that is aimed at revising our standards (or concepts), whether it admits it or not, which inevitably leads to the impoverishment of our normative resources. This side effect is, for Williams, part and parcel of reflection's theoretical aspirations. Reflection aspires to construct a theory by arriving at a single standard to be used in deliberation and evaluation. This standard is supposed to ground all other standards, or, more ambitiously, take their place. According to Williams, such an aspiration to theory can also be described as a drive toward systematicity. Although Hegel will want to keep theory and system strictly apart, he is also worried about this kind of reflection, reflection directed at the discovery of a single standard by which all others are to be assessed. And like Williams, Hegel thinks that this is the trap of theorizing.

The term "theory" appears infrequently in Hegel's texts, but whenever it does, it provides an instructive contrast with his own conception of philosophy. In his Preface to the *Philosophy of Right*, for example, Hegel criticizes philosophies of ethical life for attempting to become theories:

it might seem to be the essential task of a philosophy of the state to invent and offer *yet* another *theory* [*Theorie*], and specifically one that is new and particular. When we examine this idea and the drive suitable to it, we might well conclude that there had never been a state or constitution in the world, nor is there one now, but that we must *now* (and this "now" continues indefinitely) to start right from the beginning, and that the ethical world had been waiting only for such *present* constructions, discoveries, and proofs (PR, 15).

This passage is admittedly highly polemical and can give the impression that Hegel takes issue with *theorists*, rather than with theories. He accuses them of expecting that the world is on the edge of its seat to hear their new and unheard-of truths, so of harboring vanity and conceit. But Hegel is also articulating what he takes to be the essential feature of theorizing, independently of the self-conception of those who engage in it. The newness they promise to deliver is for Hegel internal to the theoretical approach.

According to Hegel, this theoretical approach is based on the assumption that "the business of the philosophical writer consists in discovering *truths*, speaking *truths*, and spreading *truths* and correct concepts" (my emphasis) [Wahrheiten *zu endecken,* Wahrheiten *zu sagen,* Wahrheiten *und richtige Begriffe zu verbreiten*] (PR, 13). The relevant "truths" are the correct norms or principles to be followed in social life over and above those we already do follow. While Hegel is not denying that there is a truth of the matter about which norms or principles ought to be followed in social life, he thinks that this truth "is anyway as old as it is exposed and known in public laws and in public morality and religion" (PR, 13–14). This is what theoretical approaches fail to appreciate. The aspiration to discover, speak, and spread truths can, but need not, be an explicitly political aim, namely, to delineate the rightful *laws* in contrast to the positive ones we happen to have.[10] He also mentions the identification of correct concepts as another of its supposed benefits. In any case, the problematic features that theories share is that they pit themselves against the ethical world as it is. In his words, "theories oppose themselves to that which exists and want to appear right and necessary in and for themselves" (PR, 15). This fundamental opposition between correct norm and social reality seems to

---

[10] I want to take this opportunity to address a separate matter: Hegel's insistence that the law must be universally known, which he takes to mean that it must be written down and available to all. He writes, "To hang the laws so high that no citizen can read them, as Dionysius the Tyrant did – or to bury them in an extensive apparatus of learned books, collections of verdicts based on divergent judgments and opinions, habits, or in a foreign language – is one and the same injustice [*Unrecht*]" (PR §215R). This is clearly another intervention into the "customary rights" debate, but here Hegel's point is a narrower one. He wants to say that it is unjust to punish someone for violating a law that was not formally available to her because it either too obscure (hung high, esoteric, or in a foreign language) or too implicit (to be read off of verdicts or habits). But I take this to concern *laws* only, so those rules that are administered by the state and that demarcate what counts as a crime. It does not extend to all those informal rules by which we ordinarily orient our daily activities. I am grateful to Tatjana Sheplyakova for helpful conversations about this issue.

a part of any theory, even when it admits to finding its standard *in* this reality – namely, when it isolates one standard or concept that we already employ as social participants. In other words, Hegel thinks that theories depend on a contrast between what we as a matter of fact do and what we should be doing, even when they take their standards from our practices themselves. And they introduce this contrast because they always privilege some standards over others. This, according to Hegel, makes all theories abstract, particular, and arbitrary.

When Hegel claims that theories are *abstract*, he means that the standards they espouse are derived through a process of abstraction – namely, of isolating one standard among the sea of standards to which we help ourselves when we act and deliberate, and of stripping it of any particular content so that it can be broadly employed. When he claims that theories are *particular*, he means that, even though the standard is stripped of all particular content, it is still just one standard (or a limited set of standards), isolated from all others. When Hegel claims that theories are *arbitrary*, he means that the standard is no longer embedded within the broader context that could grant them legitimacy. For Hegel, standards are never *self*-justifying, but are always justified in terms of other standards – hence his thesis that only a comprehensive system can be genuinely presupposition-less. This means that an isolated standard cannot avoid becoming a groundless presupposition, no matter how indubitable it may look. It is always possible to ask: why this standard and not some other? And the theory itself lacks the resources to answer this question.

Since this is a fairly general and fairly damning set of accusations, we can surely imagine theories that find ways around such shortcomings.[11] But my interest in Hegel's criticism is not to defend it against possible counterexamples, but to get an idea of what Hegel has in mind in order to get a better sense of his preferred alternative. To this end, let us take a look at the paradigmatic theories that are meant to exemplify these traits. Here Hegel's methodological reflections in his "Natural Law" essay are especially illuminating because this text is largely devoted to a criticism of two dominant theories – what Hegel calls "formalism" and "empiricism." At this early stage in

---

[11] It is possible that Axel Honneth's "normative reconstruction" of ethical life can meet these challenges, especially since Honneth's critical theory is significantly inspired by Hegel's *Philosophy of Right*. Honneth (2014) defined this procedure in the following way: "I will only use the term 'normative reconstruction' to refer to this notoriously misunderstood strategy. This procedure implements the normative aims of a theory of justice through social analysis, taking immanently justified values as a criterion for processing and sorting out the empirical material. ... In the context of this procedure, 'reconstruction' thus means that out of the entirety of social routines and institutions, we will only pick out those that are indispensable for social reproduction" (6). Although this procedure is deliberately selective (singling out only a subset of socially effective standards in order to generate a critical "theory"), it selects those aspects of social life that are necessary for its reproduction, so for its sustainability. In this way, Honneth's strategy comes close to Hegel's own.

his career, Hegel had not yet developed his positive conception of ethical life, though the beginnings of it emerge in statements like the following: "the ethical life of the individual is one pulse beat of the whole system and is itself the whole system" (NR, 504). In fact, this text is a testament to Hegel's effort to work out his positive conception precisely *via* criticism of the two dominant theories. So he is not developing it top down, from the perspective of a fully worked out science, but bottom up, through a critical engagement with the positions of his contemporaries.

Hegel defines formalism in the following way:

[formalism] asserts its formal principles as *a priori* and absolute, and thus [asserts] that what it cannot master by these is non-absolute and accidental, unless it helps itself by finding in the empirical generally, and from one determination to another, the formal transition of progression from the conditioned to the condition and, since the latter is in turn conditioned, so on *ad infinitum*. (NR, 443)

He seems to have in mind, among others, Fichte's theory in his *Foundations of Natural Right*, in which Fichte pursues the project of deducing, not just the concept of right, but concrete institutional constraints, from the requirements of self-consciousness. In this text, Fichte begins with an a priori principle that is purely formal because it contains no determinate information – the principle of self-positing. As he stresses extensively in his *Wissenschaftslehre*, the activity of self-positing is empty of content because it does not yet refer to any particular individual who thus posits herself. The activity of self-positing is the pure awareness that I am I, without conceiving of myself as anyone in particular. It is more basic than all other self-conceptions. And this is the principle (the I = I) from which Fichte wants to deduce the concept of right.

Though there is scholarly disagreement about the exact nature of his argument,[12] it seems to proceed roughly as follows: I cannot posit myself without "ascribing a free efficacy" to myself, i.e., without viewing myself as an agent capable of bringing about effects. The very idea of effects already makes reference to something that is not I, namely, a world of objects upon which I can exercise my agency, and other agents who impose limits on my agency by requiring their own sphere of free efficacy. Gradually, constraints are introduced as necessary conditions for self-positing, for actually *doing* it. But they are introduced as conditions for the realization of a principle whose legitimacy is not on the line. We get concrete practices back, but only as conditions for individual agency, which is taken to be of unconditional value, in need of no further vindication.

---

[12] For an illuminating discussion of the interpretive alternatives, see Nance (2012).

As we will see, Hegel's own method will on the face of it share features with Fichte's. It will also move from the abstract to the concrete, and will also be guided by considerations of what it takes to realize a given principle. It is in light of Hegel's own affinity with Fichte's method that his criticism of it is so telling. While Fichte is making the effort to redeem those practices and institutions in the actual ethical world by demonstrating that they are conditions for the realization of self-positing, he still holds on to the idea that self-positing is itself a priori. In other words, he takes his first principle to be self-legitimating, its legitimacy in no way contingent on its actualizability. While this does not make Fichte's method inconsistent, it is in fundamental disagreement with Hegel's own methodological commitment articulated in his *Doppelsatz*. As we will see in greater detail, for Hegel, the legitimacy of any principle of right depends on its actualizability. It is a rational principle, so one worth pursuing, only if it can be actualized. And this is an empirical question, one that awaits the unfolding of historical experience. So Hegel is challenging the way in which Fichte views his own starting point, his insistence that it itself is unconditioned, even if the picture of ethical life that is ultimately deduced resembles to some extent Hegel's own.

In the *Philosophy of Right*, Hegel adds a further objection, namely, that Fichte believes that he can deduce far more concreteness than is philosophically appropriate. "Fichte need not have perfected his *passport regulations* to the point of 'constructing,' as the expression ran, the requirement that the passports of suspected persons should carry not only their personal description but also their painted likeness" (PR, 25). Passport regulations, according to Hegel, belong to the domain of "externality," which means that they are conventions that can legitimately take a variety of forms. It makes no sense to attempt a philosophical justification of one form over another, by arguing, for example, that passports should *necessarily* include an image of their bearer, as Fichte does.

Despite his sympathy for Fichte's method, Hegel concludes that it is in some respects even worse off than empiricism. Hegel's treatment of empiricism is subtler, because he thinks that there is an important truth to be found in its approach, for empiricism "rightly demands that such a philosophizing should find its orientation in experience" (NR, 451). For Hegel, the characteristic trait of empiricism is that it derives its fundamental principle on the basis of empirical generalizations. He specifies that empiricists usually generalize, not over the qualities of independent agents, but over relations found in experience. Examples that Hegel gives are relations like self-preservation, love and hate, sociability, etc. And the sorts of theories this method tends to generate are contractual ones, which take these basic relational facts about us as their starting point (usually projected onto a "state of nature") and use them to ground social institutions, notably the state. These generalizations become the principles that require no further vindication, but in turn vindicate other regions of the ethical world. This already indicates a structural similarity between empiricism and formalism. Both are in the business of grounding or justifying on the basis of a fundamental principle. The difference lies primarily in how they conceive of their respective principle. Whereas formalism claims that its is a priori, empiricism admits to gleaning its from experience.

Although Hegel is no enthusiast of empiricism, he is not fully dismissive of it either. Hegel suggests that at least empiricism in its "pure" form is not as misguided as formalism, for it resists abstracting any single principle from the ethical world and in this way making it "prescriptive for the whole."[13] Empiricism is pure when "everything has equal rights with everything else and no determination, which is as real as any other, has precedence" (NR, 444). To put this a bit differently, pure empiricism does not privilege any relation (like love, sociality, self-preservation) above all others and demand that all other relations meet its measure. But this also means that "pure empiricism" is not a theory at all, since it is not involved in singling out standards of evaluation. In fact, Hegel thinks that pure empiricism has few representatives. Even what counts as the ordinary, commonsensical attitude is contaminated by reflection, and so by concepts that are bound to be one-sided. Thus empiricism is right to complain about abstractions – the problem is that it is itself affected by them.[14]

Hegel's diagnosis of theories as such emerges increasingly clearly: "This narrowing of concepts, the fixing of determinations, the elevating of one chosen aspect of appearance to universality and granting it dominance over others, has recently called itself no longer just theory, but philosophy" (NR, 451). Aside from thinking that it is philosophy when it is not, the mistake theory makes is that it fixes on specific characteristics and isolates them from the broader context in which they are embedded, taking them to be the self-legitimating standard by which all other relations should be evaluated. This also accounts for theory's prescriptive aims, which Hegel deems so unphilosophical in his *Philosophy of Right*. By fixing and isolating one characteristic (whether self-consciously culled from the ethical world or not), theories in turn demand that every domain of social life measure up to it. In this way, they do not recognize that the legitimacy of this standard depends on its embeddedness in the very

---

[13] Hegel's phrase for this is "*als das Wesentliche zum Gesetz gemacht*" (NL, 440).
[14] "[I]f determinations are fixed and their law is consistently applied to the sides elevated by empiricism, and if intuition is subordinated to them, and if generally that, which tends to be called theory, is formed, then empiricism has a right to charge these with one-sidedness" (NR, 450). Also, "[e]mpiricism would have the greatest right to assert itself against such theory and philosophy and to regard the mass of principles, purposes, laws, duties, and rights as something that is not absolute ... if it itself were to be and to remain pure." The problem is that, "when empiricism seems to go to battle with theory, it is usually revealed that the one like the other is an intuition already contaminated and superseded by reflection" (NR, 452).

ethical world from which it was abstracted, which in turn implies that it cannot be indiscriminately applied to every domain of this ethical world.

Although Hegel's own positive position emerges out of his dissatisfaction with theories of right, he does not yet have the resources to launch an "immanent critique" of such theories. This is precisely what he undertakes to do in the *Philosophy of Right* – to show that standards of right cannot be detached from one another without losing their legitimacy precisely because they lose their actualizability. What is worth noting at this point is that Hegel is not recommending that we become more self-consciously empirical and so recognize the actual ethical world as the basis of abstraction. The key is not to engage in abstraction at all. Any theorizing, whether empirical or formal, is essentially misguided, because it inevitably obscures the concrete whole.

The "Natural Law" essay is Hegel's early effort to articulate this concrete whole, written at a time when Hegel did not yet have a fully worked-out view of it. There are traces of it present in this text: the state and the necessity of war, civil society as a system of needs. But Hegel's main aim here is to suggest that there is a presupposed background that theories of right in principle cannot capture and that this background requires a different, more comprehensive perspective. He writes, "But the totality of the organic is precisely what cannot be thereby attained, and the remainder of the relation, excluded from the determinate aspect that was selected, falls under the dominion of this aspect which is elevated to be the essence and purpose of the relation" (NR, 422).[15] This is merely a negative lesson. Hegel is not yet in a position to delineate this "totality of the organic" precisely because he himself had not yet developed an alternative methodology.

The *Philosophy of Right* shares structural similarities with the "Natural Law" essay because it also begins by critically engaging approaches that Hegel will ultimately dismiss – or, to be more precise, put in their place. Abstract right and morality represent such approaches. But this later text is enriched by a deeper insight into both the problem and the solution that had plagued Hegel in the "Natural Law" essay. First, Hegel recognizes the pervasiveness of abstract reflection and so his target is no longer narrowly theories of right put forward by theorists of right. Second, Hegel launches something along the lines of an "immanent critique" of these approaches, showing how their chosen principles depend on the very background from which they have abstracted. Third, Hegel eventually lays bare this presupposed background in a way that goes beyond a mere sketch of a "totality of the organic" to which he alludes in the "Natural

---

[15] As an example he cites the effort to explain punishment by appealing to only one of the many social uses this practice has, such as moral reform or deterrence, as its justificatory ground, and thus making only one of its aspects "essential" at the expense of the rest.

Law" essay. It is here, in his *Philosophy of Right*, that we see how Hegel thinks a philosophy of right in the proper sense of the term should be conducted.

4.2 The *Doppelsatz*

When Hegel attempts to define philosophy in opposition to theory, he tends to emphasize that philosophy in the proper sense confines itself to grasping, comprehending, or understanding the ethical world:

> So this treatise, to the extent to which it contains a science of the state, is nothing other than the attempt *to comprehend and to present the state as rational*. As a philosophical text, it must be farthest away from attempting to construct a *state, as it ought to be*; the instruction, which it can contain, cannot consist in teaching the state, how it ought to be, but instead how it, as the ethical world, should be understood. (PR, 26)

But it is not obvious what Hegel takes an understanding of the ethical universe to involve. He claims that this is the sort of investigation we direct toward the natural world, because we take for granted that it possesses an "inner rationality" – that there are laws operative within it, laws that operate in concord and that form parts of a self-sustaining whole – and are content to expose this inner rationality. But he thinks that we see the ethical world as "godforsaken," as lacking a comparable structure.[16] What he advises is that we adopt a similar philosophical attitude toward the ethical world as we do toward the natural world.

That said, Hegel explicitly acknowledges the limits of his comparison. When trying to understand the laws of nature, it is only our understanding that is subject to normative constraints, and not the object of our understanding. In other words, while we can either get these laws right or wrong, the laws themselves cannot be right or wrong. As Hegel puts it, "The measure of these laws is outside of us, and our knowing adds nothing to them, does not advance them: only our knowledge of them can advance itself" (PR, 16n). But "the knowledge of right is in one respect the same, in another not" (PR, 16n). We learn ethical laws in the same way we learn the laws of nature, namely, as already there, established, and operative, whether we investigate them or not. But this divide between our knowing and its object is, when dealing with the domain of spirit, not hard-and-fast. Hegel points out that in this process of investigation we likewise discover that these laws are not "absolute," which in this context means that they are not fully independent of our attitudes toward them. Rather, they

---

[16] "About *nature* one admits that philosophy is to know [*erkennen*] it *as it is*. ... The *ethical world* in contrast, the state, reason as it actualizes itself in the element of self-consciousness, is not to enjoy the good fortune of being reason, which has in fact in this element acquired power and force, and which asserts itself in it and inhabits it [*inwohne*]" (PR, 15).

are laws (*Rechtsgesetze*) that have been "posited" (*Gesetztes*) by us in the first place.[17] Once we make this discovery, we come to think that we possess the measure that these laws must meet, rather than taking the laws as setting the measure that our understanding of them must meet. For Hegel, this is where the problems begin. This discovery introduces not only the possibility of a conflict between given principles and the dictates issued by our "inner voice," but it also allows us to grow arrogant and misled into taking our inner voice as the sole judge.

Hegel's big challenge, he tells us, is to demonstrate that the ethical world has an inner rationality as well – even if its laws are mandated by human beings in a way in which natural laws are not. It is a challenge seemingly articulated in his *Doppelsatz*: what is rational, is actual; and what is actual, is rational. This dictum has been the crux of considerable controversy in interpretations of Hegel's *Philosophy of Right*. Its most uncharitable readers have taken it to mean that the status quo (whatever laws, institutions, and practices are currently in place) must be good and so worthy of perpetuation. This "conservative" reading has come under sustained attack for misrepresenting Hegel's term "actuality." When Hegel claims that the actual is rational, he is not referring to whatever happens to exist, but only to those things that have succeeded in *actualizing* their appropriate concept.[18] Corrupt states, paradigmatically, would not be "actual" in Hegel's technical sense, even if many happen to be around, because they do not meet the standard for statehood. They are not successful actualizations of the relevant concept "state." What these "progressive" interventions have shown is that Hegel restricts his object of evaluation to something much narrower than had previously been assumed. What he seeks to vindicate are only those things that are *and* are as they ought to be.

But given Hegel's emphasis on comprehension, it is not even indisputable that he is engaging in any kind of vindication at all, which the "progressive" reading still maintains. This emphasis on comprehension has led some to conclude that Hegel's practical philosophy is in fact not meant to be practical at all, because it is not meant to direct action.[19] In a similar spirit, Robert Stern[20] has

---

[17] "But the difference is that with the laws of right [*Rechtsgesetzen*] the spirit of reflection [*Betrachtung*] arises and already the diversity of laws draws attention to the fact that they are not absolute. The laws of right are posited [*Gesetztes*], coming from human beings" (PR, 16n).

[18] Although this term "actuality" stems from his *Logic*, Hegel offers a gloss on it in the context of the *Philosophy of Right* as well. As he writes in his remark to the very first paragraph of the Introduction, "[a]ll else, apart from this actuality established through the working of the concept itself, is ephemeral existence, external contingency, opinion, unsubstantial appearance, falsity, illusion, and so forth" (PR §1R). Here he is likewise drawing this fundamental contrast between actuality and mere existence or appearance.

[19] Walsh (1969) argues that Hegel's project is better described as a "sociology of ethics" (11, 55).

[20] Stern (2006).

argued that we need to ask what Hegel means in calling something "rational" and whether it expresses affirmation on his part. Stern disputes that we should understand "rational" as a normative concept that implies justifiability. Rather, Stern argues in favor of what he calls a normatively neutral reading of the *Doppelsatz* that takes "rational" to be a methodological concept. All that Hegel means in calling the actual "rational" is that it is intelligible to reason and so suitable to be investigated by its means. It does not mean that the actual is therefore in any way *good*.

This normatively neutral reading has the advantage of being able to make sense of the *Doppelsatz*'s place in the *Philosophy of Right*. Stern is right that it would be very surprising indeed if Hegel inserted such a strong thesis in the opening pages of his work, which he usually reserves for methodological remarks.[21] Hegel after all identifies the *Doppelsatz* as the starting point of philosophical inquiry, not its conclusion. To this extent I completely agree with Stern that the *Doppelsatz* merits a methodological reading, that it has to be brought into connection with Hegel's philosophical method. But I disagree that this makes it normatively neutral. It is clear throughout the Preface that showing something to be rational, according to Hegel, means showing it to be good and so worthy of perpetuation. Consider, for example, the following two familiar passages:

The truth about right, ethical life, and the state is anyway as old as it is exhibited and known in public laws and in public morality and religion. What more does this truth require, to the extent that thinking spirit is not content to possess it in this proximate manner, but to be grasped as well, so that the content which is already rational in itself may also gain a rational form and thereby appear justified to free thinking. (PR, 13–14)

It is a great obstinacy, an obstinacy that does honor to the human being, to refuse to acknowledge in attitude anything that has not been justified by thought – and this obstinacy is the characteristic of the modern age. (PR, 27)

These passage make it is difficult to deny that Hegel thinks that a rational comprehension is meant to redeem that which it comprehends, showing it to be "justified to free thinking" or "justified by thought." These references to justification strongly suggest that Hegel thinks his account will have the implication that the ethical world merits our continued allegiance.

At the same time, I think Stern is right to deny that this is a *substantive* claim, for the *Doppelsatz* itself is meant to be trivially true: if something is

---

[21] As Stern (2006) puts it, "[Hegel] therefore does not use the introductory sections of his writings to attempt any real exposition of the book as a whole, or any defense of its conclusions; instead, he mainly uses them to deal with meta-level issues, concerning the nature of the work as a work of *philosophy*, and therefore with the question of what philosophy (in Hegel's view) is" (239).

actual (and so is as it ought to be), then it is rational (as it ought to be).[22] In the *Doppelsatz* itself Hegel is not yet advancing a hypothesis about the ethical world. What he will need to show is that the *Doppelsatz* applies to the ethical world in the first place, namely, that this world is actual because it is rational *and* that it is rational because it is actual (I will return to this second claim in a moment). Its actuality cannot be taken for granted, as if our task were merely to show that it is rational too. So Hegel is delineating his program without committing himself to a conclusion in advance, since both rationality and actuality are simultaneously at stake.

But what the *Doppelsatz* makes clear is that this is going to be an evaluative project, for to show that the ethical world is actual would also be to show that we should continue to inhabit and sustain it. So a rational comprehension of the ethical world expresses an affirmative assessment of it. In fact, the very distinction between understanding and evaluation is unsustainable in Hegel's picture. If he succeeds in exposing the "inner rationality" of the ethical world, he has simultaneously vindicated it, because he has shown that it is a successful realization of its concept. I think this way of reading the *Doppelsatz* makes much better sense of Hegel's method in the *Philosophy of Right* and sheds light on the structure of this work, since Hegel does not start with the ethical world at all. It is not his direct object, neither of neutral comprehension nor of normative evaluation. Although the ethical world is what we inhabit and so constitutes our *presupposition*, Hegel thinks that it first needs to be won back through a process by which it is shown to be actual/rational.

What I mean in saying that the *Doppelsatz* merits a methodological reading goes beyond its delineation of the task to be accomplished. The *Doppelsatz* is also meant to impose a significant constraint on Hegel's own procedure because it makes clear that the relevant standards of evaluation are themselves dependent on the actual. When Hegel writes that "what is rational is actual," he is pointing out that the rational can only prove itself rational (a *true* norm) by becoming actualized. In other words, there would be no basis for deeming a standard of assessment rational until it has passed the test of actualization, until it has shown that it can be consistently enacted. This constraint already suggests the crucial difference between Hegel's method and that which he calls

---

[22] It has become popular to privilege Hegel's alternative formulation of the *Doppelsatz* from his *Lectures on the Philosophy of Right*: "what is actual becomes rational and the rational becomes actual." See, for example, Wood 1990, 13. The emphasis on "becoming" has made this formulation more attractive because it seems to suggest an ongoing process whereby actuality is increasing in rationality and rationality in actuality. As appealing as it sounds, this formulation is unfortunately incoherent. According to Hegel's own definition of these terms, actuality cannot *become* rational – if it were not rational, it would not count as actual, and vice versa. Saying that the actual becomes rational and that the rational becomes actual is failing to recognize the triviality of the *Doppelsatz*, that the *Doppelsatz* is meant to be true by definition.

"formalism." Although a formalistic method could also proceed via considerations of actualizability (Fichte, after all, did ask himself what it would take to realize the principle of self-positing), it does not recognize that the legitimacy of its starting point hinges on it. It has often been pointed out that Hegel's method is not "transcendental," because he does not simply take something for granted, treat it as given, and then proceed to its necessary conditions. The starting point, that which is taken for granted or treated as given, is itself up for review in the process of investigating what it takes to realize it. What this will mean in the context of the *Philosophy of Right* is that the initial conception of right, which Hegel calls "abstract right," will become challenged as a self-sufficient principle from which others can be deduced. It will be compelled to cede its foundational standing in light of the necessary conditions for its actualizability.

But Hegel also denies that these conditions could be delineated in an a priori manner, which is corroborated by his objections to formalism in the "Natural Law" essay. We are in a position to know (and so to give a philosophical account of) the conditions for actualizability *because* the relevant principle has been actualized. This is the more substantive and contentious implication of the *Doppelsatz* for his method. Our knowledge of the rational, and so of the standards by which to evaluative the ethical world, is confined to the actual, and so to those standards that have been met in practice. If our knowledge were not so confined, then Hegel would have no reason *not* to engage in the kind of theorizing that he associates with formalism, which is aimed at constructing an ideal society, independently of whether a society exists that lives up to this ideal. Although Hegel is not recommending an empirical methodology either, he is particularly critical of an a priori approach, since such an approach fails to appreciate the dependence of method on its object of investigation. What this means for Hegel is that the ethical world is undergoing an objective process of actualization, a process of becoming actual/rational, and that our philosophical comprehension of the actuality/rationality of the ethical world corresponds to that stage in this developmental process.[23] Only the future unfolding of this process will show whether the current standards to which we as social participants are committed have attained their completed form, or whether they too are in need of further revision. But philosophical comprehension can do nothing to short-circuit this process and gain access to their completed form prior to their realization.[24]

---

[23] Saying that the world is in the process of becoming actual/rational is not the same as saying that the actual is becoming rational and the rational is becoming actual. So it is possible to capture the developmental unfolding of this process without prying actuality and rationality apart.

[24] Hegel addresses this issue of completeness in the *Philosophy of Right*: "Completeness means the completed collection of all individual items that belong to a sphere, and in this sense no science or body of knowledge can ever be complete. When people say that philosophy or any

So what does it mean to provide a methodological reading of the *Doppelsatz* without giving up on its normative implications? It means stressing that (1) the *Doppelsatz* as such is true by definition, but that (2) it is meant to guide inquiry by clarifying what is required for philosophical comprehension, namely, to demonstrate that your chosen object is actual/rational, and that (3) this places significant constraints on which criteria you can use in your evaluation, namely, only those that are actual. One might be tempted to characterize this as a commitment to immanent critique, but this would be misleading. Although Hegel's method is explicitly immanent (focused on the "inner rationality" of the ethical world), it is not a critical one, at least not critical of the ethical world or of its standards of assessment. Critique for Hegel is a forward-looking endeavor, oriented to overcoming contradictions in the ethical world as they arise. Philosophy, in contrast, has a backward-looking orientation. My reading of the *Doppelsatz* allows us to appreciate why this must be so. In Hegel's words, "As the *thought* of the world, [philosophy] appears only at a time when actuality has gone through its formative process and attained its completed state" (PR, 23). In short, philosophical comprehension has no recourse to rational criteria of evaluation independently of their actuality, an actuality that must first take shape. What this means is that a philosophy of right is in a position to know what is right only once right has become real, once the ethical world has attained its completed form.

4.3 Science and Right

In the very first paragraph of the Introduction, Hegel thus tells us that "the subject-matter of *the philosophical science of right* is the *Idea of right* – the concept of right and its actualization" (PR §1). This idea of the "idea of right" is clearly another expression of what is already contained in the *Doppelsatz* about the mutual implication of actuality and rationality, for it represents the unity of the concept and its realization. In this context, he stresses even more explicitly the earlier point I was making, namely, that the concept of right counts as a rational standard (or in his language, a true concept, rather than a mere abstraction) only *if it exists*. As he puts it, "The concept and its existence [*Existenz*] are two aspects [of the same thing] separate and united, like soul and body" (PR §1A). The next step, then, is to clarify what Hegel means by a philosophical "science" of right and why he thinks this science avoids the shortcomings of a formalist deduction (and empiricist induction).

> other science is incomplete, it sounds as if one has to wait until it has been supplemented, since the best could still be missing" (§216Z). He goes on to draw a comparison with a tree that continues to grow new branches without ceasing to be the same tree, concluding that "it would be foolish to refuse to plant a tree just because it might grow new branches."

Hegel's conception of a philosophical science is inseparable from his conception of a system. As he puts in the *Encyclopedia*, "A philosophizing *without system* cannot be anything scientific; moreover, such philosophizing expresses for itself more of a subjective mentality, its content is accordingly contingent. A content has its justification only as a moment of the whole, outside of which it is an ungrounded presupposition or subjective certainty" (Enz. I §14R). Hegel applies "system" to philosophical comprehension as well as to the object that is being comprehended, and in both cases it has to do with a distinct "form." One can provide a systematic account of something only if it indeed comprises a system. This underscores Hegel's claim that philosophy does not introduce anything new. Even its distinctive form has to be already present in its object of investigation.

Hegel sometimes frames this as a matter of the suitability of form to content. In his Preface, he states that "in science, the content is essentially inseparable from the *form*" (PR, 13). Philosophical comprehension makes this form explicit, but it is a form that the content must indeed possess. So what we find is not formless content. If we did, this content would not lend itself to philosophical comprehension. I previously suggested that we should think about content in the *Philosophy of Right* as referring not just to the objective institutions ethical agents inhabit, but also to the internalized principles gleaned from those institutions and to the conviction in their goodness. This is going to be a further sense in which philosophy introduces nothing new, for the systematic account of ethical life it offers is reflected in our unreflective attitudes. We treat ethical life as a system, even if we are not self-conscious that we do. At the same time, the proper object of philosophy is what Hegel calls "Objective Spirit," so ethical life in its external, institutional manifestation. Hegel wants to demonstrate, through a systematic investigation, that it constitutes the "idea of right," because it is both the concept of right and its actualization. What this means is that Hegel's *Philosophy of Right* is only successful if it can draw the ontological conclusion that the ethical world *is* indeed a system and so possesses the relevant form that allows us to give a systematic account of it. This is another way of saying that ethical life is actual/rational.

The relevant form that characterizes a system is necessity. In other words, what makes something a system is that its components stand in necessary relations with one another. When considered from the point of view of the object, necessity among components means that each part makes an indispensable, even if partial contribution to sustaining the object, allowing it to become or to continue being the sort of thing that it is. Ethical life, for example, constitutes a system only if its parts – its institutions and their underlying principles – prove crucial to its capacity for development and survival. So necessity here is understood in terms of what is needed in order to maintain living unity.[25]

---

[25] The first sentence of the "Ethical Life" chapter states: "Ethical life is the *idea of freedom* as the living good, which has its knowledge and volition in self-consciousness, and its actuality

But how does this conception of systematicity apply to a body of knowledge? What makes a philosophical account, say, of ethical life, systematic in any analogous sense? For Hegel, the answer to this question has two aspects. A systematic account of ethical life involves showing that ethical life is itself systematic, so that its parts are crucial to its development and survival. This concerns not just the structure of its object, since its mode of presentation must itself be systematic. Though it is more difficult to elucidate what this can mean, especially on the model of organic unity, Hegel suggests that such unity can also be found in a body of knowledge, not only in the object of knowledge. In other words, Hegel thinks of knowing, specifically philosophical knowing, as the unfolding of a living process.[26] So the key to understanding Hegel's systematic procedure is to see how Hegel seeks to show the development from one formulation of right to another as necessary – necessary because it constitutes a crucial step in achieving an enduring *account* of ethical life. In fact, we can only demonstrate that the object of our investigation exhibits a systematic structure, if we confine ourselves to this systematic mode of presentation. Only by adhering to this necessary development can we show our eventual object – ethical life – to be rational/actual.

Hegel states that the mode of presentation is based on the "logical spirit" (PR, 13) and calls it a "deduction" (PR §2), thus giving us reasons to think that the development from one formulation to another will involve conceptual necessity. But these statements are liable to be misunderstood. Hegel is *not* contrasting the conceptual with the empirical in the way many scholars assume.[27] So the procedure cannot be a deduction of the kind that Fichte's *Foundations of Natural Right* promises to deliver. If it were, we would be neglecting the role of actuality to which Hegel's method is tethered. The *Doppelsatz* makes clear what the constraint on conceptual comprehension is going to be, and this constraint is actuality. If the concept weren't real, if it didn't exist, we would be in no position to track its necessary development. So it is simply misguided to think of Hegel's deduction as excluding

---

through self-conscious action" (PR §142). Here Hegel suggests that ethical life is best regarded as a living being whose unity is maintained by the self-conscious actions of its members.

[26] See PG ¶2.

[27] See, for example, Dudley (2004): "Each time we discover the incorporation of an empirical contingency we would be faced with a choice: either we could conclude that the dialectical transition in question simply could not function without such an incorporation ... or we could attempt to improve upon Hegel's imperfect execution of his own philosophical project by reconstructing the transition as a strictly logical move" (9). The problem with this dilemma is that it assumes empirical considerations to be the introduction of *contingency* into Hegel's method and thus an imperfect execution of this method. But Hegel clearly thinks that experience properly understood, namely, familiarity with what is actual, can yield insight into what is rational and thus necessary.

empirical considerations.[28] In fact, it must include such considerations. Otherwise, it would not be dealing with the "idea of right." It includes such considerations as soon as it investigates what it takes for a certain formulation of right to be actualized. We move from one formulation of right to another by asking ourselves how right so conceived can become something objectively manifest. And, again, we can answer this question only to the extent to which right is something objectively manifest. So we are relying on our familiarity with actual right in our deduction of its conceptually necessary development.

In the previously cited passage about system, Hegel stresses another aspect of systematicity, which presents a challenge to his method. If you are committed to a systematic science, you are not only committed to the idea that each piece of knowledge stands in a necessary relation to every other and is thus justified as making an indispensable contribution to a living, enduring whole. You are also committed to the idea that no piece of knowledge can be adequately justified outside of those relations. In this way, Hegel denies that there is a single principle that can anchor a system, a first principle from which all others can be derived.[29] This presents Hegel with the difficulty of *how to begin* a systematic investigation, if a system can rely on no independent ground and all content has its justification only within its confines. In his reflections on philosophical method, Hegel was especially concerned to develop a presupposition-less science (the only genuine science, he thinks), to commence without helping himself to a contentious or arbitrary premise. He made this requirement explicit in his *Encyclopedia*: "But the difficulty of making a beginning arises simultaneously with the fact that a beginning as something immediate makes its presupposition, or is moreover itself such a presupposition" (Enz. I §1). This difficulty is also already present in the *Phenomenology of Spirit*, where Hegel criticizes his competitors for resting their views on presuppositions that

---

[28] Fred Neuhouser calls the transitions in the Philosophy of Right "quasi-logical" "because [they] involve more than purely conceptual analysis" (2000, 31n). This statement has caused a stir in the scholarship. Dudley (2004) contests that, "[i]f the Philosophy of Right were only quasi-logical, however, then it could not determine the structure of truly rational institutions, but instead could offer at most an account of quasi-rational institutions, or those institutions that might make sense under certain empirical conditions or certain pragmatic considerations" (8).

[29] Thus I am denying what Thompson (2001) identifies as one of Hegel's "strictures of systematicity." While I agree that, for Hegel, "the parts must stand in inferential relations to each other [and] must be individually necessary and mutually implicatory," I disagree that Hegel thinks giving an account of something requires tracing it back to a ground "by joining its various elements under the governance of an indubitable and noninferential axiom, an absolute first principle (ein erster Grundsatz)" (114). In his response, Lumsden (2001) already objected to problematic theses in Thompson's paper, for example, his claim that a systematic progression of reasoning is for Hegel an analytic one. But he does not challenge Thompson's claim that systematicity requires foundation in a first principle.

are assumed as "natural."[30] Hegel finds this deeply dogmatic, no matter how natural your starting point may seem. At the same time, we must begin, and begin somewhere. So how can we avoid falling into the same trap? A structural problem emerges in all domains for Hegel: if you want to give a philosophical account of something, an account that is essentially evaluative, you need some standard of evaluation by which you are going to assess your object. So how are you to choose your standard?[31]

Hegel suggests a solution to this problem through the image of a "circle," arguing that the test of success of a philosophical method lies in its ability to return to the point from which it departed:

> Philosophy forms a circle: it has an initial or immediate starting point, since it must begin somewhere, which it is not demonstrated and is not a result. But the starting point of philosophy is immediately relative, for it must appear at another end-point as a result. It is a sequence, which is not suspended in air, it does not begin immediately, but is rounded off within itself. (PR §2A)

Circularity is meant to enable presupposition-less-ness because it shows how a system can vindicate its own starting point, even if this starting point cannot be vindicated in advance. In the context of his *Philosophy of Right*, we begin with a standard of right without yet being in a position to see whether this standard of right is the right one. A commitment to circularity means that this starting point will have to be shown to be legitimate at the end of the procedure. It will have to be shown to be at least one legitimate formulation of right (even if it does not turn out to be right in its entirety).

This solution is inspired by Fichte, who also grappled with the difficulty of justifying his own starting point. In the Introduction to his *Wissenschaftslehre*,[32]

---

[30] For example, Hegel opens his Introduction to the *Phenomenology* with the following ironical remark: "It is a natural assumption that in philosophy, before we start to deal with its proper subject-matter, viz. the actual cognition of what truly is, one must first of all come to an understanding about cognition, which is regarded either as the instrument to get hold of the Absolute, or as the medium through which one discovers it" (PR ¶73). It is clear, I think, that Hegel is mocking the pretension that this is a "natural assumption," so one that we are justified in making without having to give a justification of it in turn.

[31] Some scholars deny that Hegel can help himself to any standard of evaluation precisely because this would be inconsistent with his method. Dudley (2004): "In fact, Hegel consistently argues that philosophy cannot, and that he does not, employ *any* criterion or norm by which to judge the rationality of social institutions (or of anything else), for the perfectly good reason that such a procedure would immediately beg the question: what justifies the application of *this* criterion or norm?" This is partly correct, because Hegel does not introduce his *own* criterion of evaluation, but takes it over from object. This, however, does not mean that we do not need a criterion of evaluation at all. It only means that this criterion must be one that is already being employed within our object (ethical life), and that the legitimacy of this criterion is at stake and can be vindicated only by the completion of the method, so that it cannot remain a mere presupposition.

[32] "If the presupposition idealism makes is correct, and if it has inferred correctly in the course of its derivations, then, as its final result (i.e. as the sum total of all of the conditions of that with

Fichte speaks in a way that suggests circularity as a test by which to assess the legitimacy of his starting point. Two philosophical options are available to us, according to Fichte. We can begin either with the subject or with the object. The challenge, then, is to see which of these two alternatives succeeds in explaining the other. His hypothesis is that starting with the subject will allow us to explain objectivity, whereas starting with the object will fail to explain subjectivity. Of course, this is only a hypothesis. He has to succeed in demonstrating that this is so in order to show his own starting point to have been the right one.

Hegel is committing himself to something similar, but he draws a different set of implications than Fichte. Hegel's method succeeds not only when it legitimates the starting point, but when it also challenges the starting point *as* a starting point, as something self-evident and self-sufficient (in Hegel's terminology, "immediate"). As Hegel puts it, philosophy must begin with something seemingly immediate, but this immediate starting point is "immediately relative," shown to be of only relative legitimacy. What this means for the science of right is that the initial formulation of right must be shown to be an inadequate conception, inadequate precisely because it cannot vindicate itself. It will call for different formulations of right in its effort at self-vindication. In this way, we will eventually have the system of right in view. Abstract right is a provisional starting point, one that the procedure itself will vindicate, but only as relative, dependent on other standards of right for its own actualizability.[33]

So Hegel, unlike Fichte, is not attempting to show that our starting point was the right starting point because it has priority over that which it allows us to subsequently derive. Hegel has abandoned in a way that is much more radical than Fichte the aspiration for a first principle that could serve as the foundation for a systematic, philosophical science. So it would not be wholly wrong to say that, for Hegel, it does not really matter *where* we begin. In fact, he sometimes suggests that the same story could have been told the other way around. He makes this explicit in the *Encyclopedia* when he comments on his chosen order of presentation, starting with "Subjective Spirit" and proceeding to "Objective Spirit": "One could say just as well that spirit is at first objective and should become subjective, as that spirit is at first subjective and has to make itself objective. Consequently the difference of subjective and objective spirit is not

---

which it began), it must arrive at the system of all necessary representations. In other words, its result must be equivalent to experience as a whole – though this equation is not established within philosophy itself, but only subsequently" (Fichte 1994, 31).

[33] A passage from the *Phenomenology* about science and system makes this point especially clear: "The genuinely *positive* exposition of the beginning is thus also, conversely, just as much a negative attitude towards it, viz. towards its initially one-sided form and being *immediate* or *purpose*" (PG ¶24).

to be seen as rigid" (Enz. III §387A). The two condition each other, make each other's actualization possible, because they are mere parts of a whole.

Although the beginning is no more than provisional, justifiable only within the system, it must nonetheless represent a version of the relevant "idea" in Hegel's technical sense. So there is an important constraint on what can serve as an adequate starting point. For Hegel, we cannot simply invoke any principle whatsoever, since it is possible that this principle will lead us astray. The criterion we invoke must be an expression of the true concept, by which he means that it must be a formulation of a genuine standard, even if initially an inadequate formulation. So the question then arises how we can be sure that our starting point is adequate in this more minimal sense and will turn out to have a place in the systematic context to be drawn from it. This presents Hegel with perhaps the toughest challenge to his method: how are we to know that our starting point does represent a version of the relevant "idea"? Even if our knowledge is initially incomplete, we still have to have some reason for thinking that thinking through this starting point will put us on the right track, because this starting point is found within the circle. In the *Philosophy of Right*, the standard in question is what Hegel calls the "free will," whose first formulation is "abstract right." So the question can then be put in the following way: how do we know that freedom has a legitimate place in a system of right and that beginning with freedom will give us access to this system?

Hegel himself offers an answer to this question, but it seems to require that we accept his philosophical project as a whole. As he puts it, the presupposition of the *Philosophy of Right* is that, if we understand what a will truly is, we will see that it is in its very nature to be free, that a "will without freedom is an empty word, just as freedom is only actual as will, as subject" (PR §4A). As Hegel admits, this is a strong assumption to make at the very outset of the *Philosophy of Right*, one whose truth is anything but self-evident. Yet Hegel rejects various standard strategies for justifying this presupposition. He denies that we can derive freedom by analyzing what is contained in the concept of the will, or by looking to our psychological attitudes like regret and guilt, or by simply asserting it as a "fact" of consciousness, all of which he seems to associate with Kant. Rather, Hegel claims, "*that* the will is free, and *what* will and freedom are – this deduction can only take place ... in connection with the whole" (PR §4R).

But what he means by the "whole" here is not the *Philosophy of Right* in its entirety. Rather, he is referring to his *Encyclopedia of the Philosophical Sciences* as the articulation of the whole system, of which the investigation of right forms only one part. He states this quite explicitly in one of his lectures: "All philosophical sciences are parts of a large whole. Philosophy has as its object the universal, the absolute. Right is one side of the manifestation of this absolute, of the divine idea" (VPR, 39). In the official text, he explains that we need to examine what precedes the introduction of right into his system – such as his discussion of intelligence and practical spirit in his "Philosophy of Subjective Spirit" – in order to find the justification for beginning with the notion of a free will. Thus it may seem highly un-Hegelian to want to treat the *Philosophy of Right* as comprising an autonomous science that swings free from his broader systematic ambitions. The only way that we can know that the free will is a fruitful starting point for the science of right is because it is the conclusion of a preceding procedure. As he states, "As a part [of philosophy], [the science of right] has a determinate *starting point*, which is the *result* and truth of what *preceded* it. Hence the concept or right, so far as its *coming into being* is concerned, falls outside of the science of right; its deduction is presupposed here and is to be taken as *given*" (PR §2).

One of the main controversies in readings of the *Philosophy of Right* concerns precisely the weight we should accord to Hegel's insistence that this text cannot vindicate its own premises, but presupposed "Subjective Spirit" for its concept of "free will," and even more importantly, the "Logic" for its methodology. Some readers worry that wedding the *Philosophy of Right* too closely to the rest of the *Encyclopedia* could mean throwing out the baby with the bathwater, since his broader systematic aspirations look far more unrealistic and indefensible than his aims in the *Philosophy of Right*.[34] Then there are those who think that any reader of the *Philosophy of Right* must take seriously its systematic place, without which it lacks adequate grounding and looks to rest on arbitrary presuppositions of its own.[35]

It is surely difficult to deny that Hegel wants to situate his science of right within the *Encyclopedia* and make the former in some important respect dependent on the latter. This is consistent with his insistence that any piece of philosophical knowledge, including knowledge about right, is going to be fully justifiable only within the whole. Moreover, there seems to be an especially strong dependence on his "Logic." As Hegel explicitly states in the *Philosophy of Right*, "Wherein consists the scientific approach of philosophy can here be presupposed from the philosophical Logic" (PR §2). Not only does Hegel remind his readers that he is going to be proceeding according to a "logical progression" and in a "logical spirit," he also wants to draw an ontological conclusion about ethical life, that it constitutes the

---

[34] As Neuhouser (2000) puts it, "most contemporary readers will be able to recognize Hegel's view as compelling if they see how it is grounded in a plausible conception of freedom, even though they may lack access to his account of how freedom can be the authoritative value of modernity or to his metaphysical arguments that self-legislating reason (a type of freedom) constitutes all reality – nature, history, and the social world as well" (4–5).

[35] For a reading that situates Hegel's *Philosophy of Right* in his broader system, see Brooks (2007).

idea of right because it is actual/rational, i.e., because it *is as it ought to be*. Many of the concepts that are necessary in order to explain Hegel's method clearly have their origin and elaboration in the "Logic," for example, "idea" and "actuality." So it would be contrary to Hegel's own self-understanding to claim that the science of right could remain scientific without relying on the achievements he takes himself to have made in the "Logic," specifically its case in favor of his scientific method.

But contrary to appearances, it is actually possible to have it both ways, to treat the science of right as an independent science without denying its embeddedness in Hegel's overall system. This possibility becomes available to us once we consider Hegel's image of a "circle of circles." Here is one articulation of it:

Each part of philosophy is a philosophical whole, a circle enclosed within itself, but the philosophical idea is therein in a particular determination or element. The individual circle therefore breaks through, because it is in itself totality, the limitation of its element and grounds a further sphere; the whole therefore presents itself as a circle of circles, of which each is a necessary moment, so that the system of their peculiar elements constitutes the whole idea, which likewise appears in each individual [circle]. (Enz. I, §15)

The system, Hegel tells us, can be conceived of as a circle of circles. Each part of philosophy exhibits a circular structure, a structure through which it can vindicate its own presuppositions, while at the same time breaking through the limits of its unique subject matter and thus initiating the next circle by presenting it with a starting point that must be vindicated next. So even though the circles stand in a circular relation to each other, each still has a unique task of vindicating its own starting point in this "relative" way (by showing it to have relative validity).

This image suggests a slightly different interpretation of circularity from the one we have been exploring. According to this interpretation, circularity is to be found not only in the relationship between different pieces of philosophical knowledge (such as "Logic," "Subjective Spirit," and "Objective Spirit"), but in the relationship between a concept and its realization, so within the relevant "idea" itself. The simplest way to put this is to say that what justifies a given concept is its realization. This means, in turn, that we can know a given concept to be a good one to the extent to which it is indeed realized. Applying this to the *Philosophy of Right* allows us to see that we can know freedom to be a true concept, if it turns out to be something real, i.e., successfully realized in ethical life. More specifically, we can know the standard represented by abstract right to be a legitimate starting point because we can show that it is something real, even though it requires a broader context for its successful realization. This again recalls Hegel's *Doppelsatz*: the rational proves rational (i.e., a good idea) through its actualization, just as the actual proves truly actual by realizing this good idea.

My aim in this section was to offer a general framework for understanding a scientific treatment of right and its relation to the systematic form that philosophy tracks in its object of investigation. As I pointed out, Hegel's method is going to have to show its difference from and superiority over formalist deduction and empiricist induction. We now have some tools for making sense of his alternative. Hegel's scientific method is not a mere deduction because it recognizes its own dependence on actuality, thus preventing it from being pure of empirical considerations. But it is not a mere induction either, for it tracks the necessary development of a concept and so can draw a distinction between what merely exists and what is strictly speaking "actual." So it can work its way forward (from concept to realization) only because it is working its way backward (from realization to concept). This approach allows Hegel to develop a science of right as a "philosophical whole," even if this science is in the end only one circle within a much bigger circle articulated in his *Encyclopedia*.

4.4 Recollection

Although Hegel's image implies that it does not really matter where we begin on the circle, since each beginning only has provisional priority over that which it precedes, there is a remarkable feature about Hegel's order of presentation, an order that is discernable throughout his works. Although Hegel aims to comprehend ethical life and claims that this is his object of evaluation, he does not begin with ethical life, nor does he immediately invoke those standards that are up to this task. Rather, he begins with an abstraction, abstract right. Next I will offer an explanation of Hegel's order of presentation that reveals what motivates the application of his method to the domain of right. This is a return to our framing question: why do we need a science of right in the first place, if it does no more than make the implicit explicit?

A famous passage from the Preface purports to express Hegel's motivations for offering a science of right:

What lies between reason as self-conscious spirit and reason as the present actuality, what separates this reason from [self-conscious spirit] and prevents the former from finding satisfaction in it, are the shackles of some abstraction, which has not been freed to the concept. To understand [*erkennen*] reason as the rose in the cross of the present and thereby to delight in [the present], this rational insight is the *reconciliation* with actuality, which philosophy grants to those who have once received the inner call to comprehend and to preserve their subjective freedom in that which is substantial, and at the same time to stand with their subjective freedom not in something particular and contingent, but in what is in and for itself.

This is also what constitutes in the more concrete sense what was described above in more abstract terms as the *unity of form and content*, for the *form* in its most concrete significance is reason as conceptual understanding [*begreifendes Erkennen*], and *content* is reason as the substantial essence of both ethical and natural actuality; the conscious identity of the two is the philosophical Idea. (PR 26–27)

According to one possible reading, Hegel is saying that his audience is failing to see that the ethical world is actual/rational. Philosophy, then, has the task of showing us that the ethical world is actual/rational, in this way allowing us to delight in it. This is a project of reconciling us with actuality by offering us rational insight into it, thus making us subjectively free.[36] There is, however, another way to read this passage, which is not incompatible with the earlier reading, but involves a different diagnosis of the present age. According to this reading, Hegel thinks that his contemporaries are confused about their own convictions. They think that they genuinely doubt whether the ethical world is actual/rational, thus demanding insight into its rationality. But as a matter of fact they do not doubt this and so already possess insight into its rationality. This may sound like a fairly serious case of false consciousness. What could be Hegel's basis for ascribing it to us? I will set this question aside for now to return to it later.

The advantage of this second reading is that it finds more textual support and that it provides a better framework for understanding Hegel's order of presentation. As far as the textual support is concerned, the first sentence of the previously cited passage is worth noting: "What lies between reason as self-conscious spirit and reason as the present world, what separates the former reason from the latter and prevents it from finding satisfaction in it, are the shackles of some abstraction, which has not been freed to the concept." Hegel is here identifying the relevant gulf as one between "self-conscious spirit" and "reason as the present actuality." This gulf emerges, he tells us, due to the

---

[36] Stern (2006) considers such an objection to his methodological gloss on the term "rational," but he argues that there is another way of construing this passage that is compatible with his neutral reading. According to Stern, rational comprehension, even in the absence of justification, embodies a kind of anti-utopianism, which is all that Hegel needs. In other words, understanding that the world is rational in this more minimal sense – i.e. rationally intelligible – is enough to prompt us to become reconciled to the world, even if it leaves open the question of whether we can endorse it. Stern adds that his neutral reading is better able to make sense of Hegel's project of reconciliation, since Hegel suggests that it is the philosopher – misled by theoretical abstractions – who is in need of reconciliation, and not the man on the street. The latter, as Hegel himself admits, finds his knowing and his willing already satisfied by the world he inhabits (PR, 16). The reading of this passage that I offer is better able to capture both aspects of this passage than Stern's – its normative and its quietistic dimension. Unlike Stern, I think philosophy seeks reconciliation by demonstrating that the ethical world is good. And we are in need of such reconciliation because we too are misled by theoretical abstractions. But Stern is right that people "on the street" – or we, in our capacity as social participants – are in some sense already reconciled because we are already convinced of its goodness.

"shackles of abstraction." So philosophy has the task of reconciling us with actuality to the extent to which abstraction has led us astray. Moreover, right after his statement about reconciliation, Hegel repeats his point about the unity of form and content. What he suggests is that, if we think of content as social institutions and of form as cognition, then philosophy is merely the *conscious* identity of the two. It does not introduce the form, only makes us conscious of it. In other words, it makes explicit what we already implicitly know, namely, that the ethical world is rational/actual. So Hegel's point about philosophical reconciliation can be understood in a different way: we must become reconciled with ourselves. Since the ethical world is something we have successfully internalized and incorporated into our ethical disposition, reconciliation with ourselves will also amount to reconciliation with the ethical world.

I hope to show that this diagnosis enables us to see why Hegel proceeds in the order that he does, specifically, why he does not begin with ethical life, but ends with it (if it is true that he could have started anywhere). The reason that Hegel cannot begin with ethical life is because ethical life, especially the principles operative in its institutions that constitute its "inner rationality," are not already in full view, even though we inhabit ethical life and heed its principles in our conduct. Ethical life is our "presupposition" (as he sometimes puts it), but one of which we are not (at least not fully) self-aware. So Hegel sets himself the task, not of justifying what we already explicitly affirm, but what lies below our reflective awareness. And this requires that we first be made aware.

This additional task becomes clearer in light of Hegel's critical attitude toward the opinions of his contemporaries. He is completely unimpressed by the fact of ethical disagreement, which others take as their point of departure, because he thinks that disagreement is merely superficial and obscures the deeper agreement expressed in what Hegel calls our "simple comportment" [*einfache Verhalten*]:

> The simple comportment of an unselfconscious disposition [*unbefangenen Gemüts*] is to stick with trusting conviction to the publicly familiar truth and to build its mode of conduct and its firm position in life on the firm foundation [of this publicly familiar truth]. Against this simple comportment may well arise the supposed difficulty of how to distinguish and discover among infinitely *different opinions* [*Meinungen*] that which is universally recognized and valid in them; and this perplexity can easily be taken for a correct and truthful earnestness about the matter. (PR, 14)

Hegel thinks that the fact that people have differing opinions about right does not really present a serious challenge that a philosophy of right must meet. He charges his former colleague Fries with taking it too seriously and developing his "ethics of conviction" in order to account for this fact. This ethical theory holds (in Hegel's uncharitable rendition) that, since we tend to disagree about what our duties are, duty must be whatever one believes one's duty to be. For

Hegel, it is fundamentally misguided to lend our opinions such credence. And when he claims that the truth about right is already widely known, he does not think that this knowledge is best reflected in people's opinions about right.

According to an Addition to the Preface, Hegel remarks that

> genuine thought is not an opinion [*Meinung*] about something, but the concept of the thing itself. Every human being has fingers and can have a brush and paint, but this does not yet make him a painter. It is the same with thinking. The thought of right is not whatever everyone has first hand, but instead correct thinking is the familiarity with and understanding of [*Kennen und Erkennen*] the thing, and our understanding should therefore be scientific. (PR, 17n)

One could read this passage as denying precisely that we do already know the truth about right. But I think there is another way to read it that makes better sense of Hegel's philosophical contribution. When he claims that the thought of right is not whatever everyone has firsthand, he is referring to the reflective understanding that people form about right – their opinions. And as we have previously seen in his critique of empiricism, what counts as common sense is for Hegel "corrupted" by processes of abstraction. As abstractions, these opinions retain some relation to right. They are abstract forms of it, so not wholly off track. At the same time, they are distortions of the familiar truth about right. This is why we need a scientific account of right, for only such an account can return us to what we know, but do not know that we know.

My proposal is that Hegel's philosophical method is best understood as a process of recollection – of retrieving a knowledge we tend to forget that we have. It is because we tend to forget that we have it that we need to employ this method. Our forgetting is what motivates Hegel's project. But as we have seen, his method is essentially evaluative. He is not interested merely in retrieving our presuppositions, but of showing us that those presuppositions are justified. In other words, Hegel wants to show us that ethical life is indeed rational/actual, as we are anyway convinced it is. I now want to explain why I believe that this process of recollection is capable of achieving this double task – of reminding us what our convictions are and showing us that we are right to have them. My suggestion goes admittedly beyond the letter of Hegel's *Philosophy of Right*, since Hegel does not mention recollection in this context. I take my cue from his association of philosophy and recollection in his earlier *Phenomenology of Spirit*, a text in which recollection is invoked in the chapter on "Absolute Knowing" as an explanation of our "phenomenological" exercise. What makes recollection especially relevant for understanding Hegel's method in the *Philosophy of Right* is that it can illuminate its order of presentation – why Hegel begins with what is most abstract and slowly makes his way back to the concrete – and its relation to the ethical world, which seems to be in no need of its practical guidance.

It might seem odd to look to the *Phenomenology of Spirit* for a statement of Hegel's conception of philosophy, given that Hegel differentiates the aims of this work from those of science proper. As Hegel himself often insisted, the *Phenomenology* presents the path to the system, whose domain we first enter with the *Encyclopedia*. At the same time, Hegel admits that "the way to science is itself already science" (PG ¶88), suggesting that its method is not going to be structurally different from the one that the *Encyclopedia* will exhibit. Both involve exposing the necessary connections within their objects of investigation. In the context of the *Phenomenology*, the object can broadly be characterized as knowing, more precisely, "actual knowing of what truly is" (PG ¶73). Hegel's aim is to show that "appearances" of knowing (configurations of consciousness and spirit) are necessary moments in an actualization process, a process of attaining "actual knowing." Thus the *Phenomenology* can be said to be a scientific account of science's own becoming [*das Werden der Wissenschaft*] (PG ¶27, 28). Absolute knowing is supposed to represent actual knowing because it is the last configuration and thus completes the series we have been tracking.[37] Thus this chapter holds the promise of teaching us what it is to know.[38] Absolute knowing also represents the transition from configurations of spirit to science proper, so we have reasons to hope that it can speak to the attitude of science toward our pre-philosophical perspectives.

As Hegel puts it, "The goal, absolute knowing, or spirit that knows itself as spirit, has as its path the recollection of spirits as they are in themselves and as they accomplish the organization of their realm" (PG ¶808). Let me provide a brief sketch of the function of recollection in the chapter on "Absolute Knowing" and in the *Phenomenology of Spirit* as a whole.[39] Although

---

[37] For an interpretation of what Hegel could mean by completion in the context of absolute knowing, see Pippin (2010), 226–227.

[38] In the Preface, Hegel states that "the goal is the insight of spirit into what knowing is" (PG ¶29).

[39] Although Hegel does not cite Plato in this context, he seems to have his doctrine of recollection in mind. This doctrine states roughly that we never acquire new knowledge, but that all learning is really a matter of remembering what we once knew and have since forgotten. In the *Meno*, Socrates invokes this doctrine in order to explain what looks like a paradox. How can you inquire into something you do not already know? Either you know it, in which case you have no further need for inquiry, or you do not know it, in which case you cannot get inquiry off the ground. Socrates attempts to solve this paradox by proposing that the soul is immortal and so has previously seen what it appears to be encountering for the first time. He famously demonstrates this by teaching the slave geometry through questions that elicit and awaken what looks to be knowledge the slave must already possess. While Hegel does not employ the notion of recollection to argue in favor of the immortality of the soul, he is reappropriating Plato's suggestion that we already possess the very knowledge we appear to be acquiring for the very first time. The significant difference, it seems to me, is that, for Hegel, this process of recollection is more than merely remembering what we once knew. It is meant to fortify this knowledge, make it less flimsy and susceptible to doubt. In fact, it seems that, for Plato, recollection can only ever be an impoverished retrieval of the kind of knowledge we possessed when we actually encountered the forms directly. Whatever we may be able to recollect within our embodied lives will fall short of this perfect knowledge we can only ever approximate. Thanks to Oksana Maksymchuk for this point.

recollection is only introduced at the very end of this work as a way of characterizing the philosophical procedure we have been applying, Hegel foreshadows its introduction by emphasizing that consciousness *forgets* what it learns throughout its experiential process of passing through various configurations.[40] The best way to understand this, I think, is that consciousness forgets that it is undergoing a process, and so that its newest configuration is a *result*.[41] In other words, it forgets the process itself, rather than what it is learning throughout it. Moreover, even if consciousness were aware of its own development, it would lack insight into the necessity that characterizes the transition from one configuration to another. While consciousness is undergoing a necessary process, it does not see it as necessary and so as rationally compelled. These are insights that absolute knowing is meant to provide. Absolute knowing does not introduce anything new because it is merely making us self-aware of something we have been doing all along, namely, partaking in a rational process of development.[42] But it does so by rehearsing this process with an emphasis on its necessity. This is why Hegel calls absolute knowing the "last configuration of spirit" and claims that it is really a form of self-knowledge, "spirit that knows itself as spirit" (PG ¶798). It is last because it yields a definitive form of self-knowledge, namely, knowledge that we have been participating in a process of genuine knowing. And this self-knowledge cannot be surpassed, even if it turns out that the process itself is not over.[43]

I have presented an admittedly very brief sketch of absolute knowing, which neglects many aspects of this configuration and its standing within the *Phenomenology*. For example, I am avoiding giving a reading of what Hegel means by "absolute." My focus here is solely on the relation between "recollection" (which is meant to provide the self-knowledge characteristic of absolute knowing) and that which it recollects, namely, the developmental process we have been forgetfully undergoing. One straightforward way to think about

---

[40] In the Preface to the *Phenomenology*, he identified recollection as the process whereby being-in-itself turns into being-for-itself, i.e., whereby we become self-conscious of something that was already true of us (PG ¶29).

[41] "Though on the one hand the first appearance of a new world is at first a whole veiled in its simplicity or the universal ground, so on the other hand is the richness of the previous existence still present in memory (*Erinnerung*) for consciousness. It misses in the newly appearing configuration the expansion and differentiation of content; but even more does it miss the development (*Ausbildung*) of form, whereby the differences are determined with certainty and are ordered in their stable relations" (PG ¶13).

[42] This is also suggested by Martin Shuster (2014), although he claims that it is the function of the second half of the *Phenomenology*, and not that of absolute knowing in particular (151).

[43] This is how I understand the sense in which absolute knowing completes the series. It involves self-knowledge about what knowing is, which is participation in an actualization process. But this does not necessarily imply that this process has come to an end, only that we now know it to be an actualization process.

this relation is to think about absolute knowing as the recollection of a *historical* development. This would mean that what we need to remember is that our contemporary forms of knowing have a history and that they evolved out of other configurations and due to their failures. This would be the added self-knowledge that absolute knowing contributes: historical self-consciousness.

But it is not difficult to see that this is at best a highly incomplete interpretation of absolute knowing. Historical self-consciousness is only one of the aims of this text and the place of history in it is by no means unambiguous.[44] Hegel does say in the chapter on "Absolute Knowing" that "the movement of carrying forward the form of its self-knowledge is the work which *actual history* [*wirkliche Geschichte*] accomplishes" (PG ¶803). He is thus making the claim that the self-knowledge of absolute knowing is a historical achievement. It is only because we have undergone an actual process of learning from experience that we are now in a position to grasp what we have undergone as a rational process. In this sense, absolute knowing is contingent on history, made possible by it. But there are at least two reasons to think that what we know when we "know absolutely" no longer possesses a historical form. This is another way of saying that the recollection involved in absolute knowing is not merely a recalling of what has happened in the order in which it happened, but a reordering of what has happened in such a way that we can discern its necessary structure. This is a connotation of the English term "recollection" (with its root of "collecting" or ordering) that is not captured by its German equivalent, *Erinnerung*.[45]

First, Hegel stresses that "comprehended history" is the translation of a historical process into a scientific form,[46] so that what looked to be a succession in time is actually a process of becoming actual/rational (in this context, of knowing). This is crucial for the evaluative conclusion it hopes to draw, that what we have is indeed actual/rational knowing. Second, and this is even more crucial,

---

[44] It has become increasingly common to argue that the *Phenomenology of Spirit* only appears to be concerned with history, but is in fact more akin to a transcendental argument that investigates the kind of presuppositions at the basis of our normative commitments. See, for example, Pippin (1989) and Forster (1998). Although Hegel is not offering a transcendental argument, he is interested in exposing the necessary conditions for actualization and wants to demonstrate that historical development is among those conditions.

[45] I am grateful to Fred Neuhouser for drawing my attention to this difference. It is worth noting that Hegel does mention gathering or collecting (*Versammlung*) in the chapter on "Absolute Knowing" (PG ¶797), which suggests that this connotation would not be off the mark.

[46] "The *goal*, absolute knowing, or spirit that knows itself as spirit, has for its path the recollection [*Erinnerung*] of the spirits as they are in themselves and as they accomplish the organization of their realm. Their preservation, regarded from the side of their free existence appearing in the form of contingency, is history; but regarded from the side of the comprehended organization [*begriffenen Organisation*], it is the *science of appearing knowing* [*Wissenschaft des erscheinenden Wissens*]" (PG ¶808).

the process that Hegel is reordering is not always one that has made a historical appearance. When he begins with "sense-certainty," he is not identifying a historically specific configuration of consciousness, but the product of the highest abstraction. "Sense-certainty" represents a "commensensical" account of knowing precisely because it is purged of all specificity and so cannot be identified as a historically embodied worldview. What is needed, then, is to "recollect" the conditions that made sense-certainty possible. These are partly historical conditions, since Hegel wants to make a case for including history in our knowledge of what knowing is. But they are more broadly the "substantial" background against which sense-certainty makes any sense as a form of knowing. Thus Hegel characterizes absolute knowing itself as the completion of a circle that shows us why and to what extent our starting point was legitimate.

> For the self-knowing spirit, just because it grasps its concept, is the immediate identity with itself, which in its difference is the *certainty of immediacy* [*Gewissheit vom Unmittelbaren*], or *sense-consciousness* [*das sinnliche Bewusstsein*] – the beginning, from which we proceeded; this release of it from its form is the highest freedom and certainty of its self-knowledge. (PG ¶806)

The *Phenomenology* as a whole can be seen as an activity of recollection not only because it involves remembering a forgotten past, but also because it involves a discovery of the background conditions needed for the realization of its starting point – what it takes for "sense-certainty" to be an actual/rational form of knowing. If we see the function of recollection in this light, it is much easier to make the transition to the *Philosophy of Right*, but also to other parts of Hegel's system,[47] and to understand why recollection is so intimately bound up with philosophical method. It involves a movement from the abstract to the concrete, even when it is retrieving principles or formulations of freedom that coexist in modern ethical life, rather than configurations that have been espoused and abandoned in our historical development. Philosophical reflection can be regarded as an activity of recollection, irrespective of its particular object (whether right or knowing), because it begins with a supposedly "commonsensical" starting point (something taken as self-evident), traces its process of becoming actual/rational, and in this way exposes the background conditions for its actuality/rationality. This activity of recollection also has the upshot of putting this immediate starting point in its place, showing it to be mediated, namely, dependent on relations to other principles. So recollection

---

[47] Hegel mentions *Erinnerung* numerous times in the opening pages of his "logic of essence." Recollection is meant to characterize the movement from "being" to "essence," but also the process of knowing this movement: "It is first through the recollection [*erinnert*] from immediate being, through this mediation, that knowledge finds essence" (WL, 13).

is another way to characterize the circularity that Hegel takes to be the test of philosophical success.

Now let me return to the science of right and connect this conception of recollection more explicitly to its aim and contribution. What I want to suggest is that the science of right has an analogous starting point to the *Phenomenology* and that its status as something self-evident has a lot to do with Hegel's diagnosis of the contemporary frame of mind. As we have seen, Hegel takes the readership to which he is addressing himself to have a distorted view of the ethical world, a view expressed in their opinions about it. He thinks his peers have detached some one principle from this ethical world and stripped it of all concrete content. Hegel identifies this principle as that of "abstract right" – the minimal conception of what constitutes a free will, according to which freedom means the ability to pursue one's personal ends in an unhindered fashion, whatever these ends happen to be. One could venture to say that, were Hegel to approach someone on the street and ask to which principle of right she is committed, she would cite some version of abstract right. So it makes sense to start with that which is most abstract, since this is where we are inclined to start, making it what is most immediate to us, what everyone has "first at hand." But it is not what our conduct reveals to be true of us. So his task is to recall this truth, knowledge of which is expressed in what we do, not what we avow.

Hegel's subsequent procedure has some remarkable features. First, although it is not meant to produce a theory of right, it borrows from both formalism and empiricism. This procedure starts with a formal principle (not far from Fichte's own) and investigates the conditions for its enactment. But in doing so, its unconditional status is put into question. It is shown to have only relative worth, requiring that it be embedded in a broader context that includes other principles that cannot be deduced from it. This is also what makes Hegel's procedure akin to empiricism, but empiricism of the "pure" sort. He is working his way back to the ethical world in its rich entirety in a way that empirical theories failed to do. Second, as an activity of recollection, Hegel's method is going to be a *critical* one. It is meant to challenge something by showing it to be inadequate, insufficient, distorted. This might come as a surprise in light of Hegel's sharp divide between our critical practices within ethical life and a philosophical grasp of ethical life. But it is important to keep in mind that what Hegel is critiquing are abstractions, the products of abstract reflection. So his object is not the social world, but our theories of (or more mundanely, opinions of) the social world. The advantage of such an approach that starts with an abstraction, rather than with *Sittlichkeit* itself, is that it can show the latter as a "result," rather than simply taking it for granted in a potentially arbitrary way. As Hegel puts it helpfully in his Introduction, "One could here raise the question why we do not begin the highest, that is, with what is concretely true. The answer is going to be that we want to see the concretely true in the form of a result, and for this it is essential first to grasp the abstract concept" (PR §32Z).

How do we move from personal freedom to contract, and eventually beyond the entire framework of abstract right? Although these transitions deserve more detailed attention, I will comment on them only schematically. I believe it is helpful to think of these transitions under the broad charge of indeterminacy. When Hegel takes up a standard of freedom such as abstract right, he asks himself what it takes to enact this standard in a way that stays true to it. We are asking ourselves whether this standard is capable of drawing the relevant distinction, say, between right and wrong. What we discover is that we cannot enact this standard without presupposing practices that invoke other standards. Without those practices and their corresponding standards, this one standard would be indeterminate, inapplicable.

This is especially vivid at the major transitions between different conceptions of freedom such as the transition from abstract right to morality. Abstract right for Hegel is the most minimal conception of the free will, according to which freedom means the ability to pursue one's ends in an unhindered fashion, whatever these ends happen to be. Neuhouser calls this "personal freedom" and stresses that what matters is that I have chosen which ends to pursue, irrespective of my reasons for doing so. Although I am saddled with a reservoir of needs and desires, I can decide which among them I will take up. As Hegel puts it, initially I only make reference to myself as an "inherently individual will of a subject [*in sich einzelner Wille eines Subjekts*]" (PR §34). But in order to attain these ends of mine, I require an external world of things that I can turn into an embodiment of my will, i.e., my property. This notion of property introduces a host of other requirements that complicate the picture of freedom at issue in abstract right. First, I discover that I need to make reference not only to things, but also to *other wills*, if I am to attain these ends of mine. Simply put, in order for something to count as my property, it must be recognized as such by others. If it were not so recognized, this thing would not be properly mine. So property presupposes contractual relations in which both parties recognize each other's things as belonging to each.

This suggests that abstract right quickly surpasses this minimal conception of what constitutes a free will, for it incorporates considerations about what kind of social world such a will would have to inhabit in order to be free in this sense. According to Hegel, actualizing the free will so conceived requires a system of rights that protects the domain of private property within which each individual will can enact her chosen ends without infringing on those of others. So even an internal account of "abstract right" inevitably unravels a more complicated structure of freedom by delineating its social conditions. But we soon discover a further limitation indicating that abstract right cannot account for freedom through its own resources, even when these resources are developed into a system of rights. At the end of his chapter, Hegel argues that contract presupposes "wrong," and so that a conception of contractual relations must be able to accommodate the possibility of breaching their terms. In the case of such a breach, we would need to appeal to a will that can adjudicate between the claims made by the conflicting parties because it itself is not embedded in contractual relations.[48] Another way to put this would be to say that we must be able to make sense of an impartial perspective and that we cannot make sense of it on the model that contract provides. Thus he concludes that personal freedom cannot be actualized without morality. So once we investigate the conditions for the upholding of contractual relations in cases where contracts have been violated, we realize that we need norms of evaluation that are not themselves contractual. This is how we win back the thinly moral standpoint.

Hegel stresses the problem of indeterminacy even more explicitly in his analysis of this moral standpoint. As we have previously seen, he takes conscience to be its highest expression because it involves a conception of freedom according to which duty is determined by the formal principle of the subjective will. In Hegel's rendition, conscience holds that my duty is whatever I believe it to be. Because conscience takes its subjective will to be a peerless authority, it cannot draw a "substantial" distinction between good and evil. What it takes to be good could as well be regarded as evil. There is no objective way to determine the difference, for conscience itself lacks the resources to tell genuine duty apart from mere opinion. As Hegel concludes, "Conscience is as formal subjectivity is simply that, to be on the verge of reverting into evil" (PR §139R). His main criticism is not that conscience is evil exactly, but that it might as well be evil because it cannot maintain the difference between good and evil. He characterizes this as a failure of determinacy:

> For the good as the substantial universal of freedom, but as still *abstract*, determinations in general as well as their principle, though a principle identical with [the good], are still required, just as for *conscience*, as only the abstract principle of determining, the objectivity and universality of its determinations is required. Both, each having elevated itself to an independent whole, become the indeterminate which *ought* to be determined. (PR §141)

This is how the indeterminacy of morality leads the way back to ethical life, recalling the context in which we are in fact capable of making the relevant distinctions.

---

[48] One of Hegel's targets in this chapter is social contract theory. Hegel argues that we cannot have a contract with the state because then there would be no higher authority to enforce the contract and a contract without such an authority would be empty. Hegel thinks this higher authority must therefore stand outside of contractual relations and first makes such relations possible.

Does this mean that ethical life is fully determinate and that it excludes any ambiguity about what should count as right and wrong, or good and evil? Although Hegel presents ethical life as the context that permits determinacy because it provides the systematic parameters within which to determine what we ought to do, he also leaves open a number of possibilities for further determination. Within this structure there could still be disputes about which specific duties ought to bind family members, coworkers, etc. This is not immediately settled by the structure itself. Moreover, this structure could be embodied in a number of different cultural contexts, thereby lending itself to a limited degree of pluralism (as discussed in the second chapter). So the answer to the question of whether ethical life yields determinate criteria of evaluation is: yes and no. It provides substantial constraints that make objective evaluation possible, but it leaves many aspects of social life, including many concrete norms, underdetermined.

The foregoing sketch gives some indication as to how it is that we move from one formulation of right to another and why we proceed in the order in which we do. The conception of freedom underpinning abstract right is not equivalent to the one Hegel ultimately endorses, though both it as well as its moral successor are meant to be preserved in his fuller account. This conception is inadequate not because it is off track, but because it captures only one principle of the free will and not yet the whole of right. So in calling it "abstract," Hegel suggests that it is the most basic picture, one that will first have to be filled in and given a concrete content, a process that will likewise radically challenge the basic tenets of abstract right and morality, notably their self-sufficiency. Considerations of determinacy are meant to expose this background against which we can employ such standards in a way that draws the relevant distinctions between right and wrong, good and evil. So Hegel is challenging the supremacy of abstract right and of morality by bringing the context in which they do function as applicable criteria of evaluation back to our attention.[49]

This last transition is the crucial step in Hegel's method, for it marks the transition from the primarily critical side of the procedure to the positive side of the science of right. Although we have now entered the domain that is supposed to correspond to our genuine convictions, Hegel thinks that he has likewise shown us why we are entitled to them. As he states at the end of the "Morality" chapter, "that this idea is the truth of the concept of freedom, this cannot be something presupposed, whether taken from feeling or elsewhere,

---

[49] Hegel is not simply charging either abstract right or morality with excessive abstraction. That would be an external criticism and one their proponents would not be compelled to accept, since right and morality are deliberately formal. The charge of indeterminacy is meant to run deeper, for it shows that abstract right and morality cannot generate content through their own criteria.

rather – in philosophy – can only be something proven [*ein Bewiesenes*]. This deduction of [the idea] is contained only in the fact that [abstract] right and moral self-consciousness show of their own accord that they regress to it as their result" (PR §141). He begins with commitments we do avow, such as those to abstract right and morality, and then proceeds to show us that these are only actual/rational in a context shaped by other commitments – such as those to social relationships and institutions. So Hegel is not merely making explicit a fact about us, namely, that we are indeed committed to the ethical world. He is also demonstrating that we are right to be committed in the ways we are, because the true object of our commitment is actual/rational.

This backward movement from the abstract to the concrete is best seen as an activity of recollection because it is tied up with Hegel's diagnosis of his present age. Hegel is employing his method in order to correct a peculiar form of confusion produced by abstraction and so represented by abstract formulations of right. These abstract formulations are expressed in what Hegel describes as opinions about right. They are not wholly misguided, since they are abstracted from the idea of right and so have their source in the true concept of right. But they are partial and incomplete without the broader normative resources to which we help ourselves when we navigate the ethical world. So there is a gulf between our actual convictions, best expressed in our unreflective comportment, and our reflective perspective generated by abstraction. And it is this gulf that Hegel's method of recollection is meant to bridge.[50]

Earlier, I admitted that such a diagnosis seems to ascribe a fairly serious case of false consciousness to his contemporaries. On what grounds can Hegel conclude that we are so self-ignorant that we do not even know what we know? A second look at the "Absolute Knowing" chapter of the *Phenomenology* can show this diagnosis to be more plausible and less paternalistic than it

---

[50] Tunick (1994) has drawn a similar comparison between the methodology between the *Phenomenology* and the *Philosophy of Right*. As he rightly points out, "as we progress, each new theory approaches asymptotically the actual world, encompassing more and more of its complexity and detail, accounting for more of our actual commitments" (324). This can be read as an alternative formulation of recollection. But Tunick misconstrues the basis of this progress. He claims that the *Philosophy of Right* is a "dialectic of experience" because it hinges on felt dissatisfaction with abstract conceptions of right. Our aim then is an account "that does not leave us in contradiction with ourselves; for we already live objective spirit, we are it, we know it implicitly...we will experience the incompleteness of any account that is not concrete enough, for in the reality portrayed in such an abstract account we will not be fully at home" (322). While this might be true, such experiences of satisfaction or dissatisfaction cannot be the basis of progress in Hegel's method. It is not even the basis of progress in the *Phenomenology*, for the *Phenomenology* relies a very different conception of experience. In any case this construal would make Hegel's method far too contingent on subjective feelings and would fail to demonstrate the necessity of the movements that lead from Abstract Right to Ethical Life.

initially seems. In a telling passage, Hegel invokes the term "recollection" in a double sense:

> As [spirit's] completion consists in knowing completely what it is, its substance, so is its knowing a *withdrawing-into-itself* [*Insichgehen*], in which it abandons its existence and cedes its shape to recollection [*Erinnerung*]. In this withdrawing-into-itself it is sunk in the night of its self-consciousness, but its vanished existence is preserved in it; and this superseded [*aufgehobenes*] existence – the previous one, but newly born from knowledge – is the new existence, a new world and shape of spirit. In it [spirit] has to start anew from [this new existence's] immediacy and to raise itself again, as if all that preceded were lost and it had learned nothing from the experience of earlier spirits. But recollection [*Er-innerung*] has preserved them and is the inner [*Innere*] and in fact higher form of the substance. (PG ¶808)

This passage is clearly playing with two different senses of recollection – recollection as *Erinnerung* and as *Er-innerung*. There is the recollection that has "preserved" experiential lessons in spite of the "night of self-consciousness" in which spirit is currently lost. In other words, Hegel is saying that we have already successfully internalized the rich content, which now strikes us as merely outer existence, a world with which we do not identify. Then there is the recollection that brings this content to light, showing us that we have already successfully internalized it, so that we are committed to a broader set of standards than our reflections reveal, standards embodied in this outer existence. This second recollection is Hegel's own philosophical aim. What he tells us is that his procedure has an "as if" structure – it operates *as if* we did not recognize ourselves (our own commitments) in the objective world, although we do. But this "as if" is not idle, because we ourselves do not know that we do. We have *internalized* this content so successfully that we have forgotten it. So we need to call to mind what we thoroughly "inwardized" precisely because we have "inwardized" it thoroughly.

This double sense of recollection has relevance to Hegel's diagnosis in the *Philosophy of Right* for it can explain the gulf between the reflective and the unreflective that motivates his method. Although I discussed this topic at far greater length in the first chapter, it is helpful to recall Hegel's picture of ethical conduct that emerges in the *Philosophy of Right*. He claims that in a rational social order (so one that is not ridden with contradictions) social participants have internalized social norms so thoroughly that they follow them habitually. He calls this a "simple identification" with ethical life, one in which following its norms has become a second nature. Although Hegel does not complete this picture in the *Philosophy of Right* itself, in his chapter on habit in the "Anthropology," he explicitly associates successful habituation with recollection in our first sense,[51] so with the thoroughgoing internalization of norms. In

---

[51] "Habit that is developed and participates in spirit as such is *recollection* [*Erinnerung*] and the *memory* [*Gedächnis*] and will be considered at a later point" (Enz. III §410R).

other words, to become habituated to follow certain rules is to no longer have to think about which rules you are following, perhaps no longer to be aware that you are following rules at all. Your behavior now exhibits an unreflective spontaneity. So it should not be surprising that we might forget what it is that we know as competent social participants as soon as we begin to reflect on our participation and so abstract away from what we are otherwise competently doing. And it should not be surprising that we might need to recollect those norms in the second sense, make them explicit to ourselves, precisely because they are so fully internalized. One could even go far as to say that the more rational a social order is and the more seamlessly its practices run, the more invisible its rationality becomes and the less available to the reflective awareness of its habituated participants.

In sum, this double sense of recollection can explain several features of Hegel's method. It can explain Hegel's reasons for thinking that his contemporaries are self-deceived, tracing this propensity to lose sight of what we implicitly know to the success of habituation in a rational/actual social order. It can explain Hegel's reasons for starting with contemporary opinions of right and returning us to ethical life as a condition for the actualization of even those commitments we are prepared to avow. And it can explain Hegel's reasons for thinking that we might need such a reminder of ethical life that brings its rationality/actuality back into view. This last feature of his method, the *need* for it, remains the most contentious, even on this account. It is still contentious, because, for Hegel, there is nothing inherently deficient in habitual conduct – at least nothing that calls for philosophical recollection. What makes habitual conduct deficient is solely its vulnerability to the influence of theory and opinion – to abstraction. On one hand, we do not need a scientific account of ethical life, as if our unreflective ways of proceeding were somehow inadequate or insufficient. On the other hand, we do need such an account, for without it, our unreflective ways of proceeding lack a defense against abstraction.

Abstraction has, first of all, raised a justificatory challenge to those practices and institutions in which we habitually participate. It has demanded that they (as a whole) justify themselves to us, that they meet our criterion of freedom. And, given the nature of abstraction, this criterion is itself an abstract one – abstracted from those practices and institutions themselves. Unsurprisingly, many of our practices and institutions will according to this course come to appear unjustified. For example, if we think that we have no reason to participate in anything that does not grant us personal freedom, then whole domains of social life – such as the family and the state – will fall short. Second, Hegel thinks that abstraction is a widespread phenomenon, that its influence is felt everywhere, even in our everyday attitudes. So this demand for comprehensive justification is not one that philosophers have first introduced. Theories of right are merely crystallizations of a milieu.[52]

It would be too quick, however, to conclude that Hegel is only a critic of abstraction and that he wishes its influence away. Although it is pernicious and confused, abstraction is not a mere misstep in our developmental process. So Hegel also welcomes the influence of abstraction because it raises the bar for what is going to count as "justified by thought" by demanding that ethical life *as a whole* prove itself rational/actual. Although our second nature expresses a conviction that the ethical world is (on the whole) rational/actual, we cannot fully justify this conviction without the aid of the philosophical method, which exposes the systematic structure of the ethical world. As I read him, Hegel does not think that, without a science of right, we are unable to justify what we are doing, when the need for it arises. So our habitual behavior already counts as an expression of genuine knowledge for him. But it cannot meet this highest demand, for as participants in ethical life we do not have a view *of* the whole in which we (for the most part) seamlessly move. The upshot of applying this method is to demonstrate that our convictions can withstand the challenge of abstraction and so to allow us to return to our unreflective ways with newfound confidence.

Hegel's project so conceived has relevance for our prior question about the place of ideology in his account. While Hegel denies that we can be subject to long-term ideological distortions, mistaking the unethical for the ethical, he admits that we can confuse ourselves about our insight into the good. This ambivalence is expressed in his verdict on "public opinion," to which I briefly return:

> A leading spirit has raised the question for public debate, *whether it is permissible to deceive a people*. One has to answer that it is impossible that a people could be deceived about its substantial basis, about the *essence* and determinate character of its spirit, but that the people can deceive *itself* about the way it knows them [*die Weise, wie es diesen weiss*] and about the way it judges its actions and events. (PR §317R)

As Hegel puts it, public opinion cannot be deceived, but it can be self-deceived. It cannot be deceived about its substantial basis, since even those

---

[52] Hegel indicates that he does not think philosophy responsible for the kinds of problems brought forth by reflection. When he cites various dualisms such as that between freedom and necessity, or between law and the heart, he remarks that "these are contrasts [*Gegensätze*], which are not simply invented through a trick of reflection [*Witz der Reflexion*] or through the school lessons of philosophy [*Schulansicht der Philosophie*], but instead the spiritual culture [*geistige Bildung*], the modern understanding, produces this contrast in the human being, which makes an amphibian out of him" (VA, 80–81). Thanks to Terry Pinkard for this passage.

who espouse such opinions *know* this basis simply by inhabiting it and moving around it with ease. But public opinion can be self-deceived about its knowledge of this basis, about *the way* that this basis is known to it, which is through habitual participation in ethical life. It is this latter self-deception, or better self-forgetfulness, that Hegel's project in the *Philosophy of Right* aspires to overcome.

4.5 Objective and Absolute Spirit

I conclude with two points about the relationship between "Objective Spirit" (the domain of right) and "Absolute Spirit" (the domain of artistic, religious, and philosophical reflection), both of which hark back to the systematic place of Hegel's *Philosophy of Right*. The first point concerns the extent to which the activities associated with "Absolute Spirit" can be regarded as a necessary condition for the actualization of "Objective Spirit." The second point concerns the extent to which "Absolute Spirit," specifically philosophical comprehension, must remain open to the activities that take place within "Objective Spirit."

In his critical engagement with Neuhouser's book, Will Dudley stresses that "far from being irrelevant to practical freedom, then, the activities treated in absolute spirit are in fact essential conditions for its actualization."[53] Dudley takes his evidence from structural features of Hegel's method. What comes next in the procedure tends to be a necessary condition for the actualization of what came before. Just as ethical life is a necessary condition for the actualization of abstract right, "Absolute Spirit" would have to be a necessary condition for the actualization of "Objective Spirit" – specifically, of the freedom that is at its core. This seems to be a very strong requirement, especially if we think of Hegel's own method as the highest articulation of "Absolute Spirit." Is Hegel saying that we cannot be fully free unless we have read the *Philosophy of Right*? It should come as no surprise that I do not think Hegel harbored such ambitions for his text. This would go against his rather modest aspiration to free us from the "shackles of abstraction," *not* to make us objectively (or even subjectively) free.[54] Such a reading of Hegel's method is also far too formulaic. Not every transition within his system needs to be seen as delineating necessary

---

[53] Dudley (2004), 8.
[54] Dudley (2004) explains the necessity of "Absolute Spirit" in the following way: "[I]n Hegel's view it is only in virtue of art, religion, and most especially philosophy that we can determine the objective institutions of freedom and subsequently educate ourselves to have the appropriate subjective dispositions toward the institutions that in fact happen to exist" (8). I do not think this can be right, since philosophy neither determines objective institutions (except retrospectively) nor educates us to have subjective dispositions toward those institutions (except perhaps in *preserving* our commitment to them in the face of abstraction).

conditions for "actualization," at least not in an analogous respect. Finally, "Absolute Spirit" is also manifest in reflective activities associated with art and religion. And, as I argued in the second chapter, reflective activities along these lines continue to have a vital role to play, even in a rational social order. So it does not mean that, without Hegel's own philosophical science, nothing that came before could be regarded as fully and adequately actualized.

But is "Absolute Spirit" dependent on "Objective Spirit" in turn? If we take Hegel's circular method seriously, he is delineating mutually necessary conditions, rather than giving us a transcendental argument for what conditions what. Although I think it would be extravagant for Hegel to argue that there could be no "Absolute Spirit" in any of its manifestation without a fully realized version of "Objective Spirit," he does think that a philosophical comprehension *of right* depends on the actualization of right, just like a philosophical comprehension *of nature* depends on the actualization of nature. In other words, if there were no rational society, we could not give a philosophical account of one, nor could we give a philosophical account of nature, if nature had never come to be. Moreover, a Science of Right must remain attentive to the developments within the objective sphere, developments it cannot guide or predict. Let me say a few final words about what I take this to mean.

Hegel concludes his methodological reflections with a familiar programmatic statement worth revisiting one final time:

To say a further word on the subject of *issuing instructions* on how the world ought to be, philosophy anyway always comes too late for it. As the *thought* of the world, it appears only at a time when actuality has finished its formative process and completed itself. This, which the concept teaches, history also necessarily shows, that it is only in the maturity of actuality that the ideal appears opposite the real and that the former reconstructs this world, grasped in its substance, in the shape of an intellectual real. When philosophy paints its gray in gray, a form of life has grown old, and with grey in grey it cannot be rejuvenated [*verjüngert*], but only understood; the owl of Minerva begins her flight only with the onset of dusk. (PR, 27–28)

Here he is once again underscoring this familiar difference between critique (or "issuing instructions") and comprehension, which is confined to actuality in a way in which critique is not. My proposal in this chapter should help clarify Hegel's reasons for insisting on this distinction. It shows that the philosophical method has certain advantages over critique precisely because it is confined to actuality, to those ideals that have stood the test of realization. But this also makes its results limited in two respects. First, it is not in a position to contribute directly to the critical enterprise, for the future is open-ended, not yet tested by reality, and so not the proper domain of philosophical comprehension. Second, it is not in a position to offer a final verdict on ethical life. The justification of it that it can offer is provisional at best, since it has access to the ideal only to the extent to which it has been realized. Philosophy cannot exclude the possibility that the current version of the ideal will come into question at a later stage of the realization process. In speaking of the "maturity of actuality," Hegel is indirectly admitting his discomfort with the prospect that actuality might not yet be mature, that the ethical world might not get be fully actual/rational (but just another stage in the process of becoming so). At the same time, his method disallows him from discounting this possibility.

He cannot discount it, for one, because his account of ethical life must incorporate the possibility of immanent critique, which is a critique that challenges the very standards by which we evaluate our institutions and practices. His account must incorporate this possibility because it cannot say in advance that no practical contradictions will emerge, contradictions that put our standards into question. So Hegel's philosophical method, even if it is not itself critical *of* ethical life, must nonetheless be compatible with critique *within* ethical life – critique that is conducted on the ground and remains sensitive to objective problems that call for normative change. But it itself can at most contribute to this enterprise in indirect ways. By reminding us of our unreflective convictions, it presents us with a wider range of resources for evaluation than abstract reflection itself can yield. And by exposing the systematic form of an actual/rational social order, it reminds us of the formal constraints on social change, if it is to give rise to a sustainable set of institutions and practices.

The unwavering thesis of Hegel's work is that, for any social order to be actual/rational, it must constitute a system, so it must be possible to offer a systematic account of it. Its concrete shape, however, remains contestable. This is something Hegel explicitly addresses when he writes, "A great old tree grows more and more branches without becoming a new tree; it would be foolish to refuse to plant a tree just because it might grow new branches" (216Z). He mentions this metaphor in a context in which he is speaking to the question of completeness, of whether a science can ever be completed. But the same can be said of its object. Just because ethical life will continue to unfold does not mean that participation in its current shape is not worth undertaking.

So even though Hegel's method is meant to be a demonstration of the actuality/rationality of the ethical world, I do not think it is possible to demonstrate it definitively – and I am not convinced that Hegel thought so either. I conclude with this mere sketch of what a consistently Hegelian position might be, with the full understanding that it is a mere sketch. Even if we grant that Hegel's method can successfully overcome the shackles of abstraction, whatever justification he can give of the concrete shape of the ethical world is going to be provisional. We are simply never in a position to rule out the possibility that our current principles will entangle us in future contradictions that show our practices to have been insufficiently actual/rational. Any particular application of the scientific procedure to the realm of reality (what Hegel calls *Realphilosophie*) is thus hostage to the test of time, to the test of experience. I believe that Hegel admitted this in his own way when he concludes the *Philosophy of Right* with a section on world history, calling world history (and not philosophy) ethical life's ultimate "court of judgment" (PR §341).

Works Cited

Abrams, M. H. (1973), *Natural Supernaturalism: Tradition and Revolution in Romantic Literature* (Norton).
Adorno, Theodor (2003), "Cultural Criticism and Society," in *Can One Live after Auschwitz?: A Philosophical Reader*, edited by R. Tiedemann, translated by R. Livingstone (Stanford University Press), 146–162.
Alznauer, Mark (2015), *Hegel's Theory of Responsibility* (Cambridge University Press).
Ameriks, Karl (2000), "The Hegelian Critique of Kantian Morality," in *Kant and the Fate of Autonomy: Problems in the Appropriation of the Critical Philosophy* (Cambridge University Press), 309–337.
Anderson, Joel (2001), "Hegel's Implicit View on How to Solve the Problem of Poverty: The Responsible Consumer and the Return of the Ethical to Civil Society," in *Beyond Liberalism and Communitarianism,* edited by Robert Williams (State University of New York Press), 185–205.
Appiah, Anthony Kwame (2007), *The Ethics of Identity* (Princeton University Press).
Aristotle (2002), *Nicomachean Ethics*, translated by Sarah Broadie and Christopher Rowe (Oxford University Press).
Avineri, Schlomi (1972), *Hegel's Theory of the Modern State* (Cambridge University Press).
Baxley, Anne Margaret (2010), *Kant's Theory of Virtue: The Value of Autocracy* (Cambridge University Press).
Benhabib, Seyla (1986), *Critique, Norm, and Utopia: A Study of the Foundations of Critical Theory* (Columbia University Press).
Boltanski, Luc (2011), *On Critique: A Sociology of Emancipation* (Polity).
Boltanski, Luc and Eve Chiapello (2007), *The New Spirit of Capitalism* (Verso).
Bristow, William (2005), "*Bildung* and the Critique of Modern Skepticism in McDowell and Hegel," in *International Yearbook of German Idealism* 3, edited by Karl Ameriks and Jurgen Stolzenberg, (De Gruyer), 179–207.
  (2007), *Hegel and the Transformation of Philosophical Critique* (Oxford University Press).
Brooks, Thom (2007), *Hegel's Political Philosophy: A Systematic Reading of the Philosophy of Right* (Edinburgh University Press).
Buchwalter, Andrew (1992), "Hegel's Concept of Virtue," *Political Theory* 20:4, 548–583.
Coetzee, J. M. (2003), *Elizabeth Costello* (Vintage).
Cohen, Joshua (1997), "The Arc of the Moral Universe," *Philosophy and Public Affairs* 26:2, 91–134.

De Beauvoir, Simone (2010), *The Second Sex*, translated by Constance Borde (Vintage).
Dreyfus, Hubert (2007), "The Return of the Myth of the Mental," *Inquiry* 50:4, 352–365.
Dudley, Will (2004), "The Systematic Context and Structure of Hegel's Social Theory: A Response to Frederick Neuhouser," *Owl of Minerva* 36:1, 3–14.
Eagleton, Terry (2016), *Culture* (Yale University Press).
  (1991), *Ideology: An Introduction* (Verso).
Emundts, Dina (2012), *Erfahren und Erkennen* (Klostermann).
Ferrarin, Alfredo (2001), *Hegel and Aristotle* (Cambridge University Press).
Fichte, J. G. (1994), *Introductions to the Wissenschaftslehre*, translated by Daniel Breazeale (Hackett).
Foer, Jonathan Safran (2009), *Eating Animals* (Penguin).
Forman, David (2010), "Second Nature and Spirit: Hegel on the Role of Habit in the Appearance of Perceptual Consciousness," *Southern Journal of Philosophy* 48:4, 325–352.
Forster, Michael (1989), *Hegel and Skepticism* (Harvard University Press).
  (1998), *Hegel's Idea of a Phenomenology of Spirit* (University of Chicago Press).
Franco, Paul (1999), *Hegel's Philosophy of Freedom* (Yale University Press).
Frankfurt, Harry (1998), "Identification and Wholeheartedness," in *The Importance of What We Care About* (Cambridge University Press), 159–176.
Fulda, Hans Friedrich (2004), "The Rights of Philosophy," in *Hegel on Ethics and Politics*, edited by Robert B. Pippin and Otfried Höffe (Cambridge University Press), 21–48.
Gadamer, Hans-Georg (1989), *Truth and Method* (Continuum).
Geiger, Ido (2007), *The Founding Act of Modern Ethical Life: Hegel's Critique of Kant's Moral and Political Philosophy* (Stanford University Press).
Geuss, Raymond (1981), *The Idea of a Critical Theory* (Cambridge University Press).
Goldstein, Joshua D. (2004), "The 'Bees Problem' in Hegel's Political Philosophy: Habit, Phronesis and the Experience of the Good," *History of Political Thought* 15:3, 481–507.
Greene, Murray (1972), *Hegel on the Soul: A Speculative Anthropology* (Martinus Nijhoff).
Hardimon, Michael (1994), *Hegel's Social Philosophy: The Project of Reconciliation* (Cambridge University Press).
Herman, Barbara (2007), "Making Room for Character," in *Moral Literacy* (Harvard University Press), 1–28.
Honneth, Axel (2014), *Freedom's Right: The Social Foundations of Democratic Life* (Columbia University Press).
  (2009), *Pathologies of Reason: On the Legacy of Critical Theory*, translated by J. Ingram (Columbia University Press).
  (2010), *The Pathologies of Individual Freedom: Hegel's Social Theory* (Princeton University Press).
Horkheimer, Max (1975), "Traditional and Critical Theory," in *Critical Theory: Selected Essays* (Continuum), 188–243.
Horstmann, Rolf-Peter (2011), "The *Phenomenology of Spirit* as a 'Transcendentalistic' Argument for a Monistic Ontology," in *Hegel's Phenomenology of Spirit: A Critical Guide*, edited by Dean Moyar and Michael Quante (Cambridge University Press), 43–62.

Ilting, Karl-Heinz (1963–1964), "Hegels Auseinandersetzung mit der Aristotelischen Politik," *Philosophisches Jahrbuch* LXXI, 38–58.
Jaeggi, Rahel (2009), "Rethinking Ideology," in *New Waves in Political Philosophy*, edited by Boudewijn de Bruin and Christopher Zurn (Palgrave Macmillan).
   (2014) *Zur Kritik von Lebensformen* (Suhrkamp).
Kant, Immanuel (2006), *Anthropology from a Pragmatic Point of View*, translated and edited by Robert Lauden (Cambridge University Press).
   (1997), *Groundwork of the Metaphysics of Morals*, edited by Mary Gregor (Cambridge University Press).
   (1999a), *Practical Philosophy*, translated and edited by Mary Gregor (Cambridge University Press).
   (1999b), *Religion within the Boundaries of Mere Reason*, translated by Allen Wood and George Di Giovanni (Cambridge University Press).
Kitcher, Patricia (2003), "What Is a Maxim?" *Philosophical Topics* 31:1–2, 215–243.
Korsgaard, Christine (1996), *The Sources of Normativity* (Cambridge University Press).
Lauer, Quentin (1983), "Religion and Culture in Hegel," in *Hegel's Philosophy of Action*, edited by Lawrence Stepelevich (Humanities Press), 103–114.
Lewis, Thomas (2008), "Speaking of Habits: The Role of Language in Moving from Habit to Freedom," *Owl of Minerva* 39:1–2, 25–53.
Lovibond, Sabina (2004), *Ethical Formation* (Harvard University Press).
Lumsden, Simon (2001), "Beyond an Ontological Foundation for the *Philosophy of Right*," *The Southern Journal of Philosophy* 39, 139–145.
MacIntyre, Alasdair (1984), *After Virtue: A Study in Moral Theory* (University of Notre Dame Press).
Malabou, Catherine (2005), *The Future of Hegel: Plasticity, Temporality, and Dialectic* (Routledge).
Markus, György (1986), "The Hegelian Conception of Culture," *Praxis International* 6:2, 113–123.
Marx, Karl (1978), *The Marx-Engels Reader*, edited by Robert Tucker (Norton).
Matz, Lou (1997), "Hegel's Missing Moral Virtues?" *British Journal for the History of Philosophy* 5:2, 321–338.
McCumber, John (1990), "Hegel on Habit," *Owl of Minerva* 21:2, 155–164.
McDowell, John (1996), *Mind and World* (Harvard University Press).
   (1998a), "Two Sorts of Naturalism," in *Mind, Value, and Reality*, 167–197.
   (1998b), "Virtue and Reason," in *Mind, Value, and Reality*, 50–73.
Melamed, Yitzhak (2001), "Leaving the Wound Visible: Hegel and Marx on the Rabble and the Problem of Poverty in Modern Society," *The Jerusalem Philosophical Quarterly* 50, 23–39.
Menke, Christoph (2010), "Autonomie und Befreiung" in *DZPhil Akademie Verlag* 58:5, 675–694.
   (2013), "Hegel's Theory of Second Nature: The 'Lapse' of Spirit," *Symposium* 17:1, 31–49.
Moland, Lydia (2011), *Hegel on Political Identity* (Northwestern University Press).
   (2003), "Inheriting, Earning, and Owning: The Source of Practical Identity in Hegel's 'Anthropology,'" *Owl of Minerva* 34:2, 139–170.
Moyar, Dean (2011), *Hegel's Conscience* (Oxford University Press).

Nance, Michael (2012), "Recognition, Freedom, and the Self in Fichte's Foundations of Natural Right," *European Journal of Philosophy* 23:2.

Neuhouser, Frederick (2009), "Desire, Recognition, and the Relation between Bondsman and Lord," in *The Blackwell Guide to Hegel's Phenomenology of Spirit*, edited by Kenneth Welstphal (Blackwell), 37–54.

(2000), *Foundations of Hegel's Social Theory: Actualizing Freedom* (Harvard University Press).

(2014), *Rousseau's Critique of Inequality: Reconstructing the Second Discourse* (Cambridge University Press).

Niedermann, Joseph (1941), *Kultur. Werden und Wandlung des Begriffs und seiner Ersatzbegriffe von Cicero bis Herder* (Firenze).

Nietzsche, Friedrich (1974), *The Gay Science*, translated by Walter Kaufmann (Random House).

Novakovic, Andreja (2015), "Gewohnheit des Sittlichen bei Hegel" in *Momente der Freiheit*, edited by Julia Christ and Titus Stahl (Klostermann), 93 – 107.

Patten, Alan (2002), *Hegel's Idea of Freedom* (Oxford University Press)

Peperzak, Adriaan (1982), "Hegels Pflichten und Tugendlehre," *Hegel-Studien* 17.

Pierce, Charles (1868), "Some Consequences of Four Incapacities," *Journal of Speculative Philosophy* 2, 140–157.

Pinkard, Terry (2012), *Hegel's Naturalism: Mind, Nature, and the Final Ends of Life* (Oxford University Press).

(1996), *Hegel's Phenomenology: The Sociality of Reason* (Cambridge University Press).

Pippin, Robert (1989), *Hegel's Idealism: The Satisfaction of Self-Consciousness* (Cambridge University Press).

(2008), *Hegel's Practical Philosophy: Rational Agency as Ethical Life* (Cambridge University Press).

(2010), "The 'Logic of Experience' as 'Absolute Knowledge' in Hegel's *Phenomenology of Spirit*," in *Hegel's Phenomenology of Spirit: A Critical Guide*, edited by Dean Moyar and Michael Quante (Cambridge University Press), 210–227.

Plato (2002), *Five Dialogues: Euthyphro, Apology, Crito, Meno, Phaedo*, translated by G. M. A. Grube (Hackett).

Pollard, Bill (2003), "Can Virtuous Actions Be both Habitual and Rational?" *Ethical Theory and Moral Practice* 6:4, 411–425.

Quante, Michael (1997), "Personal Autonomy and the Structure of the Will," in *Right, Morality, Ethical Life: Studies in G.W.H. Hegel's* Philosophy of Right. SoPhi Academic Press.

Rózsa, Erzsébet (2001), "'Bildung,' 'Reichtum,' und das Problem des Selbst: Zur Theorie des Modernen Individuums in der *'Phänomenologie des Geistes*,'" *Hegel-Jahrbuch*, 204–212.

Ryle, Gilbert (2009), "Conscience and Moral Conviction," in *Collected Essays: 1929–1968* (Routledge).

(2000), *The Concept of Mind* (University of Chicago Press).

Scheffler, Samuel (2007), "Immigration and the Significance of Culture," *Philosophy & Public Affairs* 35:2, 93–125.

Sedgwick, Sally (2012), "On Becoming Ethical: The Emergence of Freedom in Hegel's *Philosophy of Right*," in *The Freedom of Life: Hegelian Perspectives*, edited by Thomas Khurana (Der Verlag der Buchhandlung Water Koenig), 209–227.

Shuster, Martin (2014), *Autonomy after Auschwitz: Adorno, German Idealism, and Modernity* (University of Chicago Press).

Siep, Ludwig (1983), "The Aufhebung of Morality in Ethical Life," in *Hegel's Philosophy of Action*, edited by Lawrence Stepelevich (Humanities Press), 137–155.

Sophocles (1973), *Antigone*, translated by Richard Braun (Oxford University Press).

Stern, Robert (2006), "Hegel's Doppelsatz: A Neutral Reading," *Journal of the History of Philosophy* 44:2, 235–266.

(2012), *Understanding Moral Obligation: Kant, Hegel, Kierkegaard* (Cambridge University Press).

Taylor, Charles (1979), *Hegel and Modern Society* (Cambridge University Press).

Thompson, Kevin (2001), "Reason and Objective Spirit: Method and Ontology in Hegel's *Philosophy of Right*," *Southern Journal of Philosophy* 39:s, 111–137.

Tugendhat, Ernst (1986), *Self-Consciousness and Self-Determination* (MIT Press).

Tunick, Mark (2001), "Hegel on Political Identity and the Ties that Bind," in *Beyond Liberalism and Communitarianism: Studies in Hegel's* Philosophy of Right, edited by Robert Williams (State University of New York Press), 67–89.

(1994), "Hegel's Nonfoundationalism: A Phenomenological Account of the Structure of the *Philosophy of Right*," *History of Philosophy Quarterly* 11:3, 317–337.

Wallace, R. Jay (2006), "Virtue, Reason, and Principle," in *Normativity and the Will* (Clarendon Press), 241–262.

Walsh, W. H. (1969), *Hegelian Ethics* (Macmillan).

Walzer, Michael (2009), "Gesellschaftskritik und Gesellschaftstheorie," *Sozialphilosophie und Kritik*, edited by Rainer Forst, et al. (Suhrkamp), 588–607.

Wartenberg, Thomas (1982), "Poverty and the Class Structure in Hegel's Theory of Civil Society," *Philosophy and Social Criticism* 8, 169–182.

Westphal, Merold (1992), "Hegel, Human Rights, and the Hungry," in *Hegel, Freedom, and Modernity* (State University of New York Press), 19–36.

Williams, Bernard (1985), *Ethics and the Limits of Philosophy* (Harvard University Press).

Wittgenstein, Ludwig (2001), *Philosophical Investigations* (Blackwell).

Wollstonecraft, Mary (1996), *A Vindication of the Rights of Woman* (Dover).

Wood, Allen (1989), "The Emptiness of the Moral Will," *Monist* 72.

(1990), *Hegel's Ethical Thought* (Cambridge University Press).

(1993), "Hegel's Ethics," in *The Cambridge Companion to Hegel*, edited by Frederick Beiser (Cambridge University Press), 211–233.

Yeomans, Christopher (2011), *Freedom and Reflection: Hegel and the Logic of Agency* (Oxford University Press).

Index

a priori principle, 170, 171, 172, 178
Absolute Knowing, 192–194, 195, 200
Absolute Spirit, 69, 204–207
abstract right, 39, 173, 178, 184, 185, 187, 188, 196, 197–198, 199, 200, 204. *See also* right
abstract universality, 66. *See also* universality
abstraction, 6, 59, 112n12, 131, 156, 167, 190, 191, 196, 200, 202–203
   from configurations of Spirit, 126
   and cultural identity, 104
   and empiricism, 172, 173, 191
   and essence, 9
   excessive, 29, 59, 156
   and habit, 59
   and reflection, 3, 5, 21, 98, 112, 162
   and theory, 169
   and work, 96
actuality, 20, 43, 164, 165, 166, 167, 175, 177, 178, 179, 181, 187, 189, 190, 202, 205, 206
   of knowing, 165, 192
   and law, 64
   maturity of, 206
actualizability, 171, 173, 178, 184
actualization, 175, 177, 178, 180, 185, 192, 202, 204, 205
   of freedom, 3, 4, 14
   of knowledge, 14, 131, 193n43
   of Objective Spirit, 204
   of personal freedom, 198
   of right, 205
   of substance, 84, 92
Adorno, Theodor, 154n76
agricultural or substantial estate, 100, 102
alienation, 80–86, 90, 141n53, 158
   overcoming, 82
   an social identification, 75
Alznauer, Mark, 24n6
animal behavior, 22, 95
animal habits, 32
Anschauung, 89, 90
"Anthropology", 31–32, 46

habit in, 16, 26, 26n12, 27, 30, 32–38, 54, 56, 201
Antigone, 50–51, 129–133
appearance, 8, 14, 87, 105, 156, 172, 187. *See also* essence; reflection; seeming
   of goodness, 152
   of knowing, 14, 119, 192
   of legitimacy, 152
Appiah, Anthony, 75, 103
appropriate standard, 113
Aristotle, 16, 24–25, 24n8, 28, 29, 47n58, 60
   on virtue, 50
arts, 87
ascetics, 35n39
attention, 35, 36, 37, 56, 97
   excessive, 36
   and habit, 56
autonomy, 27, 54n71
Avineri, Schlomo, 135

bad habits, 36–37. *See also* habit
beautiful ethical life, 127–133, 140, 141, 146
becoming cultured, 92
becoming of Science, 13
behavior, 22, 23, 30, 102, 202
   and habit, 21, 35, 36, 203
   mechanical, 66
   obsessive-compulsive, 66–67
behavioral disposition, 21, 46, 56
being, 6, 79
being cultured, 87
Bildung, 16, 17, 70, 75, 90, 93, 95, 97, 99, 105, 138. *See also* culture; self-cultivation
   and alienation, 80–86, 90
   bondsman, 88
   civil society. *See* civil society
   of consciousness, 13
   and cosmopolitanism, distinguished, 100, 102
   cultural participation. *See* cultural participation
   and customs, 98

Bildung (cont.)
   double-aspect of, 92
   and Enlightenment, 104
   high culture, 87
   individual perspective, 77
   inorganic nature, 78
   lord, 88
   modern, 85, 101
   in *Phenomenology*, 76–80
   and productive activity, 87, 92
   and self-alienation, 81, 83
   as self-directed, 95
   and self-education, 95
   self-reflective form of, 85
   and shared standards, 98
   societal perspective, 77
   of substance, 91
   thing, 88
   universal, 99, 102
   and work, 90, 96
   world of, 81
bloodless shade, 132n37
Boltanski, Luc, 117n18, 136–137
bondsman, 87, 88, 120
bourgeoisie, 87, 94
Brown v. Board of Education, 144
business estate, 100

capitalism, 136, 143
caste system, in India, 101
categorical imperative, 29, 46, 118, 118n21, 120n25, 158
certainty, 121. *See also* sense-certainty
   and truth, 43, 122
character, 46
Chiapello, Eve, 117n18, 136–137
circularity, 31n32, 183, 187, 196
   circle of circles, 187
civil society, 76, 93–103, 110, 136, 136n44, 137, 139–142
   bourgeoisie, 94
   and cosmopolitanism, 100
   and education, 95
   estates, 100–102
   member of, 97, 102
   nobility, 94
   participation in, 98, 102
   and poverty, 18, 110, 134–136, 142, 143, 146, 147
   public features of, 99
   rationality, 95
   shared culture, 99, 102
   subjective freedom, 95
   as system of needs, 97, 98, 138, 173
   universality in, 95, 100, 138
Clark, Mamie, 145n61

codification, 60–61, 63, 64
Coetzee, J. M., 157
commitments, 15, 25, 40, 42, 48, 50, 51, 52n67, 54, 55, 59, 92, 100, 102, 103, 104, 117, 118, 132, 133, 136, 140, 143, 183, 200, 202
communitarianism, 17, 71, 72–73, 74
community
   internal differentiation, 72
   and virtue, 72, 82
compatibalism, 7n9
complete reflective awareness, 44n52
completeness, 178n24
comprehended history, 194
comprehension, 166, 175, 205
   conceptual, 18, 181
   neutral, 177
   philosophical, 2, 16, 178, 179, 180, 204, 205
   rational, 177
   and reflection, 166
conceptual thought, 2, 3
concrete freedom, 4n5
configuration, 121, 123–124, 155
   of consciousness, 14, 121, 151, 155, 192, 195
   of spirit, 14, 15, 77, 79, 126, 127–133, 146, 192, 193
conscience, 39, 39n46, 40n47, 40n48, 41n50, 44, 106n1, 107, 107n2, 198
   and conviction, 40–41
   and ethical life, 42
   and moral knowledge, 40
   sanctity of, 42
   and social norms, 40
consciousness, 55, 119, 123, 185, 193
   configuration of, 14, 40n47, 121, 151, 155, 192, 195
   false consciousness, 151, 152, 156, 189, 200
   and habit, 35, 57
   natural, 76, 126
   perceptual, 33
conservatism, 12, 147
consumption, 87, 96
continence, and virtue, 50, 60
contractual relations, 197, 198
contradictions, 13, 33, 123, 125, 131, 155n77, 158
   modern contradictions, 133–147
   practical contradiction. *See* practical contradiction
conviction
   and goodness, 41n49
   and knowledge, 51n66
cosmopolitanism, 100, 102
   and *Bildung*, distinguished, 100

Index

crime, 130–131, 132, 140, 141, 158, 159
criminals, 144
critical criticism, 110–115
   critic of, 108, 110, 112
critical reflection, 12, 21, 107, 112
   and habit, 113
   possibility of, 113
   and practical contradiction, 18, 116
   and unsustainability, 144
   value of, 110, 111
critical theory, 147–151
critique, 21, 106–110, 124
   beautiful ethical life, 127–133
   and comprehension, 205
   critical criticism, 110–115
   emancipatory effects, 153
   immanent critique, 115–125
   modern contradictions, 133–147
   and theory, 147–160
cultural community, 70, 72, 75, 101, 102
cultural formation. *See also Bildung*
   and self-cultivation, 84–85
cultural identity, 75, 103–105
cultural inheritance, 79, 86
cultural norms, 75, 86
cultural participation, 13, 16, 68, 69, 70, 75, 76, 91, 103, 106, 108
   and *Bildung*, 17, 77
   and habit, 76, 92
cultural pluralism, 73, 93, 101
   and civil society, 102
cultural self-expression, modes of, 91
culture, 13, 69
   Bildung. *See Bildung*
   and ethical life. *SeeBildung*; culture
   formation of, 92
   and habit, 70
   and tradition, difference between, 75n19
cultured person, 82, 96, 97
cultured reflection, 97–98
custom, 5, 6, 16, 17, 61, 70, 78, 79, 80, 85, 92
   and *Bildung*, 98
   centrality of, 98
   prevailing custom, 127
   shared, 99, 101, 102, 105
customary rights, 61, 64, 71, 168n10

De Beauvoir, Simone, 93
death by habit, 64–68
decisiveness, 49, 50, 51, 156, 203
deduction, 181, 188
deliberation, 21, 22, 24, 25, 53, 62, 75, 106, 127
desire, 24, 25, 28, 34, 35, 50, 85, 87, 88, 94, 96, 98, 99, 136
determinate negation, 124, 124n28
determination, 5, 33, 34–35, 54, 172
die Sache, 30, 30n25, 30n26, 59
dis-identification, 5
disposition, 24, 25, 55n72
   behavioral disposition, 21, 46, 56
   ethical disposition, 23, 25, 26, 43, 44–55, 108, 190
   political disposition, 43, 55
divine law, 50, 85, 127, 128, 129, 130, 132, 132n37
division of labor, 96
doing the right thing, 49, 50, 67
doll test, 145n61
Doppelsatz, 166, 167, 174–179, 181, 187
double-world, 82
Dreyfus, Hubert, 36n40
Dudley, Will, 183n31, 204
duty, 25, 28, 29n23, 40, 74n16, 130, 190, 198
   identifying with, 52
   and inclination, 29, 30
   and motivation, 28
   motive of, 59

Eagleton, Terry, 70n2, 152
embodied coping, 36n40
empiricism, 166, 169, 171–172, 191, 196
   and abstractions, 172, 173, 191
   pure empiricism, 172
Encyclopedia of the Philosophical Sciences, 13, 31, 32, 37, 163, 166, 167, 180, 182, 185, 186, 188, 192
enlightened self, 85
Enlightenment, 104
equality, 82, 139, 144, 145
essence, 7, 8n12, 9, 10, 51, 79, 84, 89, 105, 156. *See also* appearance
   and abstraction, 9
   defined, 8
   logic of, 6, 11
   and seeming, 8–9, 11
estates, 73, 100–102
ethical consciousness, 50n64
ethical disposition, 23, 25, 26, 44–55, 49n61, 108, 190
   definition of, 45
   and knowing, 45
   and principled living, 48
   and recognition, 45
   and reflection, 46
   and true conscience, 43
   and virtue, 46
   as whole-heartedness, 52
ethical failures, 146, 157, 158
ethical knowledge, 25, 39, 46, 60n84, 109, 127, 131
ethical laws, 1, 10, 16, 174

evaluative judgments, 83, 87, 112
excessive abstraction, 29, 59, 156
excessive attention, 36
    liberation from, 36
experiences, 116, 123, 124–125, 141, 171
external reflection, 9, 9n13, 9n14, 10
externalization, 80–86, 90

false consciousness, 151, 152, 153, 156, 189, 200
family, 74, 79, 94, 102, 127, 128, 130, 135, 139, 142, 202
fear of death, 89
Fichte, J. G., 170–171, 181, 183–184
Foer, Jonathan Safran, 159
formal conscience, 41, 43, 44, 45, 107
formal universality of willing, 99
formalism, 82, 166, 169, 172, 178, 196
    defined, 170
Forman, David, 26n12
Forster, Michael, 75n20, 81
frame of mind, 23, 25, 46, 47, 51, 110, 167, 196
Franco, Paul, 52n67
Frankfurt, Harry, 24n4
free will, 3, 7n9, 24n4, 185, 186, 196, 197, 199
    and abstraction, 6
    and reflection, 3
    unreflectiveness, 4
freedom, 3, 3n4, 44, 88n34, 129n35, 197
    abstract conceptions of, 156
    actualization of, 3, 4, 14, 198
    concrete freedom, 4n5
    and habit, 37, 56
    objective freedom, 6, 29
    personal freedom, 197, 198, 202
    subjective freedom, 3, 4, 5, 6, 14, 16, 23, 29, 30, 37, 38, 44, 64, 95, 137, 189
Fries, Jakob Friedrich, 40, 190
Fulda, Hans Friedrich, 162n2

Gadamer, Hans-Georg, 98n40
Geiger, Ido, 24
genuine identification, 90
Geuss, Raymond, 150, 153
givenness, 9, 10
Goldstein, Joshua D., 23n3
good eye, 149–150
good upbringing, and ethical disposition, 49n61
Greeks, 103, 126, 133
    culture, 85
    ethical action, 45
    ethical life, 79, 81
    polis, 20, 110, 126

habit, 4, 5, 12, 15, 20, 54, 66
    and abstract universality, 66
    and abstraction, 59
    as activity, 33
    anthropological account of, 32–38
    and attention, 56
    and behavior, 21, 35, 36, 203
    categories, 35
    compulsive, 37, 66–67
    conception of, 21
    coping with natural surroundings, 32
    death by, 64–68
    decline of, 67
    definition of, 33
    and ethical disposition, 44–55
    free activity, 37
    and freedom, 56
    of hardening, 34n37
    immediacy, 22–23
    of indifference, 34n37
    liberating, 35
    and madness, 33
    mechanical, 66
    mechanism, 30
    and motivation, 24
    negative, 35
    as physical inner necessitation, 27, 28, 30
    pragmatic point of view, 27–32
    principled habits, 56–64
    as simple identification with ethical life, 22
    of skill, 34n37
    true conscience, 38–44
    unfreedom, 37
    virtue as, 23, 24
habituation, 6, 16, 24, 25, 28, 33–34, 35n39, 44, 56, 65, 66
    excessive, 67
    and frame of mind, 25
    and inclination, 25, 28
    and political disposition, 43
    as process of appropriation, 54
    as process of liberation, 34
    and rules, 58
Hardimon, Michael, 74, 103–104, 114n14, 164
Herman, Barbara, 63n87
high culture, 87
historical self-consciousness, 194
holy wills, 28n20, 29n21
Honneth, Axel, 148, 149, 153, 155, 156, 169n11
Horkheimer, Max, 150, 151, 153
Horstmann, Rolf-Peter, 126n31
human law, 85, 127, 128, 130, 132

idea of right, 179, 180, 182, 187, 200
identity, 75, 103–105
    Hegelian and communitarian conceptions, difference between, 103

Index

Ideologiekritik, 154, 155n77
　and immanent critique, similarities between, 154
ideology, 110, 148, 151–156, 203
　critique of, 153
　as false consciousness, 151, 152
　as materially effective, 152
　and theory, 153
ignorance, forms of, 47n58
immanent critique, 17, 110, 115–125, 116n16, 126, 132, 133, 136, 146–148, 148n65, 154, 154n76, 154n77, 156, 157, 173, 179, 206
　and *Ideologiekritik*, similarities between, 154
immediacy, 11, 11n17, 22–23, 36, 96, 122, 127, 132, 133, 134, 147
immigrant communities, 105
inclination, 24, 25, 28, 50, 59, 60
　and duty, 29, 30
　and habituation, 25, 28
indeterminacy, 197, 198
individualism, 39, 102, 137
induction, 157, 179, 188
industrialization, 53, 143
inner rationality, 156, 174, 175, 177, 190
inorganic nature, 77–79, 92
instances of knowing, 121, 122
intellectual virtues, 25
intellectualism, 47, 48, 58n79
internal criticism, 133
　and immanent criticism, difference between, 116
internal rationality, 10
intuitions, 13, 109

Jaeggi, Rahel, 116, 116n16, 155n77

Kant, Immanuel, 16, 25, 28n19, 28n20, 44n53, 46, 53, 63n87, 118, 118n21, 158
　Anthropology from a Pragmatic Point of View, 27, 31, 56
　on attention, 56
　conception of virtue, 28, 44, 46, 48–49, 60
　on duty, 49
　on habit, 16, 25, 27–29, 56
　metaphysics of knowledge, 31n28
　Metaphysics of Morals, 49
　moral law, 47, 49, 50, 117
　pragmatic knowledge, definition of, 31
Kitcher, Patricia, 28n19
knowing, 11, 55, 69, 121, 174, 195. *See also* knowledge
　Absolute Knowing, 192–194, 195
　actuality, 165, 192
　appearances of, 14, 119, 192
　different ways of, 42
　and ethical disposition, 45
　instances of, 121, 122
　philosophical, 181
　universality, 95
knowledge, 14, 18, 38, 119, 122, 178, 182.
　See also knowing
　actualization of, 14
　and conviction, 51n66
　ethical knowledge, 25, 39, 46, 63n89, 109, 127, 131
　and habit, 56
　immediacy in, 132
　incorporated, 52n68
　metaphysic of, 31n28
　moral knowledge, 40
　philosophical knowledge, 186, 187
　practical knowledge, 31n30, 66, 119
　pragmatic knowledge, 31, 31n30
　self-knowledge, 193–194
　and sense-centrality, 121, 122
　and truth, 52n68
　and virtue, 47, 60
Korsgaard, Christine, 118n22, 120n25
Kultur, 70. *See also* culture

labor, 88, 89, 90, 91, 96, 100, 120
　as formative activity, 89
　and self-consciousness, 88
laws, 2, 46, 46n55, 51, 51n65, 53, 59, 64, 130n36, 168n10, 174, 175
　consistency, 62
　constraints, 61–62
　critique, 62–63
　divine law, 50, 85, 127, 128, 129, 130, 132, 132n37
　and habit, 61
　human law, 85, 127, 128, 130, 132
　moral law, 47, 48, 49, 50, 117n20
　natural law, 175
Lectures on the Philosophy of World History, 86, 97
Lewis, Thomas, 23n4, 26n12
logical progression, 186
logical spirit, 181, 186
lord, 87, 88, 89, 104, 120, 121
Lovibond, Sabina, 69n53
Lumsden, Simon, 182n29

MacIntyre, Alasdair, 72, 72n6
madness, 33
　and habit, 33
Malabou, Catherine, 32
market, 94, 136
　activity, 137
　autonomous, 135
　consequence of, 135
　modern market, 134
　participation in, 99, 101, 137

Markus, György, 85n28
marriage, 74n16
Marx, Karl, 108n6, 115, 136, 136n44, 143, 143n57, 155
Marxism, 151, 156
maxims, 28n19
McCumber, John, 37, 38
McDowell, John, 25, 26, 60, 60n82, 60n84, 63, 146
mediated immediacy, 11n17. *See also* immediacy
Menke, Christoph, 65–66
modern contradictions, 133–147
modern culture, 80, 86, 92, 103. *See also* culture
modern ethical life, 1, 18, 21, 26, 45, 51, 74, 94, 101, 106, 108, 113, 114, 126, 133–134, 136, 146, 147
modern state, 74, 98, 99
Moland, Lydia, 4n5, 54n70
moral authorship, 53n69
moral genius, 39, 45, 158
moral law, 47, 48, 49, 50, 117n20
moral norms, 117
moral reflection, 39, 42
moral theory, 11, 27, 30, 44, 111
morality, 25, 26, 38, 39, 41, 43, 44, 48, 117, 173, 197, 199, 200
　definition of, 11
　indeterminacy, 198
　perspective distinctive of, 20
　and reflection, 11, 39
motivation, 30
　and duty, 28, 29, 59
　and habit, 24
　and inclination, 25, 29
movement
　of nothing to nothing, 9
　of reflection, 7
Moyar, Dean, 39n46, 40n48, 46, 54n71, 106n1

nation, and state distinguishes between, 99
nation state, 100
natural community, 128
natural laws, 175
natural world, 174
necessity, and system, 180
Neuhouser, Frederick, 12n18, 24, 95, 96, 114n14, 186n34, 197, 204
Nietzsche, Friedrich, 52n68
nobility, 87, 94
non-rationality, 24, 25, 50
normative reconstruction, of ethical life, 169n11
normativity, dynamic view of, 46

norms, 21, 23, 121, 141, 168
　criticizing, 125
　cultural norms, 75, 86
　and habit, 27
　moral norms, 117
　rationality as, 166
　social norms, 11, 15, 17, 40, 107, 109, 119, 201

obedience, 50
objective culture, 78, 84, 86
objective freedom, 6, 29
objective institutions, 155, 164, 165, 180
objective rationality, 12
Objective Spirit, 3, 26n11, 31–32, 37, 180, 184, 204–207
objectively rational social order, 20, 23, 42, 64
objectivity, 40
　and reflection, 43
obsessive-compulsive behavior, 66–67
opinions, 40, 43, 55n72, 98, 99, 190, 191, 198
　public opinion, 53n69, 156, 203–204
optimism, 27, 157, 159

particularity, 30, 33, 40, 82, 94, 136n45, 137, 138, 139, 141, 143, 147
　as decisive factor, 40, 95
passport regulations, 171
pathologies, 33, 153, 155
patriotism, 54–55, 100
Patten, Alan, 4n6, 44n52
Peirce, Charles, 109n7
personal freedom, 197, 202
　actualization of, 198
Phenomenology of Spirit, 5, 12–15, 17, 18, 39, 50, 75, 85, 87, 93, 94, 96, 97, 102, 104, 106, 110, 115, 119, 121, 123, 125, 126, 133, 134, 140, 141, 146, 165, 182, 191, 192, 193, 195, 196, 200
　Bildung in, 76–80
philosophical knowledge, 186, 187
philosophical reconciliation, 190
philosophical reflection, 18, 70, 165, 195
philosophical science, 180, 184, 185, 205
philosophy, 115, 160, 162, 164, 172, 179, 189, 203n52, 206
Philosophy of Right, 1, 3, 4, 5, 6, 10, 11, 12, 13, 14, 15, 16, 17, 18, 20, 21, 26, 38, 54, 61, 64, 69, 73, 75, 76, 93, 94, 101, 106, 114, 123, 133, 134, 142, 155, 156, 161, 163, 164, 166, 167, 171, 172, 173, 174, 175, 176, 177, 178, 180, 183, 185, 186, 187, 191, 195, 201, 204, 207
Pinkard, Terry, 141, 142

Index

Pippin, Robert, 8n12, 85n30
pluralism, 17, 73, 132, 199
   cultural pluralism, 73, 93, 101, 102
political community, 4n5
political disposition, 43, 55
Pollard, Bill, 58n79
poverty
   and civil society, 18, 110, 134–136, 140, 142, 143, 147
   and unemployment, 143n57
practical contradiction, 115, 116, 117, 120, 120n25, 121, 124, 140, 142, 146, 147, 150, 154, 160, 206
   and critical reflection, 18, 116
   and ethical failures, 158
practical education, 96
practical identities, 118n22
practical knowledge, 31n30, 66, 119
pragmatic knowledge, 31, 31n30
pre-reflective ethical life, 23n4, 26n12
presupposition, 177, 182, 185, 190, 191
prevailing custom, 127
principled action, 50
principled habits, 56–64
principled life, 48, 51
private property, 118, 197
property, 197
   private property, 118, 197
public opinion, 53n69, 156, 203–204
   self-deceived, 204
pure empiricism, 172. *See also* empiricism

racial segregation, 144–145, 152
rational comprehension, 176, 189n36
rational reconstruction, 123–124
rational social order, 10, 12, 14, 16, 17, 20, 23, 29, 30, 41–42, 43, 44, 45, 59, 64, 69, 74, 93, 126, 127, 201, 202, 205, 206
rationality, 167, 177, 178, 179, 189, 202, 206
   of civil society, 95
   of ethical life, 1, 6, 12, 18, 45
   inner rationality, 156, 174, 175, 177, 190
   internal rationality, 10
   as norm, 166
   objective rationality, 12
reality, 81
   alien reality, 80
   and self-conception, 155
   social reality, 151, 152, 153, 156, 168
Realphilosophie, 207
reason
   as present actuality, 188
   as present world, 189
   as self-conscious spirit, 188, 189

recognition, 39, 82n26, 197
   and ethical disposition, 45
   in public life, 129
recollection, 18, 58, 165, 166, 188–204, 192n39
   and circularity, 196
   as *Erinnerung* and *Er-innerung*, 201
reconciliation, 164, 165, 188, 189, 190
reconstructive process, 123
reflection, 3, 5–12, 14, 21, 106, 167. *See also* essence; appearance; seeming
   and abstraction, 3, 5, 21, 98, 112, 162
   and comprehension, 166
   critical reflection, 12, 18, 21, 107, 110, 111, 112, 113, 116, 144
   cultured reflection, 97
   as deliberation, 22, 106
   and ethical disposition, 46
   and ethical life, 4, 11
   exercise of, 3–4
   external reflection, 9, 9n13, 9n14, 10
   and free will, 3
   and habit, 21
   immediacy, 10n15
   logic of essence, 6
   moral reflection, 39, 42
   and morality, 11
   as movement, 6
   philosophical reflection, 18, 70, 165, 195
   as restless activity, 10
   self-reflection, 5, 7, 8, 11, 14, 85
   as source of objectivity, 43
reflective activities, 205
re-habituation, 53
relation-less identity, 2, 3
relativism, 71, 73
Religion within the Bounds of Reason, 48
resistance to theory, 153
revisionary aspiration, 111
right
   abstract right, 39, 173, 178, 184, 185, 187, 188, 196, 197–198, 199, 200, 204
   actualization of, 205
   customary rights, 61, 64, 71
   idea of, 179, 180, 182, 187, 200
   and science, 18, 163, 165, 179–188, 196, 199, 203, 205
   of the subjective will, 26, 29n22, 38, 38n43, 42, 45, 107
   theories of, 167–174
Roman Law, abstract formalism of, 82
Rousseau, Jean-Jacques, 82n26
Rózsa, Erzsébet, 94n38
rule-following skepticism, 60n84
rules, 46, 58, 59, 60, 61, 67, 137, 202
Ryle, Gilbert, 58

Scheffler, Samuel, 75, 75n19, 103
Schiller, Johann Christoph Friedrich von, 50n63
science, 119n23, 161–167
   Doppelsatz, 174–179
   Objective and Absolute Spirit, 204–207
   recollection, 188–204
   and right, 18, 163, 165, 179–188, 196, 199, 203, 205
   and systematization, 162
   theories of right, 167–174
Science of Logic, 5, 6, 7n9, 10, 71, 163
seeming, 7, 7n7, 8, 8n12. *See also* appearance; reflection
   and essence, 8–9, 11
self-alienation, 81, 82, 83. *See also* alienation
self-conception, 57, 74–75, 88, 90, 91, 102, 104, 105, 129, 132, 133, 145, 155, 168, 170
self-consciousness, 40, 51, 82, 84, 88, 89, 91, 103, 131, 170, 200. *See also* consciousness
   alienation, 80
self-cultivation, 80–87, 90, 98, 101. *See also* Bildung
self-determination, 7n9. *See also* determination
self-feeling, 2, 32–33, 52, 64
self-interest, 2n3, 94, 98, 130, 136, 138
self-knowing spirit, 195
self-knowledge, 64, 90, 193–194. *See also* knowing; knowledge
self-love, 48, 48n60
self-positing, 170–171, 178
self-recognition, failure of, 82, 84
self-reflection, 5, 7, 11, 14, 85. *See also* reflection
self-relation, 6, 33
self-seeking activity, 94, 95, 129
self-standing being, 87, 88
sense-certainty, 121–123, 195
   verbal expressions of knowledge, 122
Siep, Ludwig, 38n45
simple comportment, 190
simple identification, 15, 22, 53, 112, 201
single-mindedness, 131
skeptical culture, 81
skepticism, 8, 81
   rule-following, 60n84
skills, 34, 35–36, 56–57, 58, 96. *See also* labor; work
Smith, Adam, 94, 95, 139
social contract theory, 198n48
social criticism, 17, 106, 109, 118, 142, 146, 147, 149, 154, 156, 159, 160
   and theory, 148–149

social failure, 141
social identification, 74–75
social norms, 11, 15, 17, 40, 107, 109, 119, 201
   and conscience, 40
social order, 1n2, 20, 41, 53, 68, 77, 94, 127, 130, 131, 132, 134, 140, 142, 143, 152, 153, 154, 206
   modern, 27
   rational, 10, 12, 14, 16, 17, 20, 23, 29, 30, 41–42, 43, 45, 47, 59, 64, 69, 74, 93, 106, 108, 126, 127, 201, 202, 205, 206
   unethical, 157
social participation, 7, 12, 24, 69, 135, 137
social pathology, 155. *See also* pathologies
social reality, 151, 152, 153, 156, 168
social substance, 92, 127, 128
social world, 1, 3, 6, 32, 41, 45, 53, 63, 83, 106, 108, 111, 114, 115, 127, 132, 142, 147, 149, 152, 164, 165, 196, 197
socially cultivated habits, 61
socially necessary illusions, 155, 156
Socrates, 41, 192n39
spirit, 91, 126
   configuration of, 14, 15, 77, 79, 126, 127–133, 146, 192, 193
   as substance, 77, 78
spirituality, 3, 10–11, 34, 37, 65
Staat, 73n11
state, 127, 129
   and nation, distinguishes between, 99
Stern, Robert, 28n20, 175–176, 189n36
Stoicism, 155n79
subjective freedom, 3, 4, 5, 6, 14, 16, 23, 29, 30, 37, 38, 44, 44n52, 64, 95, 137, 189
Subjective Spirit, 26n11, 31–32, 184
subjective will, 41, 198
   right of, 26, 38, 38n43, 42, 45, 107
system, 26n11, 109n8, 163, 180, 181, 206
   and necessity, 180
   of needs, 97, 98, 102, 138, 139, 173
systematic science, 167, 180, 182
systematicity, 111, 167, 181, 182

Taylor, Charles, 72–73, 100, 101
theory/ies
   as abstract, 169
   as arbitrary, 169
   and criticism, 147–160
   and ideology, 153
   particular, 169
   resistance to, 153
   of right, 161, 166, 167–174
   and social criticism, 148–149
   traditional, 150
   value of, 150

Index

thing, the, 87
Thompson, Kevin, 182n29
tics, 66–67
traditionalism, 17, 71, 73, 76
true conscience, 23, 38–44, 42n51, 45, 54, 106, 107
truth, 43, 108, 121, 168
   about right, 161, 163, 165, 176, 191
   and certainty, 122
   and knowledge, 52n68
Tugendhat, Ernst, 113–115
Tunick, Mark, 99, 99n41

uncodifiability, 60, 60n84, 61, 63, 63n89
unfreedom, 37, 65
uninhabitability, 141n53
universality, 30, 82, 102, 138, 140, 141, 143, 147
   activity aspect, 57
   and *Bildung*, 99
   civil servants estate, 100
   and civil society, 95, 100, 138
   permanent wealth, 138, 139, 141
unreflectiveness, 2n3, 4, 5, 6, 7, 11, 12, 15, 25, 42, 54, 55, 60, 64, 75, 76, 90, 92, 109, 112, 165, 180, 200, 201, 202, 203, 206
   free will, 4
unsustainability, 141–144, 157, 159, 177

virtue, 25, 45, 63n89
   of character, 24
   and commitment, 48, 53
   and community, 72
   and continence, 50
   and habit, 23, 24, 27
   as knowledge, 47
   uncodifiable, 60–61
   unity of, 46
virtuosity, 45, 63n89
virtuous agent, 60
virtuous, becoming, 53
Volk, 73n11

Walsh, W. H., 71n4
Walzer, Michael, 148–150, 153
war, 129
whole-hearted commitment, 52n67
will, 3. *See also* free will
Williams, Bernard, 110–111, 111n9, 112, 167
Wittgenstein, Ludwig, 61n84
Wollestonecraft, Mary, 151, 151n70
Wood, Allen, 20, 73, 74, 75n20, 107n4
work, 86–93, 96
   and abstraction, 96
   world as, 86n32
world history, 207
world, as work, 91

Yeomans, Christopher, 7n9